Fundamentals of Global Strategy

A Business Model Approach

Fundamentals of Global Strategy

A Business Model Approach

Cornelis A. de Kluyver

Dean and James and Shirley Rippey Distinguished Professor
Lundquist College of Business
University of Oregon

Fundamentals of Global Strategy

Copyright © Business Expert Press, LLC, 2010.

First published in 2010 by
Business Expert Press, LLC
222 East 46th Street, New York, NY 10017
www.businessexpertpress.com

ISBN-13: 978-1-60649-072-3 (paperback)
ISBN-10: 1-60649-072-9 (paperback)

ISBN-13: 978-1-60649-073-0 (e-book)
ISBN-10: 1-60649-073-7 (e-book)

10.4128/9781606490730

A publication in the Business Expert Press Strategic Management collection

Collection ISSN: 2150-9611 (print)
Collection ISSN: 2150-9646 (electronic)

Cover design by Jonathan Pennell
Interior design by Scribe Inc.

First edition: July 2010

10 9 8 7 6 5 4 3 2 1

Printed in the United States of America.

Abstract

This book looks at the opportunities and risks associated with staking out a global competitive presence and introduces the fundamentals of global strategic thinking. We define crafting a global strategy in terms of change: how a company should change and adapt its core (domestic) business model to achieve a competitive advantage as it expands globally. The conceptual framework behind this definition has three fundamental building blocks: a company's core *business model,* the various *strategic decisions* a company needs to make as it globalizes its operations, and a range of *globalization strategies* for creating a global competitive advantage.

A *business model* is defined in terms of four principal components: (a) *market participation*—who its customers are, how it reaches them and relates to them; (b) *the value proposition*—what a company offers its customers; (c) *the supply chain infrastructure*—with what resources, activities and partners it creates its offerings; and finally, (d) its *management model*—how it organizes and coordinates its operations.

Globalization requires a company to make *strategic decisions* about each component of the business model. *Market participation decisions* include choosing which specific *markets or segments* to serve, domestically or abroad; what methods of distribution to use to reach target customers; and how to promote and advertise the value proposition. Globalization decisions about the value proposition touch the full range of tangible and intangible benefits a company provides to its customers (stakeholders). Decisions about a company's *value chain infrastructure* deal with such questions as, What key *internal resources and capabilities* has the company created to support the chosen value proposition and target markets? What *partner network* has it assembled to support the business model? How are these activities organized into an overall, coherent value creation and delivery model? Finally, strategic decisions about the global *management* dimension are concerned with a company's choices about a suitable global organizational structure and decision-making process.

We use Pankaj Ghemawat's well-known *"AAA Triangle" framework* to define three generic approaches to global value creation. *Adaptation* strategies seek to increase revenues and market share by tailoring one or more components of a company's business model to suit local requirements or preferences. *Aggregation* strategies focus on achieving economies of scale or scope by creating regional or global efficiencies; they typically involve standardizing a significant portion of the value proposition and grouping together development and production processes. *Arbitrage* is about exploiting economic or other differences between national or regional markets, usually by locating separate parts of the supply chain in different places.

Key Words

Global strategy, global competitive advantage, business model, value creation, value proposition, value disciplines, market participation, supply chain infrastructure, global management model, global industry, global branding, innovation, outsourcing, offshoring

Contents

Figures

Preface

This book looks at the opportunities and risks associated with staking out a global competitive presence and introduces the fundamentals of global strategic thinking. We define crafting a global strategy in terms of change—how a company should change and adapt its core (domestic) business model to achieve a competitive advantage as it expands globally. The conceptual framework behind this definition has three fundamental building blocks: a company's core *business model*, the various *strategic decisions* a company needs to make as it globalizes its operations, and a range of *globalization strategies* for creating a global competitive advantage.

We use Pankaj Ghemawat's well-known *"AAA Triangle" framework* to describe three generic approaches to global value creation. *Adaptation* strategies seek to increase revenues and market share by tailoring one or more components of a company's business model to suit local requirements or preferences. *Aggregation* strategies focus on achieving economies of scale or scope by creating regional or global efficiencies; they typically involve standardizing a significant portion of the value proposition and grouping together development and production processes. *Arbitrage* is about exploiting economic or other differences between national or regional markets, usually by locating separate parts of the supply chain in different places.

A *business model* is simply a description of how a company does business. It has four principal components: (a) *market participation*, that is, who its customers are, how it reaches them and relates to them; (b) *the value proposition*, or, what a company offers its customers; (c) *the supply-chain infrastructure*, that is, with what resources, activities, and partners it creates its offerings; and finally, (d) its *management model, or*, how it organizes and coordinates its operations.

Globalization requires a company to make strategic decisions about each component of the business model. *Market participation decisions* include choosing which specific *markets or segments* to serve, domestically or abroad; what methods of distribution to use to reach target customers; and how to promote and advertise the value proposition.

A company's *value proposition* composes the core of its business model; it includes everything it offers its customers in a specific market or segment. This comprises not only the company's bundles of products and services—it also affects how it differentiates itself from its competitors. Globalization decisions about the value proposition therefore touch the full range of tangible and intangible benefits a company provides to its customers (stakeholders).

The *value chain infrastructure* dimension of the business model deals with such questions as, what key *internal resources and capabilities* has the company created to support the chosen value proposition and target markets; what *partner network* has it assembled to support the business model; and how are these activities organized into an overall, coherent value creation and delivery model?

Finally, the *management* dimension is concerned with a company's choices about a suitable global organizational structure and decision-making process. Creating a global mind-set is a key determinant of global success.

Organization of the Book

The book is organized in two parts. Part 1 of the book—Understanding Globalization—consists of four chapters. Chapter 1 assesses how global the world economy has become and what implications that has for companies. Chapter 2 looks at globalization at the industry level. It asks the following questions: What is a global industry? What are the driving forces behind the globalization of industries? and What explains the dominance of particular countries or regions in global industries? Chapter 3 looks at generic strategies for creating a global competitive advantage, ranging from adaptation to aggregation to arbitrage. Chapter 4 introduces the concept of a business model to define global strategy formulation as *changing or adapting a company's core (domestic) business model to achieve a competitive advantage as it globalizes its operations or presence.*

Part 2—Globalizing the Business Model—consists of six chapters. Each chapter looks at the globalization decisions that have to be made about a particular component of a company's business model or discusses a core competency associated with that component. Chapter 5 looks at decisions regarding which foreign markets to enter and why, when, and how to enter them. In other words, the chapter is about target-market selection and the timing and mode of market entry. Chapter 6 discusses the globalization of the company's core offerings and introduces the concept of a value proposition globalization matrix to guide strategic thinking. Chapter 7 addresses a related core competency: global branding. Chapter 8 looks at the globalization of the value-chain infrastructure, from research and development, to product development, to manufacturing, to distribution, to after-sale service. Chapter 9 follows this discussion with a survey of a closely related core competency: supply-chain management. Chapter 10 rounds out the business model framework by looking at the globalization of a company's management model.

Minicases and Appendices

Each chapter features a number of minicases—vignettes about real companies struggling with the issues raised in the main body of the text. They are included to provide context for the various concepts introduced, to create variety in presentation, and to challenge students to link theory to practice.

Two appendices are included in the book. The first surveys the various doctrines and regulatory frameworks that guide global trade. The second consists of suggestions for suitable case studies to accompany each chapter of the book.

Acknowledgments

Writing this book has been on my mind for almost 15 years. In the early 1990s, as Dean of the School of Business Administration at George Mason University (GMU), my friend and colleague, Stuart Malawer, distinguished Professor of Law & International Trade at GMU, invited me to coteach a course on global strategy and trade at St. Peter's College, Oxford University. This unique course brought students from different disciplines and different parts of the world together to study emerging issues in the field of international commerce. It helped me develop the approach to teaching global strategy contained in this book, which I have refined over the last 20 years.

I have others to thank. Vijay Sathe, my colleague at the Peter F. Drucker and Masatoshi Ito Graduate School of Management, and I collaborated in numerous executive programs, both in the United States and abroad. These experiences have also helped me refine the contents of this book. Mason Carpenter, the editor of this series, provided valuable feedback on a draft of this book. And, of course, I am indebted to the late Peter F. Drucker. His guidance and friendship meant a lot to me. Considered by many the "father of modern management," Peter's unique perspectives on modern capitalism and on the roles of the private sector, nonprofits, and the government have helped shape the thinking of CEOs, academics, analysts, and commentators alike. I hope this book contributes to this process.

I am also indebted to my publisher, David Parker, for his patience and encouragement. This is my second book published with Business Expert Press, testimony to the collegial and professional working relationship we have developed.

And, as aspiring authors quickly learn and seasoned writers already know, writing a book is a mammoth undertaking. Fortunately, I had a lot of encouragement along the way from my family and friends, and I take this opportunity to thank them all for letting me spend the time and for their words of encouragement. I am grateful to all of them and hope the result meets their high expectations. It goes without saying that I alone am responsible for any remaining errors or misstatements.

Cornelis A. "Kees" de Kluyver

Dean and James and Shirley Rippey
Distinguished Professor

Lundquist College of Business

University of Oregon

PART I

Understanding Globalization

Part I of this book, Understanding Globalization, has four chapters:

Chapter 1 assesses what global the world economy has become and what implications that has for companies.

Chapter 2 looks at globalization at the industry level. It asks questions such as "What is a global industry?" "What are the driving forces behind the globalization of industries?" and "What explains the dominance of particular countries or regions in global industries?"

Chapter 3 looks at generic strategies for creating a global competitive advantage ranging from adaptation to aggregation to arbitrage.

Chapter 4 introduces the concept of a business model to define global strategy formulation as changing or adapting a company's core (domestic) business model to achieve a competitive advantage as it globalizes its operations or presence.

CHAPTER 1

Competing in a Global World

To most of us, globalization—as a political, economic, social, and technological force—appears all but unstoppable. The ever-faster flow of information across the globe has made people aware of the tastes, preferences, and lifestyles of citizens in other countries. Through this information flow, we are all becoming—at varying speeds and at least in economic terms—global citizens. This convergence is controversial, even offensive, to some who consider globalization a threat to their identity and way of life. It is not surprising, therefore, that globalization has evoked counter forces aimed at preserving differences and deepening a sense of local identity.

Yet, at the same time, we increasingly take advantage of what a global economy has to offer—we drive BMWs and Toyotas, work with an Apple or IBM notebook, communicate with a Nokia phone or BlackBerry, wear Zara clothes or Nike sneakers, drink Coca-Cola, eat McDonald's hamburgers, entertain the kids with a Sony PlayStation, and travel with designer luggage. This is equally true for the buying habits of businesses. The market boundaries for IBM global services, Hewlett-Packard computers, General Electric (GE) aircraft engines, or PricewaterhouseCoopers consulting are no longer defined in political or geographic terms. Rather, it is the intrinsic value of the products and services that defines their appeal. Like it or not, we are living in a global economy.

How Global Are We?

In 1983, Theodore Levitt, the late Harvard Business School professor and editor of the *Harvard Business Review*, wrote a controversial article entitled "The Globalization of Markets." In it, he famously stated,

"The globalization of markets is at hand. With that, the multinational commercial world nears its end, and so does the multinational corporation . . . The multinational operates in a number of countries, and adjust its products and processes in each, at high relative cost. The global corporation operates with resolute constancy . . . it sells the same things in the same way everywhere"[1]

Levitt both overestimated and underestimated globalization. He did not anticipate that some markets would react against globalization, especially against Western globalization. He also underestimated the power of globalization to transform entire nations to actually embrace elements of global capitalism, as is happening in the former Soviet Union, China, and other parts of the world. He was right, however, about the importance of branding and its role in forging the convergence of consumer preferences on a global scale. Think of Coca-Cola, Starbucks, McDonald's, or Google.[2]

More than 20 years later, in 2005, Thomas Friedman, author of *The World is Flat: A Brief History of the Twenty-First Century*, had much the same idea, this time focused on the globalization of production rather than of markets. Friedman argues that a number of important events, such as the birth of the Internet, coincided to "flatten" the competitive landscape worldwide by increasing globalization and reducing the power of states. Friedman's list of "flatteners" includes the fall of the Berlin Wall; the rise of Netscape and the dot-com boom that led to a trillion-dollar investment in fiber-optic cable; the emergence of common software platforms and open source code enabling global collaboration; and the rise of outsourcing, offshoring, supply chaining, and in-sourcing. According to Friedman, these flatteners converged around the year 2000, creating "a flat world: a global, web-enabled platform for multiple forms of sharing knowledge and work, irrespective of time, distance, geography and increasingly, language."[3] And, he observed, at the very moment this platform emerged, three huge economies materialized—those of India, China, and the former Soviet Union, and "three billion people who were out of the game, walked onto the playing field."[4]

Taking a different perspective, Harvard Business School professor Pankaj Ghemawat disputes the idea of fully globalized, integrated, and homogenized future. Instead, he argues that differences between countries and cultures are larger than is generally acknowledged and that "*semiglobalization*" is the real state of the world today and is likely to remain so for the foreseeable future. To support his contention, he observes that the vast majority of all phone calls, web traffic, and investment around the world remains local; that more than 90% of the fixed investment around the world is still domestic; that while trade flows are growing, the ratio of domestic to international trade is still substantial and is likely to remain so; and, crucially, that borders and distance still matter and that it is important to take a broad view of the differences they demarcate, to identify those that matter the most in a particular industry, and to look at them not just as difficulties to be overcome but also as potential sources of value creation.[5]

Moore and Rugman also reject the idea of an emerging single world market for free trade and offer a regional perspective. They note that while companies source goods, technology, information, and capital from around the world, business activity tends to be centered in certain cities or regions around the world, and suggest that regions—rather than global opportunity—should be the focus of strategy analysis and organization. As examples, they cite recent decisions by DuPont and Procter & Gamble to roll their three separate country subsidiaries in the United States, Canada, and Mexico into one regional organization.[6]

The histories of Toyota, Wal-Mart, and Coca-Cola provide support for the diagnosis of a semiglobalized and regionally divided world. Toyota's globalization has always had a distinct regional flavor. Its starting point was *not* a grand, long-term vision of a fully integrated world in which autos and auto parts can flow freely from anywhere to anywhere else. Rather, the company anticipated expanded free-trade agreements within the Americas, Europe, and East Asia but not across them. This reflects a vision of a semiglobalized world in which neither the bridges nor the barriers between countries can be ignored.[7]

The globalization of Wal-Mart illustrates the complex realities of a more nuanced global competitive landscape (see Minicase 1.1). It has been successful in markets that are culturally, administratively, geographically, and economically closest to the United States: Canada, Mexico, and the United Kingdom. In other parts of the world, it has yet to meet its profitability targets. The point is not that Wal-Mart should not have ventured into more distant markets, but rather that such opportunities require a different competitive approach. For example, in India, which restricts foreign direct investment in retailing, Wal-Mart was forced to enter a joint venture with an Indian partner, Bharti, that operates the stores, while Wal-Mart deals with the back end of the business.

Finally, consider the history of Coca-Cola, which, in the late 1990s under chief executive officer Roberto Goizueta, fully bought into Levitt's idea that the globalization of markets (rather than production) was imminent. Goizueta embarked on a strategy that involved focusing resources on Coke's megabrands, an unprecedented amount of standardization, and the official dissolution of the boundaries between Coke's U.S. and international organizations. Fifteen years later and under new leadership, Coke's strategy looks very different and is no longer always the same in different parts of the world. In big, emerging markets such as China and India, Coke has lowered price points, reduced costs by localizing inputs and modernizing bottling operations, and upgraded logistics and distribution, especially rurally. The boundaries between the United States and international organizations have been restored, recognizing the fact that Coke faces very different challenges in America than it does in most of the rest of the world. This is because per capita consumption is an order of magnitude that is higher in the United States than elsewhere.

Minicase 1.1. The Globalization of Wal-Mart[8]

In venturing outside the United States, Wal-Mart had the option of entering Europe, Asia, or other countries in the western hemisphere. It realized that it did not have the resources—financial, organizational, and managerial—to enter all of them simultaneously and instead opted for a carefully considered, learning-based approach to market entry. During the first 5 years of its globalization (1991 to 1995), Wal-Mart concentrated heavily on establishing a presence in the Americas: Mexico, Brazil, Argentina, and Canada. This choice was motivated by the fact that the European market was less attractive to Wal-Mart as a first point of entry. The European retail industry was already mature, which meant that a new entrant would have to take market share away from an existing player. There were well-entrenched competitors such as Carrefour in France and Metro AG in Germany that would likely retaliate vigorously. Moreover, European retailers had formats similar to Wal-Mart's, which would have the effect of reducing Wal-Mart's competitive advantage. Wal-Mart might have overcome these difficulties by entering Europe through an acquisition, but the higher growth rates of the Latin American and Asian markets would have made a delayed entry into those markets extremely costly in terms of lost opportunities. In contrast, the opportunity costs of delaying acquisition-based entries into European markets were relatively small. Asian markets also presented major opportunities, but they were geographically and culturally more distant. For these reasons, as its first global points of entry, Wal-Mart chose Mexico (1991), Brazil (1994), and Argentina (1995), the countries with the three largest populations in Latin America.

By 1996, Wal-Mart felt ready to take on the Asian challenge. It targeted China, with a population of more than 1.2 billion inhabitants in 640 cities, as its primary growth vehicle. This choice made sense in that the lower purchasing power of the Chinese consumer offered huge potential to a low-price retailer like Wal-Mart. Still, China's cultural, linguistic, and geographical distance from the United States presented relatively high entry barriers, so Wal-Mart established two beachheads as learning vehicles for establishing an Asian presence. From 1992 to 1993, Wal-Mart agreed to sell low-priced products to two Japanese retailers, Ito-Yokado and Yaohan, that would market these products in Japan, Singapore, Hong Kong, Malaysia, Thailand, Indonesia, and the Philippines. Then, in 1994, Wal-Mart formed a joint venture with the C. P. Pokphand Company, a Thailand-based conglomerate, to open three Value Club membership discount stores in Hong Kong.

Once Wal-Mart had chosen its target markets, it had to select a mode of entry. It entered Canada through an acquisition. This was rational because Canada was a mature market—adding new retail capacity was unattractive—and because the strong economic and cultural similarities between the U.S. and Canadian markets minimized the need for much learning.

For its entry into Mexico, Wal-Mart took a different route. Because there were significant income and cultural differences between the U.S. and Mexican markets about which the company needed to learn, and to which it needed to tailor its operations, a greenfield start-up would have been problematic. Instead, the company chose to form a 50-50 joint venture with Cifra, Mexico's largest retailer, counting on Cifra to provide operational expertise in the Mexican market.

In Latin America, Wal-Mart targeted the region's next two largest markets: Brazil and Argentina. The company entered Brazil through a joint venture, with Lojas Americana, a local retailer. Wal-Mart was able to leverage its learning from the Mexican experience and chose to establish a 60-40 joint venture in which it had the controlling stake. The successful entry into Brazil gave Wal-Mart even greater experience in Latin America, and it chose to enter Argentina through a wholly owned subsidiary. This decision was reinforced by the presence of only two major markets in Argentina.

Global Competition's Changing Center of Gravity

The rapid emergence of a number of developing economies—notably the so-called BRIC countries (Brazil, Russia, India, and China)—is the latest development shaping the global competitive environment. The impact this development will have on global competition in the next decade is likely to be enormous; these economies are experiencing rates of growth in gross domestic product (GDP), trade, and disposable income that are unprecedented in the developed world. The sheer size of the consumer markets now opening up in emerging economies, especially in India and China, and their rapid growth rates will shift the balance of business activity far more than did the earlier rise of less populous economies such as Japan and South Korea and their handful of "new champions" that seemed to threaten the old order at the time.

This shift in the balance of business activity has redefined global opportunity. For the last 50 years, the globalization of business has primarily been interpreted as the expansion of trade from developed to emerging economies. Today's rapid rise of emerging economies means this view is no longer tenable—business now flows in both directions and increasingly from one developing economy to another. Or, as the authors of "Globality," consultants at the Boston Consulting Group (BCG), put it, business these days is all about "competing with everyone from everywhere for everything."[9]

The evidence that this latest shift in the global competitive landscape will have seismic proportions is already formidable. Consider, for example, the growing number of companies from emerging markets that appear in the *Fortune* 500 rankings of the world's biggest firms. It now stands at 62, mostly from the BRIC economies, up from 31 in 2003, and is set to rise rapidly. What is more, if current trends persist, emerging-market companies will account for one-third of the *Fortune* list within 10 years.

Look also at the recent sharp increase in the number of emerging-market companies acquiring established rich-world businesses and brands, proof that "globalization" is no longer just another word for "Americanization." For instance, Budweiser, the maker of America's favorite beer, was bought by a Belgian-Brazilian conglomerate. And several of America's leading financial institutions avoided bankruptcy only by being bailed out by the sovereign-wealth funds (state-owned investment funds) of various Arab kingdoms and the Chinese government.

Another prominent example of this seismic shift in global business is provided by Lenovo, the Chinese computer maker. It became a global brand in 2005, when it paid around $1.75 billion for the personal-computer business of one of America's best-known companies, IBM, including the ThinkPad laptop range. Lenovo had the right to use the IBM brand for 5 years, but dropped it 2 years ahead of schedule, such was its confidence in its own brand. It just squeezed into 499th place in the *Fortune* 500, with worldwide revenues of $16.8 billion last year and growth prospects many Western companies envy.

The conclusion is that this new phase of "globality" is creating huge opportunities—as well as threats—for developed-world multinationals and new champions from developing countries alike.

Globalization Pressures on Companies

Gupta, Govindarajan, and Wang identify five "imperatives" that drive companies to become more global: *to pursue growth, efficiency, and knowledge; to better meet customer needs; and to preempt or counter competition.*[10]

Growth

In many industries, markets in the developed countries are maturing at a rapid rate, limiting the rate of growth. Consider household appliances: in the developed part of the world, most households have, or have access to, appliances such as stoves, ovens, washing machines, dryers, and refrigerators. Industry growth is therefore largely determined by population growth and product replacement. In developing markets, in contrast, household penetration rates for major appliances are still low compared to Western standards, thereby offering significant growth opportunities for manufacturers.

Efficiency

A global presence automatically expands a company's scale of operations, giving it larger revenues and a larger asset base. A larger scale can help create a competitive advantage if a company undertakes the tough actions needed to convert scale into *economies of scale* by (a) spreading fixed costs, (b) reducing capital and operating costs, (c) pooling purchasing power, and (d) creating critical mass in a significant portion of the value chain. Whereas economies of scale primarily refer to efficiencies associated with supply-side changes, such as increasing or decreasing the scale of production, *economies of scope* refer to efficiencies typically associated with demand-side changes, such as increasing or decreasing the scope of marketing and distribution by entering new markets or regions or by increasing the range of products and services offered. The economic value of global scope can be substantial when serving global customers through providing coordinated services and the ability to leverage a company's expanded market power.

Knowledge

Foreign operations can be reservoirs of knowledge. Some locally created knowledge is relevant across multiple countries, and, if leveraged effectively, can yield significant strategic benefits to a global enterprise, such as (a) faster product and process innovation, (b) lower cost of innovation, and (c) reduced risk of competitive preemption. For example, Fiat developed Palio—its global car—in Brazil; Texas Instruments uses a collaborative process between Indian and U.S. engineers to design its most advanced chips; and Procter & Gamble's liquid Tide was developed as a joint effort by U.S. employees (who had the technology to suspend dirt in water), the Japanese subsidiary (who had the cleaning agents), and the Brussels operations (who had the agents that fight mineral salts found in hard water). Most companies tap only a fraction of the full potential in realizing the economic value inherent in transferring and leveraging knowledge across borders. Significant geographic, cultural, and linguistic distances often separate subsidiaries. The challenge is creating systematic and routine mechanisms that will uncover opportunities for knowledge transfer.

Customer Needs and Preferences

When customers start to globalize, a firm has little choice but to follow and adapt its business model to accommodate them. Multinationals such as Coca-Cola, GE, and DuPont increasingly insist that their suppliers—from raw material suppliers to advertising agencies to personnel recruitment companies—become more global in their approach and be prepared to serve them whenever and wherever required. Individuals are no different—global travelers insist on consistent worldwide service from airlines, hotel chains, credit card companies, television news, and others.

Competition

Just as the globalization of customers compels companies to consider globalizing their business model, so does the globalization of one or more major competitors. A competitor who globalizes early may have a first-mover advantage in emerging markets, greater opportunity to create economies of scale and scope, and an ability to cross-subsidize competitive battles, thereby posing a greater threat in the home market. The global beer market provides a good example of these forces at work. Over the past decade, the beer industry has witnessed significant consolidation, and this trend continued during 2008. On a pro forma basis, beer sales by the top 10 players now total approximately 65% of total global sales, compared to less than 40% at the start of the century. In recent major developments, the division of Scottish and Newcastle's business between Carlsberg and Heineken was completed during the first half of 2008, while InBev acquired Anheuser-Busch in November 2008. SABMiller and Molson Coors combined their operations in the United States and Puerto Rico on July 1, 2008, to form the new Miller-Coors brewing joint venture.

Minicase 1.2. Chocolatiers Look to Asia for Growth[11]

Humans first cultivated a taste for chocolate 3,000 years ago, but for India and China this is a more recent phenomenon. Compared to the sweet-toothed Swiss and Brits, both of whom devour about 24 lbs (11 kg) of chocolate per capita annually, Indians consume a paltry 5.8 oz and the Chinese, a mere 3.5 oz (165 g and 99 g, respectively).

Western chocolate makers hungry for growth markets are banking on this to change. According to market researcher Euromonitor International, in the past 5 years, the value of chocolate confectionery sales in China has nearly doubled, to $813.1 million, while sales in India have increased 64%, to $393.8 million. That is a pittance compared to the nearly $35-billion European chocolate market. But while European chocolate sales are growing a mere 1% to 2% annually, sales in the two Asian nations show no sign of slowing.

European chocolatiers are already making their mark in China. The most aggressive is Swiss food giant Nestlé, which has more than doubled its Chinese sales since 2001 to an estimated $91.5 million—still a relatively small amount. It is closing in on Mars, the longtime market leader, whose sales rose 40% during the same period to $96.7 million.

Green Tea Kisses

Nestlé's Kit Kat bar and other wafer-type chocolates are a big hit with the Chinese, helping the Swiss company swipe market share from Mars. Italy's Ferrero is another up-and-comer. It has boosted China sales nearly 79% since 2001, to $55.6 million, drawing younger consumers with its Kinder chocolate line, while targeting big spenders with the upscale Ferrero Rocher brand. Indeed, its products are so popular that they have spawned Chinese knock-offs, including a Ferrero Rocher look-alike made by a Chinese company that Ferrero has sued for alleged counterfeiting. Despite those problems, the privately owned Ferrero has steadily gained market share against third-ranked Cadbury Schweppes, whose China sales have risen a modest 26% since 2001, to $58.6 million.

Until now, U.S.-based Hershey has been a relatively small player in China. But the company has adopted ambitious expansion plans, including hooking up with a local partner to step up its distribution and introducing green-tea-flavored Hershey Kisses to appeal to Asian tastes.

Attractively Packaged

Underscoring China's growing importance, Switzerland's Barry Callebaut, a big chocolate producer that supplies many leading confectioners, opened a factory near Shanghai to alleviate pressure at a Singapore facility that had been operating at capacity. The company also inaugurated a nearby Chocolate Academy, just 1 month after opening a similar facility in Mumbai, to train local confectioners and pastry chefs in using chocolate.

Unlike China's chocolate market, India's is dominated by only two companies: Cadbury, which entered the country 60 years ago and has nearly 60% market share, and Nestlé, which has about 32% market share. The two have prospered by luring consumers with attractively packaged chocolate assortments to replace the traditional dried fruits and sugar confectioneries offered as gifts on Indian holidays, and by offering lower-priced chocolates, including bite-sized candies costing less than 3 cents.

The confectionary companies have been less successful, though, at developing new products adapted to the Indian sweet tooth. In 2005, Nestlé launched a coconut-flavored Munch bar, and Cadbury introduced a dessert called Kalakand Crème, based on a popular local sweet made of chopped nuts and cheese. Both sold poorly and were discontinued.

What Is a Global Corporation?

One could argue that a global company must have a presence in all major world markets—Europe, the Americas, and Asia. Others may define globality in terms of how globally a company sources, that is, how far its supply chain reaches across the world. Still other definitions use company size, the makeup of the senior management team, or where and how it finances its operations as their primary criterion.

Gupta, Govindarajan, and Wang suggest we define corporate globality in terms of four dimensions: a company's market presence, supply base, capital base, and corporate mind-set.[12] The first dimension—*the globalization of market presence*—refers to the degree the company has globalized its market presence and customer base. Oil and car companies score high on this dimension. Wal-Mart, the world's largest retailer, on the other hand, generates less than 30% of its revenues outside the United States. The second dimension—*the globalization of the supply base*—hints at the extent to which a company sources from different locations and has located key parts of the supply chain in optimal locations around the world. Caterpillar, for example, serves customer in approximately 200 countries around the world, manufactures in 24 of them, and maintains research and development facilities in nine. The third dimension—*globalization of the capital base*—measures the degree to which a company has globalized its financial structure. This deals with such issues as on what exchanges the company's shares are listed, where it attracts operating capital, how it finances growth and acquisitions, where it pays taxes, and how it repatriates profits. The final dimension—*globalization of the corporate mind-set*—refers to a company's ability to deal with diverse cultures. GE, Nestlé, and Procter & Gamble are examples of companies with an increasingly global mind-set: businesses are run on a global basis, top management is increasingly international, and new ideas routinely come from all parts of the globe.

In the years to come, the list of truly "global" companies—companies that are global in all four dimensions—is likely to grow dramatically. Global merger and acquisition activity continues to increase as companies around the world combine forces and restructure themselves to become more globally competitive and to capitalize on opportunities in emerging world markets. We have already seen megamergers involving financial services, leisure, food and drink, media, automobile, and telecommunications companies. There are good reasons to believe that the global mergers and acquisitions (M&A) movement is just in its beginning stages—the economics of globalization point to further consolidation in many industries. In Europe, for example, more deregulation and the EU's move toward a single currency will encourage further M&A activity and corporate restructuring.

The Persistence of Distance

Metaphors such as "the world is flat" tend to suggest that distance no longer matters—that information technologies and, in particular, global communications are shrinking the world, turning it into a small and relatively homogeneous place. But when it comes to business, that assumption is not only incorrect; it is dangerous.

Ghemawat analyzes distance between countries or regions in terms of four dimensions—*cultural, administrative, geographic,* and *economic (CAGE)*—each of which influences business in different ways.[13]

Cultural Distance

A country's culture shapes how people interact with each other and with organizations. Differences in religious beliefs, race, social norms, and language can quickly become barriers, that is, "create distance." The influence of some of these attributes is obvious. A common language, for example, makes trade much easier and therefore more likely. The impact of other attributes is much more subtle, however. Social norms—the set of unspoken principles that strongly guides everyday behavior—are mostly invisible. Japanese and European consumers, for example, prefer smaller automobiles and household appliances than Americans, reflecting a social norm that highly values space. The food industry must concern itself with religious attributes—for example, Hindus do not eat beef because it is expressly forbidden by their religion. Thus, cultural distance shapes preference and, ultimately, choice.

Administrative or Political Distance

Administrative or political distance is created by differences in governmental laws, policies, and institutions, including international relationships between countries, treaties, and membership in international organizations (see Appendix A for a brief summary). The greater the distance, the less likely it is that extensive trade relations develop. This explains the advantage that shared historical colonial ties, membership in the same regional trading bloc, and use of a common currency can confer. The integration of the European Union over the last half-century is probably the best example of deliberate efforts to reduce administrative distance among trading partners. Bad relationships can increase administrative distance, however. Although India and Pakistan share a colonial past, a land border, and linguistic ties, their long-standing mutual hostility has reduced official trade to almost nothing.

Countries can also create administrative and political distance through unilateral measures. Indeed, policies of individual governments pose the most common barriers to cross-border competition. In some cases, the difficulties arise in a company's home country. For companies from the United States, for instance, domestic prohibitions on bribery and the prescription of health, safety, and environmental policies have a dampening effect on their international businesses. More commonly, though, it is the target country's government that raises barriers to foreign competition: tariffs, trade quotas, restrictions on foreign direct investment, and preferences for domestic competitors in the form of subsidies and favoritism in regulation and procurement.

Geographic Distance

Geographic distance is about more than simply how far away a country is in miles. Other geographic attributes include the physical size of the country, average within-country distances to borders, access to waterways and the ocean, topography, and a country's transportation and communications infrastructure. Geographic attributes most directly influence transportation costs and are therefore particularly relevant to businesses with low value-to-weight or bulk ratios, such as steel and cement. Likewise, costs for transporting fragile or perishable products become significant across large distances. Intangible goods and services are affected by geographic distance as well, as cross-border equity flows between two countries fall off significantly as the geographic distance between them rises. This is a direct result of differences in information infrastructure, including telephone, Internet, and banking services.

Economic Distance

Disposable income is the most important economic attribute that creates distance between countries. Rich countries engage in proportionately higher levels of cross-border economic activity than poorer ones. The greater the economic distance between a company's home country and the host country, the greater the likelihood that it must make significant adaptations to its business model. Wal-Mart in India, for instance, would be a very different business from Wal-Mart in the United States. But Wal-Mart in Canada is virtually a carbon copy of the U.S. Wal-Mart. An exception to the distance rule is provided by industries in which competitive advantage is derived from economic arbitrage, that is, the exploitation of cost and price differentials between markets. Companies in industries whose major cost components vary widely across countries, like the garment and footwear industries, where labor costs are important, are particularly likely to target countries with different economic profiles for investment or trade. Whether or not they expand abroad for purposes of replication or arbitrage, all companies find that major disparities in supply chains and distribution channels are significant barriers to business. This suggests that focusing on a limited number of geographies may prove advantageous because of reduced operational complexity. This is evident in the home-appliance business, for instance, where companies—like Maytag—that concentrate on a limited number of geographies produce far better returns for investors than companies like Electrolux and Whirlpool, whose geographic spread has come at the expense of simplicity and profitability.

Minicase 1.3. Computer Keyboards Abroad: QWERTZ Versus QWERTY

Anyone who has traveled to Austria or Germany and has used computers there—in cybercafes, offices, or at the home of friends—will instantly recognize this dimension of "distance": *their keyboards are not the same as ours*. Once-familiar letters and symbols look like strangers, and new keys are located where they should not be.[14]

Specifically, a German keyboard has a QWERTZ layout, that is, the "Y" and "Z" keys are reversed in comparison with the U.S.-English QWERTY layout. Moreover, in addition to the "normal" letters of the English alphabet, German keyboards have the three umlauted vowels and the "sharp-s" characters of the German alphabet. The "ess-tsett" (ß) key is to the right of the zero ("0") key. (But this letter is missing on a Swiss-German keyboard, since the "ß" is not used in the Swiss variation of German.) The u-umlaut (ü) key is located just to the right of the "P" key. The o-umlaut (ö) and a-umlaut (ä) keys are to the right of the "L" key. This means, of course, that the symbols or letters that an American is used to finding where the umlauted letters are in the German version turn up somewhere else. All this is enough to bring on a major headache.

And just where the heck is that "@" key? E-mail happens to depend on it rather heavily, but on the German keyboard, not only is it NOT at the top of the "2" key but it also seems to have vanished entirely! This is surprising considering that the "at" sign even has a name in German: *der Klammeraffe* (lit., "clip/bracket monkey"). So how do you type "@"? You have to press the "Alt Gr" key plus "Q" to make "@" appear in your document or e-mail address. Ready for the Excedrin? On most European-language keyboards, the right "Alt" key, which is just to the right of the space bar and different from the regular "Alt" key on the left side, acts as a "Compose" key, making it possible to enter many non-ASCII characters. This configuration applies to PCs; Mac users will need to take an advanced course. Of course, for Europeans using a North American keyboard, the problems are reversed, and they must get used to the weird U.S. English configuration.

Global Strategy and Risk

Even with the best planning, globalization carries substantial risks. Many globalization strategies represent a considerable stretch of the company's experience base, resources, and capabilities.[15] The firm might target new markets, often in new—for the company—cultural settings. It might seek new technologies, initiate new partnerships, or adopt market-share objectives that require earlier or greater commitments than current returns can justify. In the process, new and different forms of competition can be encountered, and it could turn out that the economics model that got the company to its current position is no longer applicable. Often, a more global posture implies exposure to different cyclical patterns, currency, and political risk. In addition, there are substantial costs associated with coordinating global operations. As a consequence, before deciding to enter a foreign country or continent, companies should carefully analyze the risks involved. In addition, companies should recognize that the management style that proved successful on a domestic scale might turn out to be ineffective in a global setting.

Over the last 25 years, Western companies have expanded their activities into parts of the world that carry risks far greater than those to which they are accustomed. According to Control Risks Group, a London-based international business consultancy, multinational corporations are now active in more than 100 countries that are rated "medium" to "extreme" in terms of risk, and hundreds of billions are invested in countries rated "fairly" to "very" corrupt. To mitigate this risk, companies must understand the specific nature of the relationship between corporate globalization and geopolitics, identify the various types of risk globalization exposes them to, and adopt strategies to enhance their resilience.

Such an understanding begins with the recognition that the role of multinational corporations in the evolving global-geopolitical landscape continues to change. The prevailing dogma of the 1990s held that free-market enterprise and a liberal economic agenda would lead to more stable geopolitical relations. The decline of interstate warfare during this period also provided a geopolitical environment that enabled heavy consolidation across industries, resulting in the emergence of "global players," that is, conglomerates with worldwide reach. The economy was paramount; corporations were almost unconstrained by political and social considerations. The greater international presence of business and increasing geopolitical complexity also heightened the exposure of companies to conflict and violence, however. As they became larger, they became more obvious targets for attack and increasingly vulnerable because their strategies were based on the assumption of fundamentally stable geopolitical relations.

In recent years, the term "global player" has acquired a new meaning, however. Previously a reference exclusively to an economic role, the term now describes a company that has, however unwillingly, become a *political* actor as well. And, as a consequence, to remain a global player today, a firm must be able to survive not only economic downturns but also geopolitical shocks. This requires understanding that risk has become an endemic reality of the globalization process—that is, no longer simply the result of conflict in one country or another but something inherent in the globalized system itself.

Globalization risk can be of a *political, legal, financial-economic,* or *sociocultural nature. Political risk* relates to politically induced actions and policies initiated by a foreign government. Crises such as the September 11, 2001, terrorist attacks in the United States, the ongoing conflict in Iraq and Pakistan, instability in the Korean peninsula, and the recent global financial crisis have made geopolitical uncertainty a key component of formulating a global strategy. The effect of these events and the associated political decisions on energy, transportation, tourism, insurance, and other sectors demonstrates the massive consequences that crises, wars, and economic meltdowns, wherever and however they may take place, can have on business.

Political risk assessment involves an evaluation of the stability of a country's current government and of its relationships with other countries. A high level of risk affects ownership of physical assets and intellectual property and security of personnel, increasing the potential for trouble. Analysts frequently divide political risk into two subcategories: *global* and *country-specific risk. Global risk* affects all of a company's multinational operations, whereas *country-specific risk* relates to investments in a specific foreign country. We can distinguish between *macro* and *micro* political risk. *Macro risk* is concerned with how foreign investment in general in a particular country is affected. By reviewing the government's past use of *soft* policy instruments, such as blacklisting, indirect control of prices, or strikes in particular industries, and *hard* policy tools, such as expropriation, confiscation, nationalization, or compulsory local shareholding, a company can be better prepared for potential future government action. At the *micro* level, risk analysis is focused on a particular company or group of companies. A weak balance sheet, questionable accounting practices, or a regular breach of contracts should give rise to concerns.

Legal risk is risk that multinational companies encounter in the legal arena in a particular country. Legal risk is often closely tied to political country risk. An assessment of legal risk requires analyzing the foundations of a country's legal system and determining whether the laws are properly enforced. Legal risk analysis therefore involves becoming familiar with a country's enforcement agencies and their scope of operation. As many companies have learned, numerous countries have written laws protecting a multinational's rights, but these laws are rarely enforced. Entering such countries can expose a company to a host of risks, including the loss of intellectual property, technology, and trademarks.

Financial or economic risk in a foreign country is analogous to operating and financial risk at home. The volatility of a country's macroeconomic performance and the country's ability to meet its financial obligations directly affect performance. A nation's currency competitiveness and fluctuation are important indicators of a country's stability—both financial and political—and its willingness to embrace changes and innovations. In addition, financial risk assessment should consider such factors as how well the economy is being managed, the level of the country's economic development, working conditions, infrastructure, technological innovation, and the availability of natural and human resources.

Societal or cultural risk is associated with operating in a different sociocultural environment. For example, it might be advisable to analyze specific ideologies; the relative importance of ethnic, religious, and nationalistic movements; and the country's ability to cope with changes that will, sooner or later, be induced by foreign investment. Thus, elements such as the standard of living, patriotism, religious factors, or the presence of charismatic leaders can play a huge role in the evaluation of these risks.

Points to Remember

1. Although we often speak of global markets and a "flat" world, in reality, the world's competitive structure is best described as semi-global. Bilateral and regional trade and investment patterns continue to dominate global ones.

2. The center of gravity of global competition is shifting to the East, with China and India taking center stage. Russia and Brazil, the other two BRIC countries, are not far behind.

3. Global competition is rapidly becoming a two-way street, with new competitors from developing countries taking on traditional companies from developed nations everywhere in every industry.

4. Companies have several major reasons to consider going global: to pursue growth, efficiency, and knowledge; to better meet customer needs; and to preempt or counter competition.

5. Global companies are those that have a global market presence, supply-chain infrastructure, capital base, and corporate mind-set.

6. Although we live in a "global" world, distance still very much matters, and companies must explicitly and thoroughly account for it when they make decisions about global expansion.

7. Distance between countries or regions is usefully analyzed in terms of four dimensions: *cultural, administrative, geographic,* and *economic,* each of which influences business in different ways.

8. Even with the best planning, globalization carries substantial risks. Globalization risks can be of a *political, legal, financial-economic,* or *sociocultural nature.*

CHAPTER 2

The Globalization of Companies and Industries

"Going global" is often described in incremental terms as a more or less gradual process, starting with increased exports or global sourcing, followed by a modest international presence, growing into a multinational organization, and ultimately evolving into a global posture. This appearance of gradualism, however, is deceptive. It obscures the key changes that globalization requires in a company's mission, core competencies, structure, processes, and culture. As a consequence, it leads managers to underestimate the enormous differences that exist between managing international operations, a multinational enterprise, and managing a global corporation. Research by Diana Farrell of McKinsey & Company shows that industries and companies both tend to globalize in stages, and at each stage, there are different opportunities for and challenges associated with creating value.[1]

In the first stage (market entry), companies tend to enter new countries using business models that are very similar to the ones they deploy in their home markets. To gain access to local customers, however, they often need to establish a production presence, either because of the nature of their businesses (as in service industries like food retail or banking) or because of local countries' regulatory restrictions (as in the auto industry).

In the second stage (product specialization), companies transfer the full production process of a particular product to a single, low-cost location and export the goods to various consumer markets. Under this scenario, different locations begin to specialize in different products or components and trade in finished goods.

The third stage (value chain disaggregation) represents the next step in the company's globalization of the supply-chain infrastructure. In this stage, companies start to disaggregate the production process and focus each activity in the most advantageous location. Individual components of a single product might be manufactured in several different locations and assembled into final products elsewhere. Examples include the PC industry market and the decision by companies to offshore some of their business processes and information technology services.

In the fourth stage (value chain reengineering) companies seek to further increase their cost savings by reengineering their processes to suit local market conditions, notably by substituting lower-cost labor for capital. General Electric's (GE) medical equipment division, for example, has tailored its manufacturing processes abroad to take advantage of low labor costs. Not only does it use more labor-intensive production processes—it also designs and builds the capital equipment for its plants locally.

Finally, in the fifth stage (the creation of new markets), the focus is on market expansion. The McKinsey Global Institute estimates that the third and fourth stages together have the potential to reduce costs by more than 50% in many industries, which gives companies the opportunity to substantially lower their sticker prices in both old and new markets and to expand demand. Significantly, the value of new revenues generated in this last stage is often greater than the value of cost savings in the other stages.

It should be noted that the five stages described above do not define a rigid sequence that all industries follow. As the McKinsey study notes, companies can skip or combine steps. For example, in consumer electronics, product specialization and value chain disaggregation (the second and third stages) occurred together as different locations started to specialize in producing different components (Taiwanese manufacturers focused on semiconductors, while Chinese companies focused on computer keyboards and other components).

Understanding Industry Globalization

Executives often ask whether their industry is becoming more global and, if so, what strategies they should consider to take advantage of this development and stake out an enduring global competitive advantage. This may be the wrong question. Simple characterizations such as "the electronics industry is global" are not particularly useful. A better question is *how* global an industry is, or is likely, to become. Virtually all industries are global in some respects. However, only a handful of industries can be considered truly global today or are likely to become so in the future. Many more will remain hybrids, that is, global in some respects, local in others. *Industry globalization, therefore, is a matter of degree.* What counts is which elements of an industry are becoming global and how they affect strategic choice. In approaching this issue, we must focus on the drivers of industry globalization and think about how these elements shape strategic choice.

We should also make a distinction between *industry globalization, global competition*, and the degree to which a *company has globalized* its operations. In traditionally global industries, competition is mostly waged on a worldwide basis and the leaders have created global corporate structures. But the fact that an industry is not truly global does not prevent global competition. And a competitive global posture does not necessarily require a global reorganization of every aspect of a company's operations. Economies of scale and scope are among the most important drivers of industry globalization; in global industries, the minimum volume required for cost efficiency is simply no longer available in a single country or region. Global competition begins when companies cross-subsidize national market-share battles in pursuit of global brand and distribution positions. A global company structure is characterized by production and distribution systems in key markets around the world that enable cross-subsidization, competitive retaliation on a global basis, and world-scale volume.[2]

So why are some industries more global than others? And why do global industries appear to be concentrated in certain countries or regions? Most would consider the oil, auto, and pharmaceutical industries global industries, while tax preparation, many retailing sectors, and real estate are substantially domestic in nature. Others, such as furniture, lie somewhere in the middle. What accounts for the difference? The dominant location of global industries also poses interesting questions. Although the machine tool and semiconductor industries originated in the United States, Asia has emerged as the dominant player in most of their segments today. What accounts for this shift? Why is the worldwide chemical industry concentrated in Germany while the United States continues to dominate in software and entertainment? Can we predict that France and Italy will remain the global centers for fashion and design? These issues are important to strategists. They are also relevant as a matter of public policy as governments attempt to shape effective policies to attract and retain the most attractive industries, and companies must anticipate changes in global competition and locational advantage.

Minicase 2.1. Cemex's Globalization Path: First Cement, Then Services

When Lorenzo Zambrano became chairman and chief executive officer of Cemex in the 1980s, he pushed the company into foreign markets to protect it from the Latin American debt crisis. Now the giant cement company is moving into services.[3]

Zambrano first focused on the United States. But attempts to sell cement north of the border were greeted by hostility from producers, who convinced the U.S. International Trade Commission to levy a stiff antidumping duty. Despite a a General Agreement on Tariffs and Trade's (GATT) ruling in Cemex's favor, the company was still paying the fine a dozen years later.

Rebuffed in the world's biggest market, Zambrano turned to Spain, investing in port facilities and outmaneuvering European rivals for control of the country's two largest cement firms. When he discovered how inefficiently they were run, Zambrano sent a team of his Mexican managers to Spain to introduce his distinctive way of doing business. Called the "Cemex Way," it is a culture that blends modern, flexible management practices with cutting-edge technology.

From Spain, where profits increased from 7% to 24% during Cemex's first 2 years there, the company expanded around the globe. Blending state-of-the-art technology with the making and selling of one of the world's most basic products, Cemex has achieved remarkable customer service in some of the most logistically challenged countries. Whether Venezuela, Mexico, or the Philippines, Cemex trucks equipped with GPS navigational systems promise deliveries within 20 minutes.

After gaining a solid international footing, Zambrano went back to the United States. In 2000, he bought Houston-based Southdown Cement—one of the largest purchases ever by a Mexican company in the United States. Soon, Cemex was the biggest U.S. cement seller. In less than two decades, Zambrano had transformed Cemex from a domestic company into the world's third-largest cement firm by investing heavily and imaginatively not only in plants and equipment, which is what one would expect in the cement industry, but also in information technology and particularly in Cemex's people.

The corporation has consistently been more profitable than either of its two biggest competitors, France's Lafarge and Switzerland's Holcim. Sales in 2008 were almost $22 billion, with an operating margin of almost 12%.

Today, Cemex has a presence in more than 50 countries across 5 continents. It has an annual production capacity of close to 96 million metric tons of cement, approximately 77 million cubic meters of ready-mix concrete and more than 240 million metric tons of aggregates. Its resource base includes 64 cement plants, over 2,200 ready-mix concrete facilities, and a minority participation in 15 cement plants, and it operates 493 aggregate quarries, 253 land-distribution centers, and 88 marine terminals.

Zambrano's embrace of technology is central to Cemex's efficiency. Fiber optics link the system, and satellite communications are used to connect remote outposts. Whether at the Monterrey headquarters or on the road, the chief executive officer can tap into his computer to check kiln temperatures in Bali or cement truck deliveries in Cairo.

Because he believes many companies use technology ineffectively, Zambrano spun off Cemex's technology arm to sell its services. Organized under the CxNetworks Miami subsidiary, which is devoted to creating growth by building innovative businesses around Cemex's strengths, Zambrano formed a consulting service called Neoris. With more than half of its customers coming from outside Cemex, the operation has already become hugely profitable. It has been grouped with another start-up—Arkio, a distributor of building material products to construction companies in developing nations. "We're selling logistics," says the president of CxNetworks. "We can assure our customers that they can have the materials from our warehouse to their construction site within 48 hours."

Clustering: Porter's National Diamond

The theory of comparative economic advantage holds that as a result of natural endowments, some countries or regions of the world are more efficient than others in producing particular goods. Australia, for example, is naturally suited to the mining industry; the United States, with its vast temperate landmass, has a natural advantage in agriculture; and more-wooded parts of the world may have a natural advantage in producing timber-based products. This theory is persuasive for industries such as agriculture, mining, and timber. But what about industries such as electronics, entertainment, or fashion design? To explain the clustering of these industries in particular countries or regions, a more comprehensive theory of the geography of competition is needed.

In the absence of natural comparative advantages, industrial clustering occurs as a result of a relative advantage that is created by the industry itself.[4] Producers tend to locate manufacturing facilities close to their primary customers. If transportation costs are not too high, and there are strong economies of scale in manufacturing, a large geographic area can be served from this single location. This, in turn, attracts suppliers to the industry. A labor market is likely to develop that begins to act like a magnate for "like" industries requiring similar skills. This colocation of "like" industries can lead to technological interdependencies, which further encourage clustering. Clustering, therefore, is the natural outcome of economic forces. A good example is provided by the semiconductor industry. Together, American and Asian firms supply most of the world's needs. The industry is capital intensive, research and development costs are high, the manufacturing process is highly complex, but transportation costs are minimal. Technology interdependencies encourage colocation with suppliers, whereas cost and learning curve effects point to scale efficiencies. Clustering, therefore, is mutually advantageous.

Only when transportation costs are prohibitive or scale economies are difficult to realize—that is, when there are disincentives to clustering—do more decentralized patterns of industry location define the natural order. The appliance industry illustrates this. Companies such as GE and Whirlpool have globalized their operations in many respects, but the fundamental economics of the industry make clustering unattractive. The production of certain value-added components, such as compressors or electronic parts, can be concentrated to some extent, but the bulky nature of the product and high transportation costs make further concentration economically unattractive. What is more, advances in flexible manufacturing techniques are reducing the minimum scale needed for efficient production. This allows producers to more finely tailor their product offerings to local tastes and preferences, further thwarting the globalization of the industry.

Thus, classical economic theory tells us why clustering occurs. However, it does not fully explain why *particular* regions attract certain global industries. Porter addressed this issue using a framework he calls a "national diamond."[5] It has six components: *factor conditions, home-country demand, related and supporting industries, competitiveness of the home industry, public policy,* and *chance.*

Factor Conditions

The explanation why *particular* regions attract *particular* industries begins with the degree to which a country or region's endowments match the characteristics and requirements of an industry. Such factor conditions include natural (climate, minerals) as well as created (skill levels, capital, infrastructure) endowments. But to the extent that such factors are mobile, or can be imitated by other countries or regions, factor conditions alone do not fully explain regional dominance. In fact, the opposite is true. When a particular industry is highly profitable and barriers to entry are low, the forces of imitation and diffusion cause such an industry to spread across international borders.[6] The Japanese compete in a number of industries that originated in the United States; Korean firms imitate Japanese strategies; and Central European nations are conquering industries that were founded in Western Europe. Industries that depend on such mobile factors as capital are particularly susceptible.

Home-Country Demand

Porter's second factor is the nature and size of the demand in the home country. Large home markets act as a stimulus for industry development. And when a large home market develops before it takes hold elsewhere in the world, experienced firms have ample incentives to look for business abroad when saturation at home begins to set in. The motorcycle industry in Japan, for example, used its scale advantage to create a global presence following an early start at home.[7] Porter found that it is not just the *location* of early demand but its *composition* that matters. A product's fundamental or core design nearly always reflects home-market needs. As such, the nature of the home-market needs and the sophistication of the home-market buyer are important determinants of the potential of the industry to stake out a future global position. It was helpful to the U.S. semiconductor industry, for example, that the government was an early, sophisticated, and relatively cost-insensitive buyer of chips. These conditions encouraged the industry to develop new technologies and provided early opportunities to manufacture on a substantial scale.

Related and Supporting Industries

The presence of related and supporting industries is the third element of Porter's framework. This is similar to our earlier observation about clustering. For example, Hollywood is more than just a cluster of moviemakers—it encompasses a host of suppliers and service providers, and it has shaped the labor market in the Los Angeles area.

Competitiveness of the Home Industry

Firm strategies, the structure, and the rivalry in the home industry define the fourth element of the "national diamond" model. In essence, this element summarizes the "five forces" competitive framework described earlier. The more vigorous the domestic competition is, the more successful firms are likely to compete on a global scale. There is plenty of evidence for this assertion. The fierce rivalry that exists among German pharmaceutical companies has made them a formidable force in the global market. And the intense battle for domestic market share has strengthened the competitive position of Japanese automobile manufacturers abroad.

Public Policy and Chance

The two final components of Porter's model are public policy and chance. There can be no doubt that government policy can—through infrastructure, incentives, subsidies, or temporary protection—nurture global industries. Whether such policies are always effective is less clear. Picking "winners" in the global marketplace has never been the strong suit of governments. The chance element allows for the influence of random events such as where and when fundamental scientific breakthroughs occur, the presence of entrepreneurial initiative, and sheer luck. For example, the early U.S. domination of the photography industry is as much attributable to the fact that George Eastman (of Eastman Kodak) and Edwin Land (of Polaroid) were born here than to any other factor.

Industry Globalization Drivers

Yip identifies four sets of "industry globalization drivers" that underlie conditions in each industry that create the potential for that industry to become more global and, as a consequence, for the potential viability of a global approach to strategy.[8] *Market drivers* define how customer behavior distribution patterns evolve, including the degree to which customer needs converge around the world, customers procure on a global basis, worldwide channels of distribution develop, marketing platforms are transferable, and "lead" countries in which most innovation takes place can be identified. *Cost globalization drivers*—the opportunity for global scale or scope economics, experience effects, sourcing efficiencies reflecting differentials in costs between countries or regions, and technology advantages—shape the economics of the industry. *Competitive drivers* are defined by the actions of competing firms, such as the extent to which competitors from different continents enter the fray, globalize their strategies and corporate capabilities, and create interdependence between geographical markets. *Government drivers* include such factors as favorable trade policies, a benign regulatory climate, and common product and technology standards.

Market Drivers

One aspect of globalization is the steady convergence of customer needs. As customers in different parts of the world increasingly demand similar products and services, opportunities for scale arise through the marketing of more or less standardized offerings. How common needs, tastes, and preferences will vary greatly by product and depend on such factors as the importance of cultural variables, disposable incomes, and the degree of homogeneity of the conditions in which the product is consumed or used. This applies to consumer as well as industrial products and services. Coca-Cola offers similar but not identical products around the world. McDonald's, while adapting to local tastes and preferences, has standardized many elements of its operations. Software, oil products, and accounting services increasingly look alike no matter where they are purchased. The key to exploiting such opportunities for scale lies in understanding which elements of the product or service can be standardized without sacrificing responsiveness to local preferences and conditions.

Global customers have emerged as needs continue to converge. Large corporations such as DuPont, Boeing, or GE demand the same level of quality in the products and services they buy no matter where in the world they are procured. In many industries, global distribution channels are emerging to satisfy an increasingly global customer base, further causing a convergence of needs. Finally, as consumption patterns become more homogeneous, global branding and marketing will become increasingly important to global success.

Cost Globalization Drivers

The globalization of customer needs and the opportunities for scale and standardization it brings will fundamentally alter the economics of many industries. Economies of scale and scope, experience effects, and exploiting differences in factor costs for product development, manufacturing, and sourcing in different parts of the world will assume a greater importance as determinants of global strategy. At bottom is a simple fact: a single market will no longer be large enough to support a competitive strategy on a global scale in many industries.

Global scale and scope economics are already having far-reaching effects. On the one hand, the more the new economies of scale and scope shape the strategies of incumbents in global industries, the harder it will be for new entrants to develop an effective competitive threat. Thus, barriers to entry in such industries will get higher. At the same time, the rivalry within such industries is likely to increase, reflecting the broadening scope of competition among interdependent national and regional markets and the fact that true differentiation in such a competitive environment may be harder to achieve.

Competitive Drivers

Industry characteristics—such as the degree to which total industry sales are made up by export or import volume, the diversity of competitors in terms of their national origin, the extent to which major players have globalized their operations and created an interdependence between their competitive strategies in different parts of the world—also affect the globalization potential of an industry. High levels of trade, competitive diversity, and interdependence increase the potential for industry globalization. Industry evolution plays a role, too. As the underlying characteristics of the industry change, competitors will respond to enhance and preserve their competitive advantage. Sometimes, this causes industry globalization to accelerate. At other times, as in the case of the worldwide major appliance industry, the globalization process may be reversed.

Government Drivers

Government globalization drivers—such as the presence or absence of favorable trade policies, technical standards, policies and regulations, and government operated or subsidized competitors or customers—affect all other elements of a global strategy and are therefore important in shaping the global competitive environment in an industry. In the past, multinationals almost exclusively relied on governments to negotiate the rules of global competition. Today, however, this is changing. As the politics and economics of global competition become more closely intertwined, multinational companies are beginning to pay greater attention to the so-called nonmarket dimensions of their global strategies aimed at shaping the global competitive environment to their advantage (see the following section). This broadening of the scope of global strategy reflects a subtle but real change in the balance of power between national governments and multinational corporations and is likely to have important consequences for how differences in policies and regulations affecting global competitiveness will be settled in the years to come.

Minicase 2.2. Global Value Chains in the Automotive Industry: A Nested Structure[9]

From a geographic point of view, the world automotive industry, like many others, is in the midst of a profound transition. Since the mid-1980s, it has been shifting from a series of discrete national industries to a more integrated global industry. In the automotive industry, these global ties have been accompanied by strong regional patterns at the operational level.

Market saturation, high levels of motorization, and political pressures on automakers to "build where they sell" have encouraged the dispersion of final assembly, which now takes place in many more places than it did 30 years ago. According to Automotive News Market Data Books, while seven countries accounted for about 80% of world production in 1975, 11 countries accounted for the same share in 2005.

The widespread expectation that markets in China and India were poised for explosive growth generated a surge of new investment in these countries. Consumer preferences require that automakers alter the design of their vehicles to fit the characteristics of specific markets. They also want their conceptual designers to be close to "tuners" to see how they modify their production vehicles. These motivations led automakers to establish a series of affiliated design centers in places such as China and Southern California. Nevertheless, the heavy engineering work of vehicle development, where conceptual designs are translated into the parts and subsystems that can be assembled into a drivable vehicle, remain centralized in or near the design clusters that have arisen near the headquarters of lead firms.

The automotive industry is therefore neither fully global, consisting of a set of linked, specialized clusters, nor tied to the narrow geography of nation states or specific localities, as is the case for some cultural or service industries. Global integration has proceeded at the level of design and vehicle development as firms have sought to leverage engineering effort across regions. Examples include right- versus left-hand drive, more rugged suspension and larger gas tanks for developing countries, and consumer preferences for pick-up trucks in Thailand, Australia, and the United States.

The principal automotive design centers in the world are Detroit, Michigan, in the United States (GM, Ford, Chrysler, and, more recently, Toyota and Nissan); Cologne (Ford Europe), Rüsselsheim (Opel, GM's European division), Wolfsburg (Volkswagen), and Stuttgart (Daimler-Benz) in Germany; Paris, France (Renault); and Tokyo (Nissan and Honda) and Nagoya (Toyota) in Japan. This is just nine products sold in multiple end markets.

As suppliers have taken on a larger role in design, they have, in turn, established their own design centers close to those of their major customers in order to facilitate collaboration. On the production side, the dominant trend is regional integration, a pattern that has been intensifying since the mid-1980s for both political and technical reasons. In North America, South America, Europe, Southern Africa, and Asia, regional parts production tends to feed final assembly plants producing largely for regional markets. Political pressure for local production has driven automakers to set up final assembly plants in many of the major established market areas and in the largest emerging market countries, such as Brazil, India, and China. Increasingly, as a precondition to being considered for a new part, lead firms demand that their largest suppliers have a global presence.

Because centrally designed vehicles are manufactured in multiple regions, buyer-supplier relationships typically span multiple production regions. Within regions, there is a gradual investment shift toward locations with lower operating costs: the U.S. South and Mexico in North America; Spain and Eastern Europe in

Europe; and Southeast Asia and China in Asia. Ironically, perhaps, it is primarily local firms that take advantage of such cost-cutting investments within regions (e.g., the investments of Ford, GM, and Chrysler in Mexico), since the political pressure that drives inward investment is only relieved when jobs are created within the largest target markets (e.g., the investments of Toyota and Honda in the Unites States and Canada).

Automotive parts, of course, are more heavily traded between regions than finished vehicles. Within countries, automotive production and employment are typically clustered in one or a few industrial regions. In some cases, these clusters specialize in specific aspects of the business, such as vehicle design, final assembly, or the manufacture of parts that share a common characteristic, such as electronic content or labor intensity.

Because of deep investments in capital equipment and skills, regional automotive clusters tend to be very long-lived. To sum up the complex economic geography of the automotive industry, we can say that global integration has proceeded the farthest at the level of buyer-supplier relationships, especially between automakers and their largest suppliers. Production tends to be organized regionally or nationally, with bulky, heavy, and model-specific parts production concentrated close to final assembly plants to assure timely delivery, and with lighter, more generic parts produced at a distance to take advantage of scale economies and low labor costs. Vehicle development is concentrated in a few design centers. As a result, local, national, and regional value chains in the automotive industry are "nested" within the global organizational structures and business relationships of the largest firms. While clusters play a major role in the automotive industry, and have "pipelines" that link them, there are also global and regional structures that need to be explained and theorized in a way that does not discount the power of localization.

Globalization and Industry Structure

Yoffie suggests 5 propositions that help explain how the structure of an industry can evolve depending on, among other factors, the dynamics that shape competition in the industry and the role governments play in stimulating or obstructing the globalization process.[10]

Proposition 1 is that when industries are relatively fragmented and competitive, national environments (factors of production, domestic market and domestic demand, and so forth) will largely shape the international advantage of domestically headquartered firms and the patterns of trade. A correlate to this proposition is that in emerging industries, country advantages also play a dominant role in determining global competitive advantage.

In other words, in fragmented industries relative cost is a key determinant of global success, and since countries differ in terms of their factor costs, as long as entry barriers remain low, production will gravitate to the lowest cost, highest efficiency manufacturing location. Another way of saying this is that the presence of multinational firms, by itself, should not influence the pattern of international trade in globally competitive, fragmented industries; other things being equal, country factors determine the location of production and the direction of exports. Oligopolistic global industry structures define a very different strategic context, as the next proposition illustrates.

Proposition 2 stipulates that if an industry becomes globally concentrated with high barriers to entry, then location, activity concentration, export, and other strategic decisions by multinational companies are determined to a greater extent by the nature of the global oligopolistic rivalry. Thus, while in concentrated industries country characteristics remain important, the dynamics of the global, oligopolistic competitive climate become the principal drivers of global strategy. This is intuitive. In global oligopolies, more so than in fragmented market structures, the success of one firm is directly affected by that of a few, immediate competitors. Entry into the industry is often restricted in some way—by factors such as economies of scale or scope, high levels of capital investment, and the like, or by restrictions imposed by governments. Furthermore, in many global oligopolies, participating firms earn above-average returns, which may make the difference in cost between producing locally and exporting a less critical determinant of strategy. Opportunities to cross-subsidize businesses and geographies further reduce the importance of geography in production or export decisions. As a consequence, the moves and countermoves of direct, global competitors heavily influence company strategies. For example, it is quite common for companies to enter some other firm's home market, not just because that market is likely to generate additional profits but mainly to weaken its global competitive position. This line of reasoning directly leads to a third proposition, which relates organizational and strategic attributes of global competitors to global strategic choice.

Proposition 3 suggests that in global oligopolies, specific firm characteristics—the structure of ownership, strategies employed, and organizational factors, to name a few—directly affect strategic posture, the pattern of trade, and, sometimes, the competitiveness of nations. In global oligopolies with a relatively small number of competitors, issues such as *who* owns the resources necessary for creating value and *who* sets the global priorities take on a greater strategic significance. Executives from different cultures approach strategy differently—state-owned enterprises are often more motivated by public policy considerations, employment, and other nonprofit concerns. These differences can have a direct impact on the relative attractiveness of global strategy options. The influence of governments in global markets is captured further in the fourth proposition.

Proposition 4 suggests that extensive government intervention in global oligopolistic industries can alter the relative balance between firms of different countries—even in fragmented industries, it can alter the direction of trade and affect major corporate trade decisions. The degree and influence of government intervention varies from industry to industry. Whereas in fragmented industries the influence of governments is naturally somewhat limited by market conditions, government intervention can have a pronounced influence in industries with significant economies of scale effects or other market imperfections. For example, governments can protect "infant" industries with such characteristics. While a case can be made for the temporary protection of strategically important industries, in reality, such protection is rarely temporary. This can create a global strategic environment in which anticipating and capitalizing on the actions of governments become the driving forces of global strategy.

Proposition 5 suggests that in industries where firms make long-term commitments, corporate adjustments and patterns of trade tend to be "sticky." This fifth and final proposition addresses the issue of corporate inertia. Although the global competitive climate changes every day, choices made by multinational companies and governments tend to have an enduring impact on the industry environment. This proposition has at least two implications. First, the study of how industries evolve globally and what decisions different competitors made and how they made them is relevant to understanding what drives strategy in a particular global context. Second, the commitments already made by industry participants and governments may spell opportunity or impose constraints for years to come.

These 5 propositions define 2 important dimensions for classifying globalizing industries according to the nature of the strategic challenge they represent: *the degree of global concentration and the extent to which governments intervene.* In industries with a relatively low degree of concentration and little government intervention, the classical economic laws of *comparative advantage* are the primary drivers of international competition. Here, factor costs are a primary determinant of global competitiveness. It would seem natural, therefore, to focus on a global strategy aimed at minimizing costs. But this can be extremely difficult in a fast-changing world. Comparative country costs change continuously. In cars, semiconductors, and computers, among other industries, the comparative (cost) advantage has shifted a number of times since World War II from the United States to Japan to East Asia to Southeast Asia. What is more, there is good reason to believe it will shift again, perhaps to Africa or Latin America. And, with new technological breakthroughs, Western nations may once again become the low-cost production centers. So what should companies do? While companies should definitely take advantage of opportunities to minimize costs, especially in their initial investments, Yoffie suggests that long-term global strategic choices should emphasize *commitments to countries that are likely to act as the best platforms over time for a broad array of activities.*[11]

In globally concentrated industries where the role of governments is limited, characterized by *oligopolistic competition*, company strategies are often heavily influenced by the moves and countermoves of direct competitors. Strategies such as making significant investments in competitors' markets, regardless of their short- or medium-run profitability—which would not work in highly competitive markets—can only be explained in terms of a strategic posture aimed at maintaining a long-term global competitive balance between the various participants. Caterpillar invested heavily in Japan while Komatsu and European construction equipment manufacturing moved into the United States at a time when such moves offered limited immediate returns. In this kind of competitive environment, the potential for overglobalization—the globalization of different aspects of strategy well in advance of proven benefits—exists as the relatively small number of competitors and high barriers to entry encourage "follow-the-leader" competitive behavior. On the other hand, not responding directly to major competitors can be equally dangerous. Komatsu's challenge to Caterpillar, in part, was made possible because, early on, Caterpillar focused its strategy on keeping John Deere, International Harvester, and Dresser Industries at bay rather than on beating Komatsu. This suggests a number of strategic implications. First, while imitation cannot be the sole basis for developing strategy, in oligopolies, it may be necessary, at times, to match a competitor in order to reduce the risk of competitive disadvantage. A related implication is that in global oligopolies, companies cannot allow their competitors to have uncontested home markets in which profit sanctuaries can be used to subsidize global competitive moves. This explains Kodak's extraordinary efforts to pry open the Japanese market—it knew Fuji would be at a considerable advantage if it remained dominant in Japan. Finally, the use of alliances can make such global moves more affordable, flexible, and effective. Alliances can be powerful vehicles for rapidly entering new countries, acquiring new technologies, or otherwise supporting a global strategy at a relatively low cost.[12]

Dealing effectively with governments is a prerequisite for global success in oligopolistic industries such as telecommunications, where extensive government intervention creates a global competitive climate known as *regulated competition*. Here, nonmarket dimensions of global strategy may well be as important as market dimensions. Political involvement may be necessary to create, preserve, or enhance global competitive advantage since government regulations—whether in infant or established industries—are critical to success. As a consequence, strategy in global, regulated industries should be focused as much on shaping the global competitive environment as on capitalizing on the opportunities it offers.

Political competition, characteristic of fragmented industries with significant government intervention, also calls for a judicious mix of market and nonmarket-based strategic thinking. In contrast to regulated competition, in which government policy has a direct impact on individual companies, however, government intervention in political competition often pits one country or region of the world against another. This encourages a whole range of cooperative strategies between similarly affected players and strategic action at the country-industry level.

Finally, it is worth remembering that patterns of competition are not static. Industries evolve continuously, sometimes dramatically. Similarly, the focus of government action in different industries can change as national priorities change and the global competitive environment evolves.

Points to Remember

1. Industries and companies tend to globalize in stages, and at each stage, there are different opportunities for, and challenges associated with, creating value.

2. Simple characterizations such as "the electronics industry is global" are not particularly useful. A better question is *how* global an industry is or is likely to become; *industry globalization is a matter of degree.*

3. A distinction must be made between *industry globalization, global competition*, and the degree to which a *company has globalized* its operations. Porter explains industry clustering using a framework he calls a "national diamond." It has six components: *factor conditions, home country demand, related and supporting industries, competitiveness of the home industry, public policy,* and *chance.*

4. Yip identifies four sets of "industry globalization drivers"—underlying conditions in each industry that create the potential for that industry to become more global and, as a consequence, for the potential viability of a global approach to strategy. These drivers are *market drivers, cost drivers, competitive drivers,* and *government drivers.*

5. Yoffie offers five propositions that help explain how the structure of an industry can evolve depending on, among other factors, the dynamics that shape competition in the industry and the role

governments play in stimulating or obstructing the globalization process. These propositions define two important dimensions for classifying globalizing industries according to the nature of the strategic challenge they represent: *the degree of global concentration* and *the extent to which governments intervene.*

CHAPTER 3

Generic Strategies for Global Value Creation

In this chapter, we introduce three generic strategies for creating value in a global context—*adaptation*, *aggregation*, and *arbitrage*—and a number of variants for each.[1] This conceptualization was first introduced by Pankaj Ghemawat in his important book *Redefining Global Strategy* and, as such, is not new. In the next chapter, we extend this framework, however, by integrating these generic strategies with the proposition that global strategy formulation is about changing a company's business model to create a global competitive advantage.

Ghemawat's "AAA" Global Strategy Framework

Ghemawat so-called AAA framework offers three generic approaches to global value creation. *Adaptation* strategies seek to increase revenues and market share by tailoring one or more components of a company's business model to suit local requirements or preferences. *Aggregation* strategies focus on achieving economies of scale or scope by creating regional or global efficiencies; they typically involve standardizing a significant portion of the value proposition and grouping together development and production processes. *Arbitrage* is about exploiting economic or other differences between national or regional markets, usually by locating separate parts of the supply chain in different places.

Adaptation

Adaptation—creating global value by changing one or more elements of a company's offer to meet local requirements or preferences—is probably the most widely used global strategy. The reason for this will be readily apparent: some degree of adaptation is essential or unavoidable for virtually all products in all parts of the world. The taste of Coca-Cola in Europe is different from that in the United States, reflecting differences in water quality and the kind and amount of sugar added. The packaging of construction adhesive in the United States informs customers how many square feet it will cover; the same package in Europe must do so in square meters. Even commodities such as cement are not immune: its pricing in different geographies reflects local energy and transportation costs and what percentage is bought in bulk.

Ghemawat subdivides adaptation strategies into five categories: *variation, focus, externalization, design,* and *innovation* (Figure 3.1).

Variation strategies not only involve making changes in *products and services* but also making adjustments to *policies, business positioning,* and even *expectations for success.* The *product* dimension will be obvious: Whirlpool, for example, offers smaller washers and dryers in Europe than in the United States, reflecting the space constraints prevalent in many European homes. The need to consider adapting *policies* is less obvious. An example is Google's dilemma in China to conform to local censorship rules. Changing a company's overall *positioning* in a country goes well

Adaptation	Aggregation	Arbitrage
Variation		
		Performance Enhancement
Focus: Reduce Need for Adaptation		
	Economies of Scale	
Externalization: Reduce Burden of Adaptation		*Cost Reduction*
Design: Reduce Cost of Adaptation	*Economies of Scope*	
		Risk Reduction
Innovation: Improve on Exixting Adaptation		

Figure 3.1. AAA strategies and their variants.

beyond changing products or even policies. Initially, Coke did little more than "skim the cream" off big emerging markets such as India and China. To boost volume and market share, it had to reposition itself to a "lower margin–higher volume" strategy that involved lowering price points, reducing costs, and expanding distribution. Changing *expectations* for, say, the rate of return on investment in a country, while a company is trying to create a presence is also a prevalent form of variation.

A second type of adaptation strategies uses a *focus* on particular *products, geographies, vertical stages* of the value chain, or *market segments* as a way of reducing the impact of differences across regions. A *product* focus takes advantage of the fact that wide differences can exist *within* broad product categories in the degree of variation required to compete effectively in local markets. Ghemawat cites the example of television programs: action films need far less adaptation than local newscasts. Restriction of *geographic* scope can permit a focus on countries where relatively little adaptation of the domestic value proposition is required. A *vertical* focus strategy involves limiting a company's direct involvement to specific steps in the supply chain while outsourcing others. Finally, a *segment* focus involves targeting a more limited customer base. Rather than adapting a product or service, a company using this strategy chooses to accept the reality that without modification, their products will appeal to a smaller market segment or different distributor network from those in the domestic market. Many luxury good manufacturers use this approach.

Whereas focus strategies overcome regional differences by narrowing scope, externalization strategies transfer—through *strategic alliances, franchising, user adaptation,* or *networking*—responsibility for specific parts of a company's business model to partner companies to accommodate local requirements, lower cost, or reduce risk. For example, Eli Lilly extensively uses *strategic alliances* abroad for drug development and testing. McDonald's growth strategy abroad uses *franchising* as well as company-owned stores. And software companies heavily depend on both *user adaptation and networking* for the development of applications for their basic software platforms.

A fourth type of adaptation focuses on *design* to reduce the cost of, rather than the need for, variation. Manufacturing costs can often be achieved by introducing design *flexibility* so as to overcome supply differences. Introducing standard production *platforms* and *modularity* in components also helps to reduce cost. A good example of a company focused on design is Tata Motors, which has successfully introduced a car in India that is affordable to a significant number of citizens.

A fifth approach to adaptation is *innovation*, which, given its crosscutting effects, can be characterized as improving the effectiveness of adaptation efforts. For instance, IKEA's flat-pack design, which has reduced the impact of geographic distance by cutting transportation costs, has helped that retailer expand into 3 dozen countries.

Minicase 3.1. McDonald's McAloo Tikki[2]

When Ray Kroc opened his first McDonald's in Des Plaines, Illinois, he could hardly have envisioned the golden arches rising 5 decades later in one of the oldest commercial streets in the world. But McDonald's began dreaming of India in 1991, a year after opening its first restaurant in China. The attraction was obvious: 1.1 billion people, with 300 million destined for middle-class status.

But how do you sell hamburgers in a land where cows are sacred and 1 in 5 people are vegetarian? And how do you serve a largely poor consumer market that stretches from the Himalayas to the shores of the Indian Ocean? McDonald's executives in Oak Brook struggled for years with these questions before finding the road to success.

McDonald's has made big gains since the debut of its first two restaurants in India, in Delhi and Mumbai, in October 1996. Since then, the fast-food chain has grown to more than 160 outlets. The Indian market represents a small fraction of McDonald's $24 billion in annual revenues. But it is not insignificant because the company is increasingly focused on high-growth markets. "The decision to go in wasn't complicated," James Skinner, McDonald's chief executive officer, once said. "The complicated part was deciding what to sell."

At first, McDonald's path into India was fraught with missteps. First, there was the nonbeef burger made with mutton. But the science was off: mutton is 5% fat (beef is 25% fat), making it rubbery and dry. Then there was the french fry debacle. McDonald's started off using potatoes grown in India, but the local variety had too much water content, making the fries soggy. Chicken kabob burgers? Sounds like a winner except that they were skewered by consumers. Salad sandwiches were another flop: Indians prefer cooked foods.

If that was not enough, in May 2001, the company was picketed by protesters after reports surfaced in the United States that the chain's fries were injected with beef extracts to boost flavor—a serious infraction for vegetarians. McDonald's executives in India denied the charges, claiming their fries were different from those sold in America.

But the company persevered, learned, and succeeded. It figured out what Indians wanted to eat and what they would pay for it. It built, from scratch, a mammoth supply chain—from farms to factories—in a country where elephants, goats, and trucks share the same roads. To deal with India's massive geography, the company divided the country into two regions: the north and east, and the south and west. Then it formed 50-50 joint ventures with two well-connected Indian entrepreneurs: Vikram Bakshi, who made his fortune in real estate, runs the northern region; and Amit Jatia, an entrepreneur who comes from a family of successful industrialists, manages the south.

Even though neither had any restaurant experience, this joint-venture management structure gave the company what it needed: local faces at the top. The two entrepreneurs also brought money: before the first restaurant opened, the partners invested $10 million into building a workable supply chain, establishing distribution centers, procuring refrigerated trucks, and finding production facilities with adequate hygiene. They also invested $15 million in Vista Processed Foods, a food processing plant outside Mumbai. In addition, Mr. Jatia, Mr. Bakshi, and 38 staff members spent an entire year in the Indonesian capital of Jakarta studying how McDonald's operated in another Asian country.

Next, the Indian executives embarked on basic-menu research and development (R&D). After awhile, they hit on a veggie burger with a name Indians could understand: the McAloo Tikki (an "aloo tikki" is a cheap potato cake locals buy from roadside vendors).

The lesson in the McDonald's India case: local input matters. Today, 70% of the menu is designed to suit Indians: the Paneer Salsa Wrap, the Chicken Maharaja Mac, the Veg McCurry Pan. The McAloo, by far the best-selling product, also is being shipped to McDonald's in the Middle East, where potato dishes are popular. And in India, it does double duty: it not only appeals to the masses; it is also a hit with the country's 200 million vegetarians.

Another lesson learned from the McDonald's case: vegetarian items should not come into contact with nonvegetarian products or ingredients. Walk into any Indian McDonald's and you will find half of the employees wearing green aprons and the other half in red. Those in green handle vegetarian orders. The red-clad ones serve nonvegetarians. It is a separation that extends throughout the restaurant and its supply chain. Each restaurant's grills, refrigerators, and storage areas are designated as "veg" or "non-veg." At the Vista Processed Foods plant, at every turn, managers stressed the "non-veg" side was in one part of the facility, and the "vegetarian only" section was in another.

Today, after many missteps, one can truly imagine the ghost of Ray Kroc asking Indians one of the greatest questions of all time—the one that translates into so many cultures: "You want fries with that?" Yes, Ray, they do.

Aggregation

Aggregation is about creating *economies of scale* or *scope* as a way of dealing with differences (see Figure 3.1). The objective is to exploit similarities among geographies rather than adapting to differences but stopping short of complete standardization, which would destroy concurrent adaptation approaches. The key is to identify ways of introducing economies of scale and scope into the global business model without compromising local responsiveness.

Adopting a *regional* approach to globalizing the business model—as Toyota has so effectively done—is probably the most widely used aggregation strategy. As discussed in the previous chapter, *regionalization* or *semiglobalization* applies to many aspects of globalization, from investment and communication patterns to trade. And even when companies do have a significant presence in more than one region, competitive interactions are often regionally focused.

Examples of different *geographic* aggregation approaches are not hard to find. Xerox centralized its purchasing, first regionally, later globally, to create a substantial cost advantage. Dutch electronics giant Philips created a global competitive advantage for its Norelco shaver product line by centralizing global production in a few strategically located plants. And the increased use of global (corporate) branding over product branding is a powerful example of creating economies of scale and scope. As these examples show, geographic aggregation strategies have potential application to every major business model component.

Geographic aggregation is not the only avenue for generating economies of scale or scope. The other, nongeographic dimensions of the CAGE framework introduced in Chapter 1—*cultural, administrative, geographic*, and *economic*—also lend themselves to aggregation strategies. Major book publishers, for example, publish their best sellers in but a few languages, counting on the fact that readers are willing to accept a book in their second language (*cultural* aggregation). Pharmaceutical companies seeking to market new drugs in Europe must satisfy the regulatory requirements of a few selected countries to qualify for a license to distribute throughout the EU (*administrative* aggregation). As for *economic* aggregation, the most obvious examples are provided by companies that distinguish between developed and emerging markets and, at the extreme, focus on just one or the other.

Minicase 3.2. Globalization at Whirlpool Corporation[3]

The history of globalization at the Whirlpool Corporation—a leading company in the $100-billion global home-appliance industry—illustrates the multitude of challenges associated with globalizing a business model. Whirlpool manufactures appliances across all major categories—including fabric care, cooking, refrigeration, dishwashing, countertop appliances, garage organization, and water filtration—and has a market presence in every major country in the world. It markets some of the world's most recognized appliance brands, including Whirlpool, Maytag, KitchenAid, Jenn-Air, Amana, Bauknecht, Brastemp, and Consul. Of these, the Whirlpool brand is the world's top-rated global appliance brand and ranks among the world's most valuable brands. In 2008, Whirlpool realized annual sales of approximately $19 billion, had 70,000 employees, and maintained 67 manufacturing and technology research centers around the world.

In the late 1980s, Whirlpool Corporation set out on a course of growth that would eventually transform the company into the leading global manufacturer of major home appliances, with operations based in every region of the world. At the time, Dave Whitwam, Whirlpool's chairman and CEO, had recognized the need to look for growth beyond the mature and highly competitive U.S. market. Under Mr. Whitwam's leadership, Whirlpool began a series of acquisitions that would give the company the scale and resources to participate in global markets. In the process, Whirlpool would establish new relationships with millions of customers in countries and cultures far removed from the U.S. market and the company's roots in rural Benton Harbor, Michigan.

Whirlpool's global initiative focused on establishing or expanding its presence in North America, Latin America, Europe, and Asia. In 1989, Whirlpool acquired the appliance business of Philips Electronics N.V., which immediately gave the company a solid European operations base. In the western hemisphere, Whirlpool expanded its longtime involvement in the Latin America market and established a presence in Mexico as an appliance joint-venture partner. By the mid-1990s, Whirlpool had strengthened its position in Latin America and Europe and was building a solid manufacturing and marketing base in Asia.

In 2006, Whirlpool acquired Maytag Corporation, resulting in an aligned organization able to offer more to consumers in the increasingly competitive global marketplace. The transaction created additional economies of scale. At the same time, it expanded Whirlpool's portfolio of innovative, high-quality branded products and services to consumers.

Executives knew that the company's new scale, or global platform, that emerged from the acquisitions offered a significant competitive advantage, but only if the individual operations and resources were working in concert with each other. In other words, the challenge is not in buying the individual businesses—the real challenge is to effectively integrate all the businesses together in a meaningful way that creates the leverage and competitive advantage.

Some of the advantages were easily identified. By linking the regional organizations through Whirlpool's common systems and global processes, the company could speed product development, make purchasing increasingly more efficient and cost-effective, and improve manufacturing utilization through the use of common platforms and cross-regional exports.

Whirlpool successfully refocused a number of its key functions to its global approach. Procurement was the first function to go global, followed by technology and product development. The two functions shared much in common and have already led to significant savings from efficiencies. More important, the global focus has helped reduce the number of regional manufacturing platforms worldwide. The work of these two functions, combined with the company's manufacturing footprints in each region, has led to the development of truly global platforms—products that share common parts and technologies but offer unique and innovative features and designs that appeal to regional consumer preferences.

Global branding was next. Today, Whirlpool's portfolio ranges from global brands to regional and country-specific brands of appliances. In North America, key brands include Whirlpool, KitchenAid, Roper by Whirlpool Corporation, and Estate. Acquired with the company's 2002 purchase of Vitromatic S.A., brands Acros and Supermatic are leading names in Mexico's domestic market. In addition, Whirlpool is a major supplier for the Sears, Roebuck and Co. Kenmore brand. In Europe, the company's key brands are Whirlpool and Bauknecht. Polar, the latest addition to Europe's portfolio, is the leading brand in Poland. In Latin America, the brands include Brastemp and Consul. Whirlpool's Latin American operations include Embraco, the world's leading compressor manufacturer. In Asia, Whirlpool is the company's primary brand and the top-rated refrigerator and washer manufacturer in India.

Arbitrage

A third generic strategy for creating a global advantage is *arbitrage* (see Figure 3.1). Arbitrage is a way of exploiting differences, rather than adapting to them or bridging them, and defines the original global strategy: buy low in one market and sell high in another. Outsourcing and offshoring are modern day equivalents. Wal-Mart saves billions of dollars a year by buying goods from China. Less visible but equally important absolute economies are created by greater differentiation with customers and partners, improved corporate bargaining power with suppliers or local authorities, reduced supply chain and other market and nonmarket risks, and through the local creation and sharing of knowledge.

Since arbitrage focuses on exploiting differences between regions, the CAGE framework described in Chapter 1 is of particular relevance and helps define a set of substrategies for this generic approach to global value creation.

Favorable effects related to country or place of origin have long supplied a basis for *cultural arbitrage*. For example, an association with French culture has long been an international success factor for fashion items, perfumes, wines, and foods. Similarly, fast-food products and drive-through restaurants are mainly associated with U.S. culture. Another example of cultural arbitrage—real or perceived—is provided by Benihana of Tokyo, the "Japanese steakhouse." Although heavily American—the company has only one outlet in Japan out of more than 100 worldwide—it serves up a theatrical version of teppanyaki cooking that the company describes as "Japanese" and "eatertainment."

Legal, institutional, and political differences between countries or regions create opportunities for *administrative* arbitrage. Ghemawat cites the actions taken by Rupert Murdoch's News Corporation in the 1990s. By placing its U.S. acquisitions into holding companies in the Cayman Islands, the company could deduct interest payments on the debt used to finance the deals against the profits generated by its newspaper operations in Britain. Through this and other similar actions, it successfully lowered its tax liabilities to an average rate of less than 10%, rather than the statutory 30% to 36% of the three main countries in which it operated: Britain, the United States, and Australia. By comparison, major competitors such as Disney were paying close to the official rates.[4]

With steep drops in transportation and communication costs in the last 25 years, the scope for *geographic* arbitrage—the leveraging of geographic differences—has been diminished but not fully eliminated. Consider what is happening in medicine, for example. It is quite common today for doctors in the United States to take X-rays during the day, send them electronically to radiologists in India for interpretation overnight, and for the report to be available the next morning in the United States. In fact, reduced transportation costs sometimes create new opportunities for geographic arbitrage. Every day, for instance, at the international flower market in Aalsmeer, the Netherlands, more than 20 million flowers and 2 million plants are auctioned off and flown to customers in the United States.

As Ghemawat notes, in a sense, all arbitrage strategies that add value are "economic." Here, the term *economic* arbitrage is used to describe strategies that do not directly exploit *cultural, administrative,* or *geographic differences.* Rather, they are focused on leveraging differences in the costs of labor and capital, as well as variations in more industry-specific inputs (such as knowledge) or in the availability of complementary products.[5]

Exploiting differences in labor costs—through outsourcing and offshoring—is probably the most common form of economic arbitrage. This strategy is widely used in labor-intensive (garments) as well as high-technology (flat-screen TV) industries. Economic arbitrage is not limited to leveraging differences in labor costs alone, however. Capital cost differentials can be an equally rich source of opportunity.

Minicase 3.3. Indian Companies Investing in Latin America? To Serve U.S. Customers? [6]

Indian investment in Latin America is relatively small but growing quickly. Indian firms have invested about $7 billion in the region over the last decade, according to figures released by the Latin American division of India's Ministry of External Affairs in New Delhi. The report projects that this amount will easily double in the next few years.

As India has become a magnet for foreign investment, Indian companies themselves are looking abroad for opportunities, motivated by declining global trade barriers and fierce competition at home. Their current focus is on Latin America, where hyperinflation and currency devaluation no longer dominate headlines.

Like China, India is trying to lock up supplies of energy and minerals to feed its rapidly growing economy. Indian firms have stakes in oil and natural gas ventures in Colombia, Venezuela, and Cuba. In 2006, Bolivia signed a deal with New Delhi-based Jindal Steel and Power, Ltd., which plans to invest $2.3 billion to extract iron ore and to build a steel mill in that South American nation.

At the same time, Indian information technology companies are setting up outsourcing facilities to be closer to their customers in the West. Tata Consultancy Services is the leader, employing 5,000 tech workers in more than a dozen Latin American countries.

Indian manufacturing firms, accustomed to catering to low-income consumers at home, are finding Latin America a natural market. Mumbai-based Tata Motors, Ltd., has formed a joint venture with Italy's Fiat to produce small pickup trucks in Argentina. Generic drug makers, such as Dr. Reddy's, are offering low-cost alternatives in a region where U.S. and European multinationals have long dominated.

The Indian government has carefully positioned India as a partner, rather than a rival out to steal the region's resources and jobs, a common worry about China. Mexico has been particularly hard-hit by China's rise. The Asian nation's export of textiles, shoes, electronics, and other consumer goods has cost Mexico tens of thousands of manufacturing jobs, displaced it as the second-largest trading partner with the United States, and flooded its domestic market with imported merchandise. In 2006, Mexico's trade deficit with China was a record $22.7 billion, but China has invested less than $100 million in the country since 1994, according to the Bank of Mexico.

Mexico's trading relationship with India, albeit small, is much more balanced. Mexico's trade deficit with India was just under half a billion dollars in 2006, and Indian companies have invested $1.6 billion here since 1994—or about 17 times more than China—according to Mexico's central bank.

Some of that investment is in basic industries and traditional *maquiladora* factories making goods for export. For example, Mexico's biggest steel plant is owned by ArcelorMittal. Indian pharmaceutical companies, too, are finding Latin America to be attractive for expansion. Firms including Ranbaxy Laboratories, Ltd., Aurobindo Pharma, Ltd., and Cadila Pharmaceuticals, Ltd., have sales or manufacturing operations in the region.

Which "A" Strategy Should a Company Use?

A company's financial statements can be a useful guide for signaling which of the "A" strategies will have the greatest potential to create global value. Firms that heavily rely on branding and that do a lot of advertising, such as food companies, often need to engage in considerable adaptation to local markets. Those that do a lot of R&D—think pharmaceutical firms—may want to aggregate to improve economies of scale, since many R&D outlays are fixed costs. For firms whose operations are labor intensive, such as apparel manufacturers, arbitrage will be of particular concern because labor costs vary greatly from country to country.

Which "A" strategy a company emphasizes also depends on its globalization history. Companies that start on the path of globalization on the supply side of their business model, that is, that seek to lower cost or to access new knowledge, first typically focus on aggregation and arbitrage approaches to creating global value, whereas companies that start their globalization history by taking their value propositions to foreign markets are immediately faced with adaptation challenges. Regardless of their starting point, most companies will need to consider all "A" strategies at different points in their global evolution, sequentially or, sometimes, simultaneously.

Nestlé's globalization path, for example, started with the company making small, related acquisitions outside its domestic market, and the company therefore had early exposure to adaptation challenges. For most of their history, IBM also pursued an adaptation strategy, serving overseas markets by setting up a mini-IBM in each target country. Every one of these companies operated a largely local business model that allowed it to adapt to local differences as necessary. Inevitably, in the 1980s and 1990s, dissatisfaction with the extent to which country-by-country adaptation curtailed opportunities to gain international scale economies led to the overlay of a regional structure on the mini-IBMs. IBM aggregated the countries into regions in order to improve coordination and thus generate more scale economies at the regional and global levels. More recently, however, IBM has also begun to exploit differences across countries (arbitrage). For example, it has increased its work force in India while reducing its headcount in the United States.

Procter & Gamble's (P&G) early history parallels that of IBM, with the establishment of mini-P&Gs in local markets, but it has evolved differently. Today, the company's global business units now sell through market development organizations that are aggregated up to the regional level. P&G has successfully evolved into a company that uses all three "A" strategies in a coordinated manner. It adapts its value proposition to important markets but ultimately competes—through global branding, R&D, and sourcing—on the basis of aggregation. Arbitrage, while important—mostly through outsourcing activities that are invisible to the final consumer—is less important to P&G's global competitive advantage because of its relentless customer focus.

From A to AA to AAA[7]

Although most companies will focus on just one "A" at any given time, leading-edge companies—such as General Electric (GE), P&G, IBM, and Nestlé, to name a few—have embarked on implementing two, or even all three of the "A"s. Doing so presents special challenges because there are inherent tensions between all three foci. As a result, the pursuit of "AA" strategies, or even an "AAA" approach, requires considerable organizational and managerial flexibility.

Pursuing Adaptation and Aggregation

P&G started out with a focus on adaptation. Attempts to superimpose aggregation across Europe first proved difficult and, in particular, led to the installation of a matrix structure throughout the 1980s, but the matrix proved unwieldy. So, in 1999, the then CEO, Durk Jager, announced another reorganization whereby global business units (GBUs) retained ultimate profit responsibility but were complemented by geographic market development organizations (MDOs) that actually managed the sales force as a shared resource across GBUs. The result was disastrous. Conflicts arose everywhere, especially at the key GBU-MDO interfaces. The upshot: Jager departed after less than a year in office.

Under his successor, A. G. Lafley, P&G has enjoyed much more success, with an approach that strikes a better balance between adaptation and aggregation and that makes allowances for differences across general business units and markets. For example, the pharmaceuticals division, with distinct distribution channels, has been left out of the MDO structure. Another example: in emerging markets, where market development challenges are huge, profit responsibility continues to rest with country managers.

Aggregation and Arbitrage

VIZIO, founded in 2002 with only $600,000 in capital by entrepreneur William Wang to create high quality, flat panel televisions at affordable prices, has surpassed established industry giants Sony Corporation and Samsung Electronics Company to become the top flat-panel high definition television (HDTV) brand sold in North America. To get there, VIZIO developed a business model that effectively combines elements of aggregation and arbitrage strategies. VIZIO's contract manufacturing model is based on aggressive procurement sourcing, supply-chain management, economies of scale in distribution.

While a typical flat-screen television includes thousands of parts, the bulk of the costs and ultimate performance are a function of two key components: the panel and the chipset. Together, these two main parts account for about 94% of the costs. VIZIO's business model therefore focuses on optimizing the cost structure for these component parts. The vast majority of VIZIO's panels and chipsets are supplied by a handful of partners. Amtran provides about 80% of VIZIO's procurement and assembly work, with the remaining 20% performed by other ODMs, including Foxconn and TPV Technology.

One of the cornerstones of VIZIO's strategy is the decision to sell through wholesale clubs and discount retailers. Initially, William Wang was able to leverage his relationships at Costco from his years of selling computer monitors. VIZIO's early focus on wholesale stores also fit with the company's value position and pricing strategy. By selling through wholesale clubs and discount stores, VIZIO was able to keeps its prices low. For VIZIO, there is a two-way benefit: the prices of its TVs are comparatively lower than those from major manufacturers at electronics stores, and major manufacturers cannot participate as fully as they would like to at places like Costco.

VIZIO has strong relationships with its retail partners and is honored to offer them only the most compelling and competitively priced consumer electronics products. VIZIO products are available at valued partners including Wal-Mart, Costco, Sam's Club, BJ's Wholesale Club, Sears, Dell, and Target stores nationwide along with authorized online partners. VIZIO has won numerous awards including a number-one ranking in the *Inc.* 500 for "Top Companies in Computers and Electronics," *Good Housekeeping's* "Best Big-Screens," *CNET's* "Top 10 Holiday Gifts," and *PC World's* "Best Buy," among others.[8]

Arbitrage and Adaptation

An example of a strategy that simultaneously emphasizes arbitrage and adaptation is investing heavily in a local presence in a key market to the point where a company can pass itself off as a "local" firm or "insider." A good example is provided by Citibank in China. The company, part of Citigroup, has had an intermittent presence in China since the beginning of the 20th century. A little more than 100 years later, in 2007, it was one of the first foreign banks to incorporate locally in China. The decision to incorporate locally was motivated by the desire to increase Citibank's status as an "insider"; with local incorporation, the Chinese government allowed it to extend its reach, expand its product offerings, and become more closely engaged with its local customers in the country.

China's decision in 2001 to become a member of the World Trade Organization (WTO) was a major factor in Citibank's decision to make a greater commitment to the Chinese market. Prior to China' joining the WTO, the banking environment in China was fairly restrictive. Banks such as Citibank could only give loans to foreign multinationals and their joint-venture partners in local currency, and money for domestic Chinese companies could only be raised in offshore markets. These restrictions made it difficult for foreign banks to gain a foothold in the Chinese business community.

Once China agreed to abide by WTO trading rules, however, banks such as Citibank had significantly greater opportunities: they would be able to provide local currency loans to blue-chip Chinese companies and would be free to raise funds for them in debt and equity markets within China. Other segments targeted by Citibank included retail credit cards and home mortgages. These were Citibank's traditional areas of expertise globally, and a huge potential demand for these products was apparent.

Significant challenges remained, however. Competing through organic growth with China's vast network of low-cost domestic banks would be slow and difficult. Instead, in the next few years, it forged a number of strategic alliances designed to give it critical mass in key segments. The first consisted of taking a 5% stake in China's ninth-largest bank, SPDB, a move that allowed Citibank to launch a dual-currency credit card that could be used to pay in *renminbi* in China and in foreign currencies abroad. In the following years, Citibank steadily increased its stake to the maximum 20% allowed under Chinese law and significantly expanded its product portfolio.

In June 2007, Citibank joined forces with Sino-U.S. MetLife Insurance Company, Ltd., to launch an investment unit-linked insurance product. In July of 2008, the company announced the launch of its first debit card. Simultaneously, it signed a deal with China's only national bankcard association, which allowed Citibank's debit cardholders to enjoy access to the association's vast network in China. The card would provide Chinese customers with access to over 140,000 ATMs within China and 380,000 ATMs in 45 countries overseas. Customers could also use their debit cards with over 1 million merchants within China and in 27 other countries. Today, Citibank is one of the top foreign banks operating in China, with a diverse range of products, eight corporate and investment bank branches, and 25 consumer bank outlets.[9]

Developing an AAA Strategy

There are serious constraints on the ability of any one company to use all three "A"s simultaneously with great effectiveness. Such attempts stretch a firm's managerial bandwidth, force a company to operate with multiple corporate cultures, and can present competitors with opportunities to undercut a company's overall competitiveness. Thus, to even contemplate an "AAA" strategy, a company must be operating in an environment in which the tensions among adaptation, aggregation, and arbitrage are weak or can be overridden by large-scale economies or structural advantages, or in which competitors are otherwise constrained. Ghemawat cites the case of GE Healthcare (GEH). The diagnostic imaging industry has been growing rapidly and has concentrated globally in the hands of three large firms, which together command an estimated 75% of revenues in the business worldwide: GEH, with 30%; Siemens Medical Solutions (SMS), with 25%; and Philips Medical Systems (PMS), with 20%. This high degree of concentration is probably related to the fact that the industry ranks in the 90th percentile in terms of R&D intensity.

These statistics suggest that the aggregation-related challenge of building global scale has proven particularly important in the industry in recent years. GEH, the largest of the three firms, has consistently been the most profitable, reflecting its success at aggregation through (a) economies of scale (e.g., GEH has higher total R&D spending than its competitors, but its R&D-to-sales ratio is lower), (b) acquisition prowess (GEH has made nearly 100 acquisitions under Jeffrey Immelt before he became GE's CEO), and (c) economies of scope (the company strives to integrate its biochemistry skills with its traditional base of physics and engineering skills; it finances equipment purchases through GE Capital).

GEH has even more clearly outpaced its competitors through arbitrage. It has recently become a global product company by rapidly migrating to low-cost production bases. By 2005, GEH was reportedly more than halfway to its goals of purchasing 50% of its materials directly from low-cost countries and locating 60% of its manufacturing in such countries.

In terms of adaptation, GEH has invested heavily in country-focused marketing organizations. It also has increased customer appeal with its emphasis on providing services as well as equipment—for example, by training radiologists and providing consulting advice on postimage processing. Such customer intimacy obviously has to be tailored by country. And, recently, GEH has cautiously engaged in some "in China, for China" manufacture of stripped-down, cheaper equipment, aimed at increasing penetration there.

Pitfalls and Lessons in Applying the AAA Framework

There are several factors that companies should consider in applying the AAA framework. Most companies would be wise to *focus on one or two of the "A"s*—while it is possible to make progress on all three "A"s, especially for a firm that is coming from behind, companies (or, more often to the point, businesses or divisions) usually have to focus on one or, at most, two "A"s in trying to build competitive advantage. Companies should also *make sure the new elements of a strategy are a good fit organizationally.* If a strategy does embody substantially new elements, companies should pay particular attention to how well they work with other things the organization is doing. IBM has grown its staff in India much faster than other international competitors (such as Accenture) that have begun to emphasize India-based arbitrage. But quickly molding this work force into an efficient organization with high delivery standards and a sense of connection to the parent company is a critical challenge: failure in this regard might even be fatal to the arbitrage initiative. Companies should also *employ multiple integration mechanisms.* Pursuit of more than one of the "A"s requires creativity and breadth in thinking about integration mechanisms. Companies should also *think about externalizing integration.* Not all the integration that is required to add value across borders needs to occur within a single organization. IBM and other firms have shown that some externalization can be achieved in a number of ways: joint ventures in advanced semiconductor research, development, and manufacturing; links to, and support of, Linux and other efforts at open innovation; (some) outsourcing of hardware to contract manufacturers and services to business partners; IBM's relationship with Lenovo in personal computers; and customer relationships governed by memoranda of understanding rather than detailed contracts. Finally, companies should *know when not to integrate.* Some integration is always a good idea, but that is not to say that more integration is always better.

Points to Remember

1. There are three generic strategies for creating value in a global context: *adaptation, aggregation,* and *arbitrage.*

2. *Adaptation* strategies seek to increase revenues and market share by tailoring one or more components of a company's business model to suit local requirements or preferences. *Aggregation* strategies focus on achieving economies of scale or scope by creating regional or global efficiencies. These strategies typically involve standardizing a significant portion of the value proposition and grouping together development and production processes. *Arbitrage* is about exploiting economic or other differences between national or regional markets, usually by locating separate parts of the supply chain in different places.

3. Adaptation strategies can be subdivided into five categories: *variation, focus, externalization, design,* and *innovation.*

4. Aggregation strategies revolve around generating *economies of scale or scope.* The other nongeographic dimensions of the CAGE framework introduced in Chapter 1—*cultural, administrative, geographic,* and *economic*—also lend themselves to aggregation strategies.

5. Since arbitrage focuses on exploiting differences between regions, the CAGE framework also defines a set of substrategies for this generic approach to global value creation.

6. A company's financial statements can be a useful guide for signaling which of the "A" strategies will have the greatest potential to create global value.

7. Although most companies will focus on just one "A" at any given time, leading-edge companies such as GE, P&G, IBM, and Nestlé,

to name a few, have embarked on implementing two, or even all three, of the "A"s.

8. There are serious constraints on the ability of any one company to simultaneously use all three "A"s with great effectiveness. Such attempts stretch a firm's managerial bandwidth, force a company to operate with multiple corporate cultures, and can present competitors with opportunities to undercut a company's overall competitiveness.

9. Most companies would be wise to (a) focus on one or two of the "A"s, (b) make sure the new elements of a strategy are a good fit organizationally, (c) employ multiple integration mechanisms, (d) think about externalizing integration, and (e) know when not to integrate.

CHAPTER 4

Global Strategy as Business Model Change

Every company has a *core (domestic) strategy*, although it may not always be explicitly articulated. This strategy most likely evolved over time as the company rose to prominence in its domestic market and reflects key choices about what value it provides to whom and how, and at what price and cost. At any point in time, these choices are reflected in the company's primary *business model*, a conceptual framework that summarizes how a company creates, delivers, and extracts value. A *business model* is therefore simply a description of how a company does business. As shown in Figure 4.1, it describes who its customers are, how it reaches them and relates to them (*market participation*); what a company offers its customers (*the value proposition*); with what resources, activities, and partners it

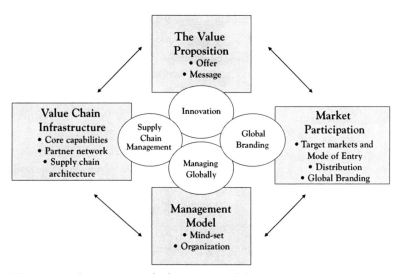

Figure 4.1. Components of a business model.

creates its offerings (*value chain infrastructure*); and, finally, how it organizes and manages its operations (*global management model*).

Components of a Business Model

A company's *value proposition* composes the core of its business model; it includes everything it offers its customers in a specific market or segment. This comprises not only the company's bundles of products and services but also how the company differentiates itself from its competitors. A value proposition therefore consists of the full range of tangible and intangible benefits a company provides to its customers (stakeholders).

The *market participation* dimension of a business model has three components. It describes what specific *markets or segments* a company chooses to serve, domestically or abroad; what methods of distribution it uses to reach its customers; and how it promotes and advertises its value proposition to its target customers.

The *value chain infrastructure* dimension of the business model deals with such questions as, what key *internal resources and capabilities* has the company created to support the chosen value proposition and target markets; what *partner network* has it assembled to support the business model; and how are these activities organized into an overall, coherent value creation and delivery model?

The *global management* submodel summarizes a company's choices about a suitable global organizational structure and management policies. Global organization and management style are closely linked. In companies that are organized primarily around global product divisions, management is often highly centralized. In contrast, companies operating with a more geographic organizational structure are usually managed on a more decentralized basis.

It used to be that each industry was characterized by a single dominant business model. In such a landscape, competitive advantage was won mainly through better execution, more efficient processes, lean organizations, and product innovation. While execution and product innovation obviously still matter, they are no longer sufficient today.

Companies are now operating in industries that are characterized by multiple and coexisting business models. Competitive advantage is increasingly achieved through focused and innovative business models.

Consider the airline, music, telecommunications, or banking industries. In each one, there are different business models competing against each other. In the airline industry, for example, there are the traditional flag carriers, the low-cost airlines, the business-class-only airlines, and the fractional private-jet-ownership companies. Each business model embodies a different approach to achieving a competitive advantage.

Southwest Airlines' business model, for example, can be described as offering customers an alternative to traveling by car, bus, or train by giving them a no-frills flight service, enhanced through complementary activities. Southwest's business model differs from those of other major U.S. airlines along several dimensions. It is about more than low fares, point-to-point connections, and the use of a standardized fleet of aircraft. A key differentiating factor is the way Southwest treats its employees—putting them first with profit-sharing and empowerment programs. Another is the fun experience Southwest creates on board and in the terminal, with jokes, quizzes, and the relaxed behavior of the cabin crew and ground staff. Yet another is the legendary care and attention Southwest puts into its customer service. Not surprisingly, Southwest's demonstrably successful business model has spawned numerous imitators around the world, including Ryanair, EasyJet, JetBlue, and Air Arabia.

Apple provides an example of why it is useful to focus on a company's overall business model rather than individual components such as products, markets, or suppliers. While it is tempting to think of the iPod as a successful product, it is, in fact, much more. Less visible than redefining the size, look, and functionality of an MP3 player, Apple's real innovation was creating a digital rights management system that could satisfy the intellectual property concerns of the music industry while simultaneously creating a legal music download service that would satisfy consumers. Thus, Apple's real breakthrough was not good product design, it was the creation of a revolutionary business model—one that allowed people to find and legally download high-quality music files extremely easily but that would not allow the pirating of entire albums. Put differently, the iPod was the front-end of a very smart and highly differentiated platform that worked for both the music industry and the consumer. That platform, the iTunes Music Store—which now also offers digital music videos, television shows, iPod games, and feature-length movies—is at the very heart of Apple's strategic move into consumer electronics, allowing more recent Apple products like the iPhone and Apple TV to sync with PCs as easily as the iPod. In fact, iTunes is the trojan horse with which Apple plans to capture a significant share of the home entertainment market.

Describing a company's business strategy in terms of its business model allows explicit consideration of the logic or architecture of each component and its relationship to others as a set of designed *choices* that can be changed. Thus, thinking holistically about every component of the business model—and systematically challenging orthodoxies within these components—significantly extends the scope for innovation and improves the chances of building a sustainable competitive advantage.

Global Strategy as Business Model Change

When a company decides to expand into foreign markets, it must take its business model apart and consider the impact of global expansion on every single component of the model. For example, with respect to its value proposition, a company must decide whether or not to modify its company's core strategy as it moves into new markets. This decision is intimately linked to a choice of what markets or regions to enter and why. Once decisions have been made about the *what* (the value proposition) and *where* (market coverage) of global expansion, choices need to be made about the *how*—whether or not to adapt products and services to local needs and preferences or standardize them for global competitive advantage; whether or not to adopt a uniform market positioning worldwide; which value-adding activities to keep in-house, which to outsource, and which to relocate to other parts of the world—and so on. Finally, decisions need to be made about how to organize and manage these efforts on a global basis. Together, these decisions define a company's global strategic focus on a continuum from a truly global orientation to a more local one. *Crafting a global strategy therefore is about deciding how a company should change or adapt its core (domestic) business model to achieve a competitive advantage as the firm globalizes its operations.*

Linking Pankaj Ghemawat's *generic strategy framework* for creating a global competitive advantage, introduced in the Chapter 3, with the above *business model* concept and the full array of *globalization decisions* a company faces when it evaluates its global options, defines the global strategy formulation (conceptual) framework shown in Figure 4.2. Generic value creation options need to be evaluated for each business model component to address a range of globalization decisions.

Part 2 of this book is organized using this framework, with chapters devoted to the globalization of the different parts of the business model or the skills needed to do so. Before we embark on this journey, the balance of this chapter is devoted to introducing the concept of *value disciplines*—generic strategic foci for creating value for customers and the key in defining a company's value proposition—and its implications for the other components of the business model.

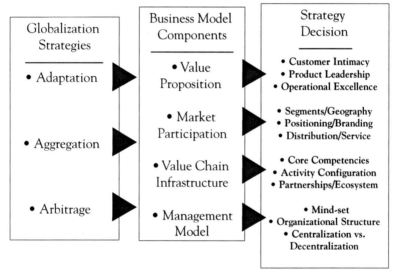

Figure 4.2. Global strategy: A conceptual framework.

Minicase 4.1. Microsoft in China[1]

Consider the challenges Microsoft faced in going to China. Today, Bill Gates is a local hero. On a recent visit he met with four members of the Politburo in a single day; most executives would count themselves lucky to talk with one of China's top leaders. Last spring, President Hu Jintao toured the Microsoft campus in Redmond, Washington, and was treated to a dinner at Gates's home.

It has not always been this way. Microsoft stumbled for years after entering China in 1992 and lost money there for over a decade. It finally became apparent that almost none of the success factors that drove the company's performance in the United States and Europe applied to China. To succeed there, Microsoft had to become the "un-Microsoft," pricing at rock bottom instead of charging hundreds of dollars for its Windows operating system and Microsoft Office applications; abandoning the public-policy strategy it used elsewhere of protecting its intellectual property at all costs; and closely partnering with the government instead of fighting it, as in the United States—a decision that has opened the company to criticism from human rights groups.

The story begins 15 years ago, when Microsoft sent a couple of sales managers into China from Taiwan. Their mission was to sell software at the same prices the company charged elsewhere. It did not work. The problem was not brand acceptance—everyone was using Windows. But no one was paying. Counterfeit copies could be bought on the street for a few dollars. Market share simply did not translate into revenue.

Microsoft fought bitterly to protect its intellectual property. It sued other companies for illegally using its software but lost regularly in court. Country managers came and went—five in one 5-year period. Two of them later wrote books criticizing the company. One, Juliet Wu, whose *Up Against the Wind* became a local best seller, wrote that Microsoft heartlessly sought sales by any means, that its antipiracy policy was needlessly heavy-handed, and that her own efforts to help bosses in Redmond understand China had been rebuffed.

To add insult to injury, Beijing's city government started installing free open-source Linux operating systems on workers' PCs. (The Chinese Academy of Sciences promoted a version called Red Flag Linux.) Meanwhile, security officials were troubled that government and military operations depended on Microsoft software made in the United States.

In 1999, Gates sent a senior executive, who headed the company's public-policy efforts, to figure out why Microsoft was so hated. After extensive investigation, the executive concluded that Microsoft's business model in China was wrong: the company had assigned executives that were too junior, selling was overemphasized, and the company's business practices did not recognize the importance of collaborating with the government.

In response, Gates sent 25 of Microsoft's 100 vice presidents on a weeklong "China Immersion Tour." The company hired former Secretary of State Henry Kissinger for advice and to open doors. And it told leaders that Microsoft wanted to help China develop its own software industry, an urgent government priority. The company even commissioned a McKinsey study for Chinese officials in 2001 that, among other things, recommended improving the protection of intellectual property.

The company also initiated talks with Chinese security officials to convince them that Microsoft's software was not a secret tool of the U.S. government. As a result, in 2003, the company offered China and 59 other countries the right to look at the fundamental source code for its Windows operating system and to substitute certain portions with their own software—something Microsoft had never allowed in the past. Now when China uses Windows in sensitive applications—such as in the president's office and in its missile systems—it can install its own cryptography.

The opening of a research center in Beijing in 1998 proved to be a real turning point. Created because Gates was impressed with the quality of the country's computer scientists, the laboratory helped Microsoft revamp its image. It began accumulating an impressive record of academic publications, helped lure back smart émigré scientists, and contributed key components to globally released products like the Vista operating system. The lab soon became, according to local polls, the most desirable place in the country for computer scientists to work.

Microsoft executives had also concluded that China's weak intellectual property enforcement laws meant its usual pricing strategies were doomed to fail. Arguing that while it was terrible that people in China pirated so much software, Gates decided that if they were going to pirate anybody's software, he would certainly prefer it be Microsoft's.

In hindsight, it is clear that tolerating piracy turned out to be Microsoft's best long-term strategy, and that it is the reason Windows is used on an estimated 90% of China's almost 200 million PCs. Competing with Linux is easier when there is piracy than when there is not: you can get the real thing, and you get it at the same price. In China's back alleys, Linux often costs more than Windows because it requires more disks. And Microsoft's own prices have dropped so low, it now sells a $3 package of Windows and Office to students.

In 2003, Microsoft took a quantum leap forward in China by hiring Tim Chen, who had been running Motorola's China subsidiary. Chen arrived with entrée to the corridors of power and a practiced understanding of how a Western company could succeed in China. He kept up the blitz of initiatives. Microsoft made Shanghai a global center to respond to customer e-mails. It began extensive training programs for teachers and software entrepreneurs. And it began to work with the ministry of education to finance 100 model computer classrooms in rural areas.

These actions served to change the perception that Microsoft had mainly come to promote antipiracy and to sue people and demonstrated that it had a long-term vision. In the following years, Microsoft invested substantially in China and even invited officials to help decide in which local software and outsourcing companies it should invest. By doing so, it successfully leveraged the synergy that existed between the need of the Chinese economy to have local software capability and the company's need for an ecosystem of companies using its technology and platform. At the same time, the Chinese government started thinking more like Microsoft: it required central, provincial, and local governments to begin using legal software. The city of Beijing now pays for software its employees had previously pirated.

In another boost for Microsoft, last year, the government required local PC manufacturers to load legal software on their computers. Lenovo, the market leader, had been shipping as few as 10% of its PCs that way, and even U.S. PC makers in China were selling many machines "naked." Another mandate requires gradual legalization of the millions of computers in state-owned enterprises. As a consequence, the number of new machines shipped with legal software nationwide has risen from about 20% to more than 50% in recent years.

Value Disciplines and Business Models

A business model—and a company's principal value proposition in particular—is shaped by the firm's underlying value creation strategy or *value discipline*, a term coined by Michael Treacy and Fred Wiersema to describe different ways companies can differentiate itself from competitors.[2] A value discipline is more than just a benefit statement—it is a statement of strategic focus and provides a context for a company to set its corporate vision and objectives, to target its most profitable customers, and to focus and align its activities.

In contrast to more traditional market segmentation strategies, which group customers by geography, product mix, or demographics, value disciplines segment customers according to the full range of benefits that are most valuable to them. Specifically, Treacy and Wiersema identify three generic value disciplines: *operational excellence, customer intimacy*, and *product leadership*.

A strategy of *operational excellence* is defined by a relentless focus on providing customers with reliable products or services at competitive prices and delivered with minimal difficulty or inconvenience. Dell Inc., for instance, is a master of operational excellence. Dell has shown buyers of electronics that they do not have to sacrifice quality or state-of-the-art technology in order to buy PCs, printers, or other products easily and inexpensively. By selling to customers directly, building to order rather than to inventory, and creating a disciplined, extremely low-cost culture, Dell has been able to undercut its competitors in price yet provide high-quality products and service. Other leaders in operational excellence include Wal-Mart, Jet Blue, ING bank, and Federal Express.

Companies pursuing operational excellence are relentless in seeking ways to minimize overhead costs, to eliminate intermediate production steps, to reduce transaction and other "friction" costs, and to optimize business processes across functional and organizational boundaries. They focus on delivering their products or services to customers at competitive prices and with minimal inconvenience. Because they build their entire businesses around these goals, these organizations do not look or operate like other companies pursuing other value disciplines.

An operationally excellent company proactively designs its entire business model for its targeted customer segments, paying particular attention to speed, efficiency, and cost. This includes critically reevaluating business processes, reassessing the complete supply chain, and reaching out to suppliers, distributors, and customers to create a larger, more integrated approach to meeting customer needs.

Achieving market leadership through operational excellence requires the development of a business model that pervades the entire organization. Thus, becoming operationally excellent is a challenge not just for the manufacturing department but for the entire company. And while operationally excellent companies are focused on cost and efficiency, they are not necessarily the lowest cost producer or supplier. The notion that an operationally excellent company is fixated on costs and cost cutting, has a rigid command and control organization, and is focused on plant and internal efficiencies is a limited view that seriously misstates the intent and goals of operational excellence.

Minicase 4.2. Air Arabia Leads the World in Operational Excellence[3]

In April of 2009, Air Arabia, the first and largest low-cost carrier (LCC) in the Middle East and North Africa, announced that it was recognized by Airbus, one of the world's leading aircraft manufacturers, for achieving the highest operational utilization in the world. This is the fourth consecutive year that Air Arabia maintained the lead among all global airlines operating Airbus A320 aircraft. According to the latest reports from Airbus, Air Arabia achieved the highest aircraft utilization in 2008, with 99.8% operational reliability.

Operational excellence and service reliability are integral to Air Arabia's success. In selecting Air Arabia for its operational excellence rankings, Airbus conducted a detailed technical analysis of all carriers in the segment. Air Arabia recorded the highest indicators for operational reliability and aircraft utilization reflecting the carrier's extremely high maintenance and technical standards.

Currently, Air Arabia has a fleet of 16 Airbus A320 aircraft and has already placed an order of 44 additional Airbus A320s. By the end of 2009, Air Arabia expected to add two more aircraft and increase its fleet size to 18.

Air Arabia (PJSC), listed on the Dubai Financial Market, is the Middle East and North Africa's leading low-cost carrier. Air Arabia commenced operations in October 2003 and currently operates a fleet of 16 new Airbus A320 aircraft, currently serving 44 destinations across the Middle East, North Africa, South Asia, and Central Asia through its main hub in Sharjah, United Arab Emirates.

Air Arabia is modeled after leading American and European low-cost airlines, and its business model is customized to accommodate local preferences. Its main focus is to make air travel more convenient through Internet bookings and through offering the lowest fares in the market along with the highest levels of safety and service standards.

A focus on *customer intimacy*, the second value discipline, means segmenting and targeting markets precisely and then tailoring offerings to exactly match the demands of those niches. Companies that excel in customer intimacy combine detailed customer knowledge with operational flexibility so they can respond quickly to almost any need, from customizing a product to fulfilling special requests. As a consequence, these companies engender tremendous customer loyalty. Nordstrom, the department store, for example, is better than any other company in its market of customer service and getting the customer precisely the product or information he or she wants.

While companies pursuing operational excellence concentrate on the operational side of their business models, those pursuing a strategy of customer intimacy continually tailor and shape products and services to fit an increasingly fine definition of the customer. This can be expensive, but customer-intimate companies are willing to take a long-term perspective and invest to build lasting customer loyalty. They typically look at the customer's lifetime value to the company, not the value of any single transaction. This is why employees in these companies will do almost anything—with little regard for initial cost—to make sure that each customer gets exactly what he or she really wants. Nordstrom is a good example of such a company. A few years ago, Home Depot was known for its customer intimacy; more recently, however, it has strayed from this strategic focus.

Customer-intimate companies understand the difference between profit or loss on a single transaction and profit over the lifetime of their relationship with a single customer. Most companies know, for instance, that not all customers require the same level of service or will generate the same revenues. Profitability, then, depends in part on maintaining a system that can identify, quickly and accurately, which customers require what level of service and how much revenue they are likely to generate. Sophisticated companies now routinely use a telephone-computer system capable of recognizing individual customers by their telephone numbers when they call. Such systems allow differential levels of service for different customer groups. Clients with large accounts and frequent transactions are routed to their own senior account representative; those who typically place only an occasional order are referred to a more junior employee or a call center. In either case, the customer's file appears on the representative's screen before the phone is answered. What is more, such a system allows the company to direct specific value-added services or products to specific groups of clients.

Some years ago, Kraft USA decided to strengthen its focus on customer intimacy and created the capacity to tailor its advertising, merchandising, and operations in a single store, or in several stores within a supermarket chain, to the needs of those stores' particular customers. To do so, it had to develop new information systems and analytical capabilities and educate its sales force to create multiple, so-called micromerchandising programs for a chain that carries its products. In other words,

Kraft first had to change itself: it had to create the organization, build the information systems, and educate and motivate the people required to pursue a strategy of customer intimacy.

Like most companies that pursue customer intimacy, Kraft decentralized its marketing operations in order to empower the people actually dealing with the customer. Today, Kraft salespeople are trained and rewarded to work with individual store managers and regional managers to create customized promotional programs. To do so, the company gives them the data they need to make recommendations to store managers and to shape promotional programs such as consumer purchases by store, category, and product and their response to past price and other promotions. At corporate headquarters, Kraft trade marketing teams sort and integrate information from multiple sources to supply the sales force with a menu of programs, products, value-added ideas, and selling tools. For instance, the trade marketing team sorted all shoppers into six distinct groups, with names such as "full-margin shoppers," "planners and dine-outs," and "commodity shoppers."

Minicase 4.3. Customer Intimacy at the Four Seasons[4]

Isadore Sharp, one of four children of Polish parents who immigrated to Toronto before his birth in 1931, opened his first hotel—the Four Seasons Motor Hotel—in 1961 with 125 affordable rooms in a rather seedy area outside the core of downtown Toronto.

At that time, a would-be hotelier had two choices. He could build a small motel with fewer than 200 rooms and simple amenities at relatively low cost. The alternative was a large downtown hotel catering to business travelers. Such hotels usually had at least 750 guest rooms and extensive amenities, including conference facilities, multiple restaurants, and banquet rooms. Each type of hotel had its advantages as well as distinct drawbacks. For all its comfort and intimacy, the small motel was not an option for the business traveler who needed a well-appointed meeting room or state-of-the-art communications facilities. Large hotels produced a big enough pool of revenues to fund the features the market demanded but tended to be cold and impersonal.

But after opening his fourth hotel, Sharp decided to experiment and combine the best of the small hotel with the best of the large hotel. He envisioned a medium-sized hotel, big enough to afford an extensive array of amenities but small enough to maintain a sense of intimacy and personalized service. Sharp reasoned that if the Four Seasons offered distinctly better service than its competitors, it could charge a substantial premium, boosting revenue per room to the point where it could offer top-of-the-line amenities. Before he could ask guests to pay a superpremium room rate, though, Sharp understood that he would have to offer them an entirely different kind of service.

Luxury, at that time, was chiefly defined in terms of architecture and décor. Sharp decided to redefine luxury as service—a support system to fill in for the one left at home and the office. Four Seasons became the first to offer shampoo in the shower; 24-hour room service; bathrobes; cleaning and pressing; a two-line phone in every guest room; a big, well-lighted desk; and 24-hour secretarial services. Defying the traditional approach in the industry, which was to set a relatively fixed standard of physical and service quality across the entire chain, Sharp made sure each city's Four Seasons reflected the local color and culture.

To free up capital and focus its senior management on providing service rather than managing real estate and financing, Four Seasons also became the first big hotel company to manage, rather than own, the hotel facilities that bore its name.

Redefining the way it treated its own employees also helped sharpen Four Seasons' customer focus. Rather than treating its employees as disposable, Four Seasons distinguished itself by hiring more for attitude than experience, by establishing career paths and promotion from within, and by paying as much attention to employee concerns as guest complaints. It pushed responsibility down and encouraged self-discipline by setting high performance standards and holding people accountable, adhering to the company's credo, "generating trust." Significantly, Four Seasons has no separate customer service department. Each employee at the Four

Seasons is not just a member of the customer service department but is in charge of it.

Today, with 73 hotels in 31 countries, and with 25 properties under development, Four Seasons is considerably larger than the next biggest luxury player. Condé Nast Traveler ranks 18 Four Seasons hotels in its global "Top 100" list, more than 3 times the next most-cited chain. A Four Seasons signifies that a city has become a global destination.

Finally, *product leadership*, the third discipline, means offering customers leading-edge products and services that consistently enhance the customer's use or application of the product, thereby making rivals' goods obsolete. Companies that pursue product leadership are innovation-driven, and they constantly raise the bar for competitors by offering more value and better solutions. Product leaders work with three basic principles. First, they focus on creativity; constant innovation is the key to their success. They look for new ideas inside as well as outside the company, have an "experimentation is good" mind-set, and reward risk taking. Second, they know that in order to be successful, they must be fast in capitalizing on new ideas; they know how to commercialize new ideas quickly. To do so, all their business and management processes have to be engineered for speed. Third, product leaders must relentlessly pursue new solutions to the problems that their own latest product or service has just solved. In other words, if anyone is going to render their technology obsolete, they prefer to do it themselves.

Examples of companies that use product leadership as a cornerstone of their strategies include BMW, Intel, Apple, and Nike. These companies have created and maintain a culture that encourages employees to bring ideas into the company and, just as important, they listen to and consider these ideas, however unconventional and regardless of the source. In addition, product leaders continually scan the landscape for new product or service possibilities; where others see glitches in their marketing plans or threats to their product lines, companies that focus on product leadership see opportunity and rush to capitalize on it.

Product leaders avoid bureaucracy at all costs because it slows commercialization of their ideas. Managers make decisions quickly since, in a product leadership company, it is often better to make a wrong decision than to make a late or not at all. That is why these companies are prepared to decide today, then implement tomorrow. Moreover, they continually look for new ways—such as concurrent engineering—to shorten their cycle times. Japanese companies, for example, succeed in automobile innovation because they use concurrent development processes to reduce time to market. They do not have to aim better than competitors to score more hits on the target because they can take more shots from a closer distance.

Product leaders are their own fiercest competitors. They continually cross a frontier, then break more new ground. They have to be adept at rendering obsolete the products and services that they have created because they realize that if they do not develop a successor, another company will. Apple and other innovators are willing to take the long view of profitability, recognizing that whether they extract the full profit potential from an existing product or service is less important to the company's future than maintaining its product leadership edge and momentum. These companies are never blinded by their own successes.

Finally, product leaders also possess the infrastructure and management systems needed to manage risk well. For example, each time Apple ventures into an untapped area, it risks millions of dollars as well as its reputation. It takes that chance, though, in part because its hybrid structure allows it to combine the economies of scale and resource advantages of a multibillion-dollar corporation with the cultural characteristics of a startup company.

Figure 4.3 depicts *strategic focus* in terms of the three value disciplines discussed here and summarizes how each responds to a particular set of competitive drivers and customer needs.

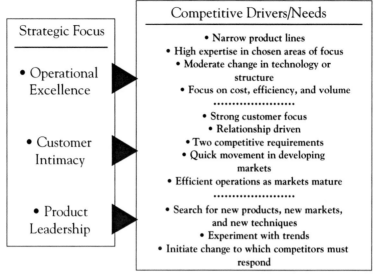

Figure 4.3. Choosing a value proposition: Value disciplines.

Minicase 4.4. How Apple Maintains Product Leadership[5]

How does Apple consistently redefine each market it enters by creating products that leapfrog the competition? First, it takes *clarity of purpose and resolve*: it may take years to cultivate new skills and build the right new product. Second, a significant *investment in infrastructure is required*: for example, Apple supports a dedicated innovation team. Third, consistently redefining markets requires *strategic clarity*: innovating effectively means creating your own opportunities in a crowded marketplace to avoid both mediocrity and commoditization. Fourth, *patience is essential*: creativity does not always follow the clock. False starts and the occasional flop are part of the process and must not only be tolerated but be sources of learning. Fifth, *strong leadership is a prerequisite*: innovation does not happen by committee. Visionaries with effective management skills are hard to find, but they are a critical ingredient for success.

Clarity of Purpose and Resolve

Apple's company motto, "Think Different," provides a hint at how Apple maintains focus and its introspective, self-contained operating style that is capable of confounding competitors and shaking up entire industries. Internally, Apple barely acknowledges competition. It is the company's ability to think differently about itself that keeps Apple at the head of the pack. Current and past employees tell stories about products that have undergone costly overhauls just to improve one simple detail. Other products are canceled entirely because they do not fit in or do not perform up to par. Apple's culture has codified a habit that is good for any company to have but is especially valuable for firms that make physical things: stop, step back from your product, and take a closer look. Without worrying about how much work you have already put into it, is it really as good as it could be? Apple constantly asks that question.

Infrastructure Investment

From the outside, Apple's offices look like those of just about any large modern American corporation. Having outgrown its headquarters campus in Cupertino, California, Apple now has employees in other buildings scattered across the town and around the world. Size and sprawl are formidable challenges that most companies do not manage very well, either by splintering into disorganized, undisciplined communities or by locking employees into tight, stifling bureaucracies. Apple tends toward the latter, but it does so in a unique way that generally (but not always) plays to its advantage. At its worst, Apple's culture is characterized by paranoia: employees are notoriously secretive and continuously fear being fired or sued for speaking to anyone outside the company. This obsession with secrecy does give Apple an element of surprise in the marketplace. But this comes at a high cost. Apple's corporate culture came under scrutiny recently after an employee of a foreign supplier—reportedly under suspicion for leaking the prototype of a new iPhone—committed suicide in Shenzhen, China.

Beyond the secrecy, which affects everyone, Apple's approach is hardly one-size-fits-all. Rank-and-file employees are often given clear-cut directives and close supervision. Proven talent gets a freer hand, regardless of job title.

Strategic Clarity

Over time, Apple has built a seasoned management team to support bold new product initiatives. The team's guiding principles include the following:

1. *Ignore fads.* Apple held off building a cheap miniature laptop to respond to the "netbook" fad because these devices do not offer good margins. Instead, it released the ultrathin, ultraexpensive Air, a product more in line with its own style.
2. *Do not back down from fights you can win.* Apple is a tough partner and a ruthless enemy. In 2007, Apple pulled NBC's television programs from the iTunes Store after the network tried to double the prices consumers pay to download shows. NBC backed down within days, and, ever since, giant media conglomerates have been hesitant to face off with Apple over pricing.
3. *Flatten sprawling hierarchies.* Companies with extended chains of authority tend to plod when it is time to act. Most of the decisions at Apple come from its chief executive officer, Steve Jobs, and his immediate deputies.
4. *Pay less attention to market research and competitors.* Most firms develop their products based on information obtained from consumer focus groups and imitation of successful products from other companies. Apple does neither, as the iPod and iPhone clearly demonstrate.
5. *Empower your most valuable employees to do amazing work.* Apple takes meticulous care of a specific group of employees known as the "creatives." Its segmented, stratified organizational structure—which protects and coddles its most valuable, productive employees—is one of the company's most formidable assets. One example is Apple's Industrial Design Group (IDG), the

team that gives Apple products their distinctive, glossy look. Tucked away within Apple's main campus, the IDG is a world unto itself. It is also sealed behind unmarked, restricted-access doors. Within the IDG, employees operate free from outside distractions and interference. But despite their favored status, Apple's creatives still have no more insight into the company's overall operations than an army private has into the Pentagon. At Apple, new products are often seen in their complete form by only a small group of top executives. This, too, works as a strength for Apple: instead of a sprawling bureaucracy that new products have to be pushed through, Apple's top echelon is a small, tightly knit group that has a hand in almost every important decision the company makes.

Patience

Apple's corporate culture is different because the company dances to a rhythm of its own making. Although its rising stock has become a vital part of many portfolios, Apple cancels, releases, and updates products at its own speed, seemingly irrespective of market conditions or competitive pressure. Apple does not telegraph its moves, either: the iPod and iPhone, both iconic products, each began as rumors that Apple seemed determined to quash.

Strong Leadership

New adherents to the cult of Steve Jobs may be surprised to hear this: the most iconic Apple laptop, the original PowerBook, was released in 1991 after Jobs had been absent for 6 years. Jobs was not responsible for this enduring innovation. So does that mean Steve Jobs is irrelevant? Or is Jobs—and his maniacal focus on building insanely great products—a necessary ingredient of Apple's success? It is said that great leaders are made by their circumstances and that their great deeds actually reflect the participation of thousands, or even millions, of people. In the case of Apple, there would be no Mac, no iPod, and no iPhone without the efforts of thousands of engineers and vast numbers of consumers who were looking for products that better served their needs. That said, Jobs is an imposing figure, and if he was "made" by his circumstances, that process took many years. Remember that the first edition of Steve Jobs—the young inventor who, at 21, created Apple Computer—was not the visionary we know today. Instead, after 9 years at Apple's helm, the young Steve Jobs was ousted because of his aggressive, take-no-prisoners personality, which created a poisonous, unproductive atmosphere when it pervaded the company.

Today's Steve Jobs seems to have learned how to focus that aggressive, take-no-prisoners personality more shrewdly and to great effect. While he is still an essential part of Apple's success, the company has also institutionalized many of Jobs' values to such an extent that Apple is now far less dependent on him. Tim Cook, for example, functioned effectively as acting CEO when Jobs was on sick leave recently. But questions remain. So long as the overwhelming personality of Jobs is present, can anyone really grow into that position? Only when Jobs permanently steps back from his role will we really be able to determine how well Apple has learned the lessons he has taught.

Choosing a Value Discipline or Selecting a Target Market?

Choosing a value discipline and selecting a particular set of customers to serve are two sides of the same coin. Customers seeking *operational excellence* define value on the basis of price, convenience, and quality, with price the dominant factor. They are less particular about what they buy than they are about getting it at the lowest possible price and with the least possible hassle. They are unwilling to sacrifice low price or high convenience to acquire a product with a particular label or to obtain a premium service. Whether they are consumers or industrial buyers, they want high quality goods and services, but, even more, they want to get them cheaply or easily or both. These customers like to shop for retail goods at discount and membership warehouse stores, and they are comfortable buying directly from manufacturers. When they buy a car, they seek basic transportation, and when they buy or sell stocks, they use discount brokers.

Consumers seeking *customer intimacy* are far more concerned with obtaining precisely what they want or need. The specific features and benefits of the product or the way the service is delivered are far more important to them than any reasonable price premium or purchase inconvenience they might incur. Chain stores—whether in the food, book, or music business—that customize their inventories to match regional or even neighborhood tastes serve this category of customer. Other retailers and catalogers attract this customer type by offering the largest imaginable range of products. They typically do not carry just one version of a product or a single brand but many versions or multiple brands.

Finally, customers attuned to *product leadership* crave new, different, and unusual products. As clothing buyers, they are primarily interested in fashion and trends. In an industrial context, they are buyers who value state-of-the-art products or components because their own customers demand the latest technology from them. If they are service companies, they want suppliers that help them seize breakthrough opportunities in their own markets. They also like to be the first to adopt new technologies, whether BlackBerrys, new cell phones, or large flat-screen TVs.

Market Leadership and Value Disciplines

The research by Treacy and Wiersema revealed that companies that push the boundaries of one value discipline while meeting industry standards in the other two often gain a significant lead—one that competitors have difficulty overcoming.[6] A key reason is that value-discipline leaders do not just tailor their products and services to their customers' preferences but align *their entire business model* to serve a chosen value discipline. This makes it much harder for competitors to copy them, thus providing them with a more enduring competitive advantage.

Companies in different industries that pursue the same value discipline share many characteristics. The business models of Federal Express, Southwest Airlines, and Wal-Mart, for example, are notably similar because they all pursue operational excellence. Someone working at FedEx, therefore, would likely be very comfortable at Wal-Mart, and vice versa. Similarly, the systems, structures, and cultures of product leaders such as Apple in electronics, Johnson & Johnson in health care and pharmaceuticals, and Nike in sport shoes have a great deal in common. But across disciplines, the similarities end. Employees from Wal-Mart do not fit well with the value propositions, management styles, and cultures at Nike or Nordstrom.

When a company decides to go global and is faced with the challenge of adapting its business model to the needs of a foreign market, a key question is how easily the underlying value discipline "travels" or whether the company has to embrace a different strategic focus to succeed. Adapting a business model within a particular value discipline at which the company excels is decidedly easier than creating a new business model based on another value discipline that the company has not previously focused on, as the following minicase attests to.

Minicase 4.5. Dell in Asia: Adapt or Change? [7]

From direct sales to retail and staid designs to sexy, Dell is speeding up its reinvention drive in Asia, with the region now earmarked as its bellwether for computer sales worldwide. The company considers countries such as China still "underdeveloped" information technology (IT) markets that offer ample opportunity for growth. To tap into this sales potential, the company is shedding some of the attributes that have defined its modus operandi in the past two decades. Dell has traditionally designed its business around selling to larger corporations, but it is diversifying to leverage Asia's exploding PC user base.

First, the pioneer of direct selling by phone and over the Internet has struck retail agreements across the region, including tie-ups with electronics mega stores such as Gome in China and Courts in Singapore and a partnership with Tata Croma in India. The channel push is crucial to the company's attempt to catch up in the cutthroat regional consumer and small and midsized business markets where Hewlett-Packard (HP) and Lenovo have long had a retail presence.

Second, to create a following, the company is supplementing its retail push with a radical shift in product design that now focuses on form as opposed to the functional and low-cost attributes that Dell has typically emphasized. For example, the firm is selling selected Dell laptops with an unusual color palette of blue, pink, and red. Soon, the company will even allow customers to print their own photos and pictures onto its notebooks. Beyond hardware and aesthetic components, Dell also allows consumers to personalize the content of their PCs, including the preloading of popular movies on selected products.

And third, while Dell previously relied on Asian companies primarily for manufacturing, it is increasingly using the region for higher-value activities such as product design. Four out of five of its new global design centers are based in the region. Its Singapore facility focuses on the company's imaging portfolio of monitors, televisions, and printers; its Bangalore counterpart is responsible for software development and enterprise solutions; the company's Taiwan design centre focuses on laptop and server development; and its China unit concentrates on developing desktop systems and PC-related services.

Points to Remember

1. Every company has a *core (domestic) strategy*, although it may not always be explicitly articulated.
2. A *business model* is therefore simply a description of how a company does business. It describes who its customers are and how it reaches them and relates to them (*market participation*); what a company offers its customers (*the value proposition*); with what resources, activities, and partners it creates its offerings (*value chain infrastructure*); and, finally, how it organizes its operations (*implementation model*).
3. Competitive advantage is increasingly achieved through focused and innovative business models.

4. Crafting a global strategy is about deciding how a company should change or adapt its core (domestic) business model to achieve a competitive advantage as the firm globalizes its operations.

5. A business model is shaped by a company's underlying value creation strategy or *value discipline*. A value discipline is a statement of strategic focus and provides a context for a company to set its corporate vision and objectives, to target its most profitable customers, and to focus and align its activities.

6. Three generic value disciplines are *operational excellence, customer intimacy,* and *product leadership*. A strategy of *operational excellence* is defined by a relentless focus on providing customers with reliable products or services at competitive prices and delivered with minimal difficulty or inconvenience. A focus on *customer intimacy*, the second value discipline, means segmenting and targeting markets precisely and then tailoring offerings to match exactly the demands of those niches. And *product leadership*, the third discipline, means offering customers leading-edge products and services that consistently enhance the customer's use or application of the product, thereby making rivals' goods obsolete.

7. Choosing a value discipline and selecting a particular set of customers to serve are two sides of the same coin.

8. Companies that push the boundaries of one value discipline while meeting industry standards in the other two often gain a significant lead—one that competitors have difficulty overcoming.

PART II

Globalizing the Business Model

Part II, Globalizing the Business Model, consists of six chapters:

Chapter 5 looks at decisions regarding which foreign markets to enter why, when, and how. In other words, the chapter is about target market selection and the timing and mode of market entry.

Chapter 6 discusses the globalization of the company's core offerings and introduces the concept of a value proposition globalization matrix to guide strategic thinking.

Chapter 7 addresses a related core competency: global branding.

Chapter 8 looks at the globalization of the value chain infrastructure—from R&D to product development to manufacturing to distribution to after-sale service.

Chapter 9 follows with a survey of a closely related core competency: supply chain management.

Chapter 10 rounds out the business model framework by looking at the globalization of a company's management model.

CHAPTER 5

Target Markets and Modes of Entry

Market participation decisions—selecting global target markets, entry modes, and how to communicate with customers all over the world—are intimately related to decisions about how much to adapt the company's basic value proposition. The choice of customers to serve in a particular country or region and with a particular culture determines how and how much a company must adapt its basic value proposition. Conversely, the extent of a company's capabilities to tailor its offerings around the globe limits or broadens its options to successfully enter new markets or cultures. In this chapter, we look at the first two of these decisions: selecting target markets around the world and deciding how best to enter them. In Chapter 6, we introduce a framework for analyzing choices about adapting a company's basic value proposition. In Chapter 7, we take up global branding, one of a company's primary vehicles for communicating with customers all over the world (Figure 5.1).

Target Market Selection

Few companies can afford to enter all markets open to them. Even the world's largest companies such as General Electric or Nestlé must exercise strategic discipline in choosing the markets they serve. They must also decide when to enter them and weigh the relative advantages of a direct or indirect presence in different regions of the world. Small and midsized companies are often constrained to an indirect presence; for them, the key to gaining a global competitive advantage is often creating a worldwide resource network through alliances with suppliers, customers, and, sometimes, competitors. What is a good strategy for one company, however, might have little chance of succeeding for another.

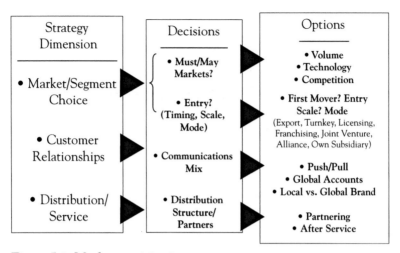

Figure 5.1. Market participation.

The track record shows that picking the most attractive foreign markets, determining the best time to enter them, and selecting the right partners and level of investment has proven difficult for many companies, especially when it involves large emerging markets such as China. For example, it is now generally recognized that Western carmakers entered China far too early and overinvested, believing a "first-mover advantage" would produce superior returns. Reality was very different. Most companies lost large amounts of money, had trouble working with local partners, and saw their technological advantage erode due to "leakage." None achieved the sales volume needed to justify their investment.

Even highly successful global companies often first sustain substantial losses on their overseas ventures, and occasionally have to trim back their foreign operations or even abandon entire countries or regions in the face of ill-timed strategic moves or fast-changing competitive circumstances. Not all of Wal-Mart's global moves have been successful, for example—a continuing source of frustration to investors. In 1999, the company spent $10.8 billion to buy British grocery chain Asda. Not only was Asda healthy and profitable, but it was already positioned as "Wal-Mart lite." Today, Asda is lagging well behind its number-one rival, Tesco. Even though Wal-Mart's UK operations are profitable, sales growth has been down in recent years, and Asda has missed profit targets for several quarters running and is in danger of slipping further in the UK market.

This result comes on top of Wal-Mart's costly exit from the German market. In 2005, it sold its 85 stores there to rival Metro at a loss of $1 billion. Eight years after buying into the highly competitive German market, Wal-Mart executives, accustomed to using Wal-Mart's massive market muscle to squeeze suppliers, admitted they had been unable to attain the economies of scale it needed in Germany to beat rivals' prices, prompting an early and expensive exit.

What makes global market selection and entry so difficult? Research shows there is a pervasive the-grass-is-always-greener effect that infects global strategic decision making in many, especially globally inexperienced, companies and causes them to overestimate the attractiveness of foreign markets.[1] As noted in Chapter 1, "distance," broadly defined, unless well-understood and compensated for, can be a major impediment to global success: cultural differences can lead companies to overestimate the appeal of their products or the strength of their brands; administrative differences can slow expansion plans, reduce the ability to attract the right talent, and increase the cost of doing business; geographic distance impacts the effectiveness of communication and coordination; and economic distance directly influences revenues and costs.

A related issue is that developing a global presence takes time and requires substantial resources. Ideally, the pace of international expansion is dictated by customer demand. Sometimes it is necessary, however, to expand ahead of direct opportunity in order to secure a long-term competitive advantage. But as many companies that entered China in anticipation of its membership in the World Trade Organization have learned, early commitment to even the most promising long-term market makes earning a satisfactory return on invested capital difficult. As a result, an increasing number of firms, particularly smaller and midsized ones, favor global expansion strategies that minimize direct investment. Strategic alliances have made vertical or horizontal integration less important to profitability and shareholder value in many industries. Alliances boost contribution to fixed cost while expanding a company's global reach. At the same time, they can be powerful windows on technology and greatly expand opportunities to create the core competencies needed to effectively compete on a worldwide basis.

Finally, a complicating factor is that a global evaluation of market opportunities requires a multidimensional perspective. In many industries, we can distinguish between *"must"* markets—markets in which a company must compete in order to realize its global ambitions—and *"nice-to-be-in"* markets—markets in which participation is desirable but not critical. "Must" markets include those that are critical from a *volume* perspective, markets that define *technological leadership*, and markets in which key *competitive* battles are played out. In the cell phone industry, for example, Motorola looks to Europe as a primary competitive battleground, but it derives much of its technology from Japan and sales volume from the United States.

Measuring Market Attractiveness

Four key factors in selecting global markets are (a) a *market's size and growth rate*, (b) a particular country or region's *institutional contexts*, (c) a region's *competitive environment*, and (d) a market's *cultural, administrative, geographic*, and *economic distance* from other markets the company serves.

Market Size and Growth Rate

There is no shortage of country information for making market portfolio decisions. A wealth of country-level economic and demographic data are available from a variety of sources including governments, multinational organizations such as the United Nations or the World Bank, and consulting firms specializing in economic intelligence or risk assessment. However, while valuable from an overall investment perspective, such data often reveal little about the prospects for selling products or services in foreign markets to local partners and end users or about the challenges associated with overcoming other elements of distance. Yet many companies still use this information as their primary guide to market assessment simply because country market statistics are readily available, whereas real product market information is often difficult and costly to obtain.

What is more, a country or regional approach to market selection may not always be the best. Even though Theodore Levitt's vision of a global market for uniform products and services has not come to pass, and global strategies exclusively focused on the "economics of simplicity" and the selling of standardized products all over the world rarely pay off, research increasingly supports an alternative "global segmentation" approach to the issue of market selection, especially for branded products. In particular, surveys show that a growing number of consumers, especially in emerging markets, base their consumption decisions on attributes beyond direct product benefits, such as their perception of the global brands behind the offerings.

Specifically, research by John Quelch and others suggests that consumers increasingly evaluate global brands in "cultural" terms and factor three global brand attributes into their purchase decisions: (a) what a global brand signals about quality, (b) what a brand symbolizes in terms of cultural ideals, and (c) what a brand signals about a company's commitment to corporate social responsibility. This creates opportunities for global companies with the right values and the savvy to exploit them to define and develop target markets across geographical boundaries and create strategies for "global segments" of consumers. Specifically, consumers who perceive global brands in the same way appear to fall into one of four groups:

1. *Global citizens* rely on the global success of a company as a signal of quality and innovation. At the same time, they worry whether a company behaves responsibly on issues like consumer health, the environment, and worker rights.
2. *Global dreamers* are less discerning about, but more ardent in their admiration of, transnational companies. They view global brands as quality products and readily buy into the myths they portray. They also are less concerned with companies' social responsibilities than global citizens.
3. *Antiglobals* are skeptical that global companies deliver higher-quality goods. They particularly dislike brands that preach American values and often do not trust global companies to behave responsibly. Given a choice, they prefer to avoid doing business with global firms.
4. *Global agnostics* do not base purchase decisions on a brand's global attributes. Instead, they judge a global product by the same criteria they use for local brands.[2]

Companies that use a "global segment" approach to market selection, such as Coca-Cola, Sony, or Microsoft, to name a few, therefore must manage two dimensions for their brands. They must strive for superiority on basics like the brand's price, performance, features, and imagery, and, at the same time, they must learn to manage brands' global characteristics, which often separate winners from losers. A good example is provided by Samsung, the South Korean electronics maker. In the late 1990s, Samsung launched a global advertising campaign that showed the South Korean giant excelling, time after time, in engineering, design, and aesthetics. By doing so, Samsung convinced consumers that it successfully competed directly with technology leaders across the world, such as Nokia and Sony. As a result, Samsung was able to change the perception that it was a down-market brand, and it became known as a global provider of leading-edge technologies. This brand strategy, in turn, allowed Samsung to use a global segmentation approach to making market selection and entry decisions.

Institutional Contexts[3]

Khanna and others developed a five-dimensional framework to map a particular country or region's institutional contexts. Specifically, they suggest careful analysis of a country's (a) *political and social systems*, (b) *openness*, (c) *product markets*, (d) *labor markets*, and (e) *capital markets*.

A country's political system affects its product, labor, and capital markets. In socialist societies like China, for instance, workers cannot form independent trade unions in the labor market, which affects wage levels. A country's social environment is also important. In South Africa, for example, the government's support for the transfer of assets to the historically disenfranchised native African community has affected the development of the capital market.

The more open a country's economy, the more likely it is that global intermediaries can freely operate there, which helps multinationals function more effectively. From a strategic perspective, however, openness can be a double-edged sword: a government that allows local companies to access the global capital market neutralizes one of the key advantages of foreign companies.

Even though developing countries have opened up their markets and grown rapidly during the past decade, multinational companies struggle to get reliable information about consumers. Market research and advertising are often less sophisticated and, because there are no well-developed consumer courts and advocacy groups in these countries, people can feel they are at the mercy of big companies.

Recruiting local managers and other skilled workers in developing countries can be difficult. The quality of local credentials can be hard to verify, there are relatively few search firms and recruiting agencies, and the high-quality firms that do exist focus on top-level searches, so companies scramble to identify middle-level managers, engineers, or floor supervisors.

Capital and financial markets in developing countries often lack sophistication. Reliable intermediaries like credit-rating agencies, investment analysts, merchant bankers, or venture capital firms may not exist, and multinationals cannot count on raising debt or equity capital locally to finance their operations.

Emerging economies present unique challenges. Capital markets are often relatively inefficient and dependable sources of information, scarce while the cost of capital is high and venture capital is virtually nonexistent. Because of a lack of high-quality educational institutions, labor markets may lack well-trained people requiring companies to fill the void. Because of an underdeveloped communications infrastructure, building a brand name can be difficult just when good brands are highly valued because of lower product quality of the alternatives. Finally, nurturing strong relationships with government officials often is necessary to succeed. Even then, contracts may not be well enforced by the legal system.

Competitive Environment

The number, size, and quality of competitive firms in a particular target market compose a second set of factors that affect a company's ability to successfully enter and compete profitably. While country-level economic and demographic data are widely available for most regions of the world, competitive data are much harder to come by, especially when the principal players are subsidiaries of multinational corporations. As a consequence, competitive analysis in foreign countries, especially in emerging markets, is difficult and costly to perform and its findings do not always provide the level of insight needed to make good decisions. Nevertheless, a comprehensive competitive analysis provides a useful framework for developing strategies for growth and for analyzing current and future primary competitors and their strengths and weaknesses.

Minicase 5.1. Which BRIC Countries?
A Key Challenge for Carmakers[4]

Today, automobile manufacturers face a critical challenge: deciding which BRIC countries (Brazil, Russia, India, and China) to bet on. In each, as per capita income rises, so will per capita car ownership—not in a straight line but in classic "S-curve" fashion. Rates of vehicle ownership stay low during the first phases of economic growth, but as the GDP or purchasing power of a country reaches a level of sustained broad prosperity, and as urbanization reshapes the work patterns of a country, vehicle sales take off. But that is about where the similarities end. Each of the four BRIC nations has a completely different set of market and industry dynamics that make decision choices about which countries to target, including making difficult decisions about which markets to avoid, extremely difficult.

For one thing, vehicle manufacturing is a high-profile industry that generates enormous revenue, employs millions of people, and is often a proxy for a nation's manufacturing prowess and economic influence. Governments are extensively involved in regulating or influencing virtually every aspect of the product and the way the industry operates—including setting emissions and safety standards, licensing distributors, and setting tariffs and rules about how much manufacturing must take place locally. This reality makes the job of understanding each market and appreciating the differences more vital. For example, a summary overview of the BRIC nations reveals the differences among these markets and the operating complexities in all of them.

Brazil, with Russia, is one of the smaller BRIC countries, with 188 million people (by comparison, China and India each have more than 1 billion, Russia has 142 million). Yet car usage is already relatively high: 104 cars in use per 1,000 people, nearly 10 times the rate of usage in India, according to the *Economist*

Intelligence Unit. Because of this, growth projections for Brazil are relatively low—more in line with developed nations than with the other BRIC countries. Projections made by the industry research firm Global Insight show that sales will grow just 2% until 2013, underperforming even the U.S. market's projected growth rate.

On the plus side, Brazil is socioeconomically stable, with increasing wealth and a maturing finance system that is helping to propel growth among rural, first-time buyers who prefer compact cars. Few domestic brands exist, as the market is dominated by GM, Ford, Fiat, and Volkswagen. Prompted by generous government incentives, high import taxes, and exchange rate risks, foreign automakers have invested significantly in Brazil, which has thus become an unrivaled production hub for the rest of South America. Brazilian consumers live in a country with large rural areas and very rough terrain; they demand fairly large, SUV-like cars, made with economical small engines and flex-fuel power trains friendly to the country's biofuel industry. When a Latin American family buys its first automobile, chances are it was made in Brazil.

Russia, even though it is the smallest of the BRIC countries in population, has the highest auto adoption of the four: 213 cars in use per 1,000 people. (Western Europe, by comparison, has 518, according to the *Economist Intelligence Unit*.) Yet Global Insight expects future sales growth to average 6.5% from 2008 to 2013, far outpacing Brazil (2%), Western Europe (1.2%), and Japan and Korea (0.2%).

Given Russia's proximity to Europe, consumer preferences there are more akin to those of the developed markets than to those of China or India, and expensive, status-enhancing European models remain popular, although European safety features, interior components, and electronics are often stripped out to reduce costs. For vehicle manufacturers, the attractions of the Russian market include an absence of both local partnership requirements and significant local competitors. But there is high political risk. So far, the Russian government has permitted foreign carmakers to operate relatively freely, but the Kremlin's history of meddling in private enterprise and undercutting private ownership worries some executives. These concerns were heightened in November 2008, when Russia implemented tariffs against car imports in hopes of avoiding layoffs that might spark labor unrest among the country's 1.5 million car industry workers.

India has 1.1 billion people, but its level of car adoption is still low, with only 11 cars in use per 1,000 people. The upside is higher potential growth: among the BRIC countries, India is expected to have the fastest-growing auto sales, almost 15% per year until 2013, according to Global Insight. Sales of subcompact cars are strong, even during the global recession. The popularity of these small cars combines with India's energy shortages and the country's chronic pollution to provide foreign carmakers with an ideal opportunity to further develop electric power-train technologies there.

Until the early 1990s, foreign automobile manufacturers were mostly shut out of India. That has changed radically. Today, foreign automakers are welcomed and the government promotes foreign ownership and local manufacturing with tax breaks and strong intellectual property protection. And because foreign companies were shut out for a long period of time, India has capable manufacturers and suppliers for foreign vehicle manufacturers to partner with. Local competition is strong but is thus far concentrated among three players: Maruti Suzuki India, Ltd., Tata, and the Hyundai Corporation, which is well established in India.

China is almost as large as the other three combined in total auto sales and production. Its overall auto usage is just 18 cars per 1,000 households, but annual sales growth until 2013 is expected to be almost 10%. Its size and growth potential make China a dominant force in the industry going forward; new models and technologies developed there will almost certainly become available elsewhere.

But the Chinese government plays a central role in shaping the auto industry. Current ownership policies mandate that foreign vehicle manufacturers enter into 50-50 joint ventures with local automakers, and poor intellectual property rights enforcement puts the design and engineering innovations of foreign car companies at constant risk. At the same time, to cope with energy shortages and rampant pollution, the Chinese government is strongly encouraging research and development on alternative power trains, including electric cars and gasoline-electric hybrids. As a result, Chinese car companies may develop significant power-train capabilities ahead of their competitors.

Like their Indian counterparts, Chinese car companies have outpaced global automakers in developing cars specifically for emerging markets. A few Western companies, like Volkswagen AG, which has sold its Santana models in China through a joint venture (Shanghai Volkswagen Automotive Company) since 1985, are competitive. Some Chinese carmakers, like BYD Company, aspire to become global leaders in the industry. But many suffer from a talent shortage and inexperience in managing across borders. This may prompt them to acquire all or part of distressed Western automobile companies in the near future or to hire skilled auto executives from established companies and their suppliers.

In short, each of the four BRIC nations has a completely different set of market and industry dynamics. And the same is true for the other developing nations. Meanwhile, the number of autos in use in the developing world is projected to expand almost six-fold by 2018.

Cultural, Administrative, Geographic, and Economic Distance

Explicitly considering the four dimensions of *distance* introduced in Chapter 1 can dramatically change a company's assessment of the relative attractiveness of foreign markets. In his book *The Mirage of Global Markets*, David Arnold describes the experience of Mary Kay Cosmetics (MKC) in entering Asian markets. MKC is a direct marketing company that distributes its products through independent "beauty consultants" who buy and resell cosmetics and toiletries to contacts either individually or at social gatherings. When considering market expansion in Asia, the company had to choose: enter Japan or China first? Country-level data showed Japan to be the most attractive option by far: it had the highest per capita level of spending on cosmetics and toiletries of any country in the world, disposable income was high, it already had a thriving direct marketing industry, and it had a high proportion of women who did not participate in the work force. MKC learned, however, after participating in both markets, that the market opportunity in China was far greater, mainly because of economic and cultural distance: Chinese women were far more motivated than their Japanese counterparts to boost their income by becoming beauty consultants. Thus, the entrepreneurial opportunity represented by what MKC describes as "the career" (i.e., becoming a beauty consultant) was a far better predictor of the true sales potential than high-level data on incomes and expenditures. As a result of this experience, MKC now employs an additional business-specific indicator of market potential within its market assessment framework: the average wage for a female secretary in a country.[5]

MKC's experience underscores the importance of analyzing distance. It also highlights the fact that different product markets have different success factors: some are brand-sensitive while pricing or intensive distribution are key to success in others. Country-level economic or demographic data do not provide much help in analyzing such issues; only locally gathered marketing intelligence can provide true indications of a market's potential size and growth rate and its key success factors.

Minicase 5.2. Tata Making Inroads Into China[6]

Not content with just India, Mumbai-based Tata Group, the maker of the $2,500 Nano small car, is developing a small car for China. The platform is being designed and developed by a joint Indian and Chinese team based in China. The alliance won a new project for the complete design and development of a vehicle platform for a leading original equipment manufacturer for a small car for the China's domestic market. The team is integrating components in automotive modules to radically improve manufacturability and bring down total cost.

Meanwhile, in 2009, Nanjing Tata AutoComp Systems began supplying automotive interior products to Shanghai General Motors and Changan Ford Automobile Company Products, including plastic vents, outlet parts, and cabin air-ventilation grilles. In the same year, Nanjing Tata began supplying General Motors Corporation in Europe. Eventually, the plant will supply global automakers in North America and Europe as well as emerging markets such as China.

Nanjing Auto is a wholly owned subsidiary of Tata AutoComp Systems, which is the automotive part manufacturing arm of India's Tata Motors. The company has 30 manufacturing facilities, mainly in India, and production capabilities in automotive plastics and engineering. It also has 15 joint ventures with Tier 1 supplier companies, mainly in India.

The company has almost completed construction of the 280,000-square-foot Nanjing plant at a cost of approximately $15 million. The first phase included capacity to make parts for air vents, handles, cupholders, ashtrays, glove boxes, and floor consoles. When completed, the plant will have double the current capacity and will also produce instrument panels, door panels, and larger parts. The plant is operated by local Chinese employees; only a few managers are Indian.

In its bid to become a $1 billion global automotive supplier by 2008, Tata AutoComp had to expand into China. Total passenger car sales in India in 2007 were slightly more than 1.4 million units; in China, the number was more than 5.2 million units, according to data from Automotive Resources Asia, a division of J.D. Power and Associates. Tata Motors sold 221,256 passenger cars in India in 2007. In the same year, Shanghai General Motors sold 495,405 cars. "We see huge potential in China. To us, China is not just a manufacturing base, but a window to the global market. Our investments are keeping this promising future in mind,'" says the Tata AutoComp's chief executive officer.

Entry Strategies: Modes of Entry

What is the best way to enter a new market? Should a company first establish an export base or license its products to gain experience in a newly targeted country or region? Or does the potential associated with first-mover status justify a bolder move such as entering an alliance, making an acquisition, or even starting a new subsidiary? Many companies move from exporting to licensing to a higher investment strategy, in effect treating these choices as a learning curve. Each has distinct advantages and disadvantages.

Exporting is the marketing and direct sale of domestically produced goods in another country. Exporting is a traditional and well-established method of reaching foreign markets. Since it does not require that the goods be produced in the target country, no investment in foreign production facilities is required. Most of the costs associated with exporting take the form of marketing expenses.

While relatively low risk, exporting entails substantial costs and limited control. Exporters typically have little control over the marketing and distribution of their products, face high transportation charges and possible tariffs, and must pay distributors for a variety of services. What is more, exporting does not give a company firsthand experience in staking out a competitive position abroad, and it makes it difficult to customize products and services to local tastes and preferences.

Licensing essentially permits a company in the target country to use the property of the licensor. Such property is usually intangible, such as trademarks, patents, and production techniques. The licensee pays a fee in exchange for the rights to use the intangible property and possibly for technical assistance as well.

Because little investment on the part of the licensor is required, licensing has the potential to provide a very large return on investment. However, because the licensee produces and markets the product, potential returns from manufacturing and marketing activities may be lost. Thus, licensing reduces cost and involves limited risk. However, it does not mitigate the substantial disadvantages associated with operating from a distance. As a rule, licensing strategies inhibit control and produce only moderate returns.

Strategic alliances and *joint ventures* have become increasingly popular in recent years. They allow companies to share the risks and resources required to enter international markets. And although returns also may have to be shared, they give a company a degree of flexibility not afforded by going it alone through direct investment.

There are several motivations for companies to consider a partnership as they expand globally, including (a) facilitating market entry, (b) risk and reward sharing, (c) technology sharing, (d) joint product development, and (e) conforming to government regulations. Other benefits include political connections and distribution channel access that may depend on relationships.

Such alliances often are favorable when (a) the partners' strategic goals converge while their competitive goals diverge; (b) the partners' size, market power, and resources are small compared to the industry leaders; and (c) partners are able to learn from one another while limiting access to their own proprietary skills.

The key issues to consider in a joint venture are ownership, control, length of agreement, pricing, technology transfer, local firm capabilities and resources, and government intentions. Potential problems include (a) conflict over asymmetric new investments, (b) mistrust over proprietary knowledge, (c) performance ambiguity, that is, how to "split the pie," (d) lack of parent firm support, (e) cultural clashes, and (f) if, how, and when to terminate the relationship.

Ultimately, most companies will aim at building their own presence through company-owned facilities in important international markets. *Acquisitions* or *greenfield* start-ups represent this ultimate commitment. Acquisition is faster, but starting a new, wholly owned subsidiary might be the preferred option if no suitable acquisition candidates can be found.

Also known as *foreign direct investment* (FDI), acquisitions and greenfield start-ups involve the direct ownership of facilities in the target country and, therefore, the transfer of resources including capital, technology, and personnel. Direct ownership provides a high degree of control in the operations and the ability to better know the consumers and competitive environment. However, it requires a high level of resources and a high degree of commitment.

Minicase 5.3. Coca-Cola and Illycaffé[7]

In March 2008, the Coca-Cola company and Illycaffé Spa finalized a joint venture and launched a premium ready-to-drink espresso-based coffee beverage. The joint venture, Ilko Coffee International, was created to bring three ready-to-drink coffee products—Caffè, an Italian chilled espresso-based coffee; Cappuccino, an intense espresso, blended with milk and dark cacao; and Latte Macchiato, a smooth espresso, swirled with milk—to consumers in 10 European countries. The products will be available in stylish, premium cans (150 ml for Caffè and 200 ml for the milk variants). All three offerings will be available in 10 European Coca-Cola Hellenic markets including Austria, Croatia, Greece, and Ukraine. Additional countries in Europe, Asia, North America, Eurasia, and the Pacific were slated for expansion into 2009.

The Coca-Cola Company is the world's largest beverage company. Along with Coca-Cola, recognized as the world's most valuable brand, the company markets four of the world's top five nonalcoholic sparkling brands, including Diet Coke, Fanta, Sprite, and a wide range of other beverages, including diet and light beverages, waters, juices and juice drinks, teas, coffees, and energy and sports drinks. Through the world's largest beverage distribution system, consumers in more than 200 countries enjoy the company's beverages at a rate of 1.5 billion servings each day.

Based in Trieste, Italy, Illycaffé produces and markets a unique blend of espresso coffee under a single brand leader in quality. Over 6 million cups of Illy espresso coffee are enjoyed every day. Illy is sold in over 140 countries around the world and is available in more than 50,000 of the best restaurants and coffee bars. Illy buys green coffee directly from the growers of the highest quality Arabica through partnerships based on the mutual creation of value. The Trieste-based company fosters long-term collaborations with the world's best coffee growers—in Brazil, Central America, India, and Africa—providing know-how and technology and offering above-market prices.

Entry Strategies: Timing

In addition to selecting the right mode of entry, the timing of entry is critical. Just as many companies have overestimated market potential abroad and underestimated the time and effort needed to create a real market presence, so have they justified their overseas' expansion on the grounds of an urgent need to participate in the market early. Arguing that there existed a limited window of opportunity in which to act, which would reward only those players bold enough to move early, many companies made sizable commitments to foreign markets even though their own financial projections showed they would not be profitable for years to come. This dogmatic belief in the concept of a first-mover advantage (sometimes referred to as "pioneer advantage") became one of the most widely established theories of business. It holds that the first entrant in a new market enjoys a unique advantage that later competitors cannot overcome (i.e., that the competitive advantage so obtained is structural and therefore sustainable).

Some companies have found this to be true. Procter & Gamble (P&G), for example, has always trailed rivals such as Unilever in certain large markets, including India and some Latin American countries, and the most obvious explanation is that its European rivals were participating in these countries long before P&G entered. Given that history, it is understandable that P&G erred on the side of urgency in reacting to the opening of large markets such as Russia and China. For many other companies, however, the concept of pioneer advantage was little more than an article of faith and was applied indiscriminately and with disastrous results to country-market entry, to product-market entry, and, in particular, to the "new economy" opportunities created by the Internet.

The "get in early" philosophy of pioneer advantage remains popular. And while there are clear examples of its successful application—the advantages gained by European companies from being early in "colonial" markets provide some evidence of pioneer advantage—first-mover advantage is overrated as a strategic principle. In fact, in many instances, there are disadvantages to being first. First, if there is no real first-mover advantage, being first often results in poor business performance, as the large number of companies that rushed into Russia and China attests to. Second, pioneers may not always be able to recoup their investment in marketing required to "kick start" the new market. When that happens, a "fast follower" can benefit from the market development funded by the pioneer and leapfrog into earlier profitability.[8]

This ability of later entrants to free-ride on the pioneer's market development investment is the most common source of first-mover disadvantage and suggests two critical conditions necessary for real first-mover advantage to exist. First, there must be a scarce resource in the market that the first entrant can acquire. Second, the first mover must be able to lock up that scarce resource in such a way that it creates a barrier to entry for potential competitors. A good example is provided by markets in which it is necessary for foreign firms to obtain a government permit or license to sell their products. In such cases, the license, and perhaps government approval, more generally, may be a scarce resource that will not be granted to all comers. The second condition is also necessary for first-mover advantage to develop. Many companies believed that brand preference created by being first constituted a valid source of first-mover advantage, only to find that, in most cases, consumers consider the alternatives available at the time of their first purchase, not which came first.

Minicase 5.4. Starbucks' Global Expansion[9]

Starbucks' decision to expand abroad came after an extended period of exclusive focus on the North American market. From its founding in 1971, it grew to almost 700 stores by 1995, all within the United States and Vancouver, Canada. It was not until the next decade that Starbucks made its first entry into international markets. By 2006, Starbucks operated approximately 11,000 stores, with 70% in the United States and 30% in international markets, and international revenue had grown to almost 20% of Starbucks' total revenue. Starbucks offered the same basic coffee menu internationally as it did in the United States; however, the range of food products and other items, such as coffee mugs stocked, varied somewhat according to local customs and tastes.

Along with many other companies that pursue global expansion, Starbucks continually faces questions about where and how to further increase its global presence. Should the emphasis be on growth in existing countries or on increasing the number of countries in which it has a presence? How important is the fact that international markets so far have proven less profitable than the U.S. and Canadian markets?

Starbucks in Japan. Interestingly, Starbucks' first foreign move (i.e., outside the United States and Canada) was a joint venture in Japan. At the time, Japan had the second largest economy in the world and was consistently among the top five coffee importers in the world.

The decision to use a joint venture to enter Japan followed intense internal debate. Concerns among senior executives centered on Starbucks' lack of local knowledge, and questions were raised about the company's ability to attract the local talent necessary to grow the Japanese business quickly enough. Starbucks was acutely aware that there were significant differences between doing business in Japan and in the United States and that it might not have enough experience to be successful on its own.

Among other factors, operating costs were predicted to be double those of North America, and Starbucks would have to pay to ship coffee to Japan from its roasting facility in Kent, Washington (near Seattle). In addition, retail space in Tokyo was 2 to 3 times as expensive as in Seattle. Just finding rental space in such a populous city might prove to be a tremendous challenge. Starbucks concluded it needed to form an alliance with a local group that had experience with complex operations and real estate.

Starbucks executives worried that a licensing deal would not be the right solution. Specifically, they were concerned about possible loss of control and insufficient knowledge transfer to learn from the experience. A joint venture was thought to be a better answer, and, after a long search, Starbucks approached Sazaby, Inc., operators of upscale retail and restaurant chains, whose president had approached Starbucks years earlier about the potential of opening Starbucks stores in Japan. Similarity in values, culture, and community-development goals between Starbucks and Sazaby were important considerations in concluding the 50-50 deal. The two companies were equally represented on the board of directors of the newly created Starbucks

Coffee Japan. Starbucks was the sole decision-making power in matters relating to brand, product line advertising, and corporate communications, while decisions regarding real-estate operational issues and human resources were handled by Sazaby. Despite strong local competition, the venture was successful from the start. By fiscal year 2000, Starbucks Coffee Japan became profitable more than 2 years ahead of plan.

Starbucks in the United Kingdom. Unlike its expansion into Asia and (later) the Middle East, Starbucks chose to enter the United Kingdom through acquisition rather than partnerships. Speed was a major factor in Starbucks' decision to enter the fast-growing UK market by acquisition. In addition, the culture, language, legal environment, management practices, and labor economics in the United Kingdom were considered sufficiently similar to those that Starbucks' management already knew. This meant that a 100%-owned UK subsidiary could be successfully established from the outset. In May 1998, Starbucks acquired the Seattle Coffee Company, which had a presence in the United Kingdom for some time. This fast-growing chain was modeled on its own style of operations and, at the time of the purchase, had 56 retail units. The Seattle Coffee Company was an attractive acquisition target because of its focus: relatively small market capitalization and established retail units. By 2005, Starbucks had 469 stores in the United Kingdom, which made it the third largest country, after the United States and Japan, to serve Starbucks coffee.

Licensing in China. In a number of developing markets, including China, Starbucks chose to enter into minority share licensing agreements with high-quality, experienced local partners in order to minimize market-entry risks. Under these agreements, the local partners absorbed the capital costs (real estate, store construction) of bringing the Starbucks brand abroad. This eliminated the need for substantial general and administrative expenses by Starbucks and enabled it to establish a presence in foreign markets much more quickly than it would have if it had to invest its own capital and absorb start-up losses.

Risk was also a major consideration when Starbucks looked to enter China. While offering high-volume opportunities in an untapped coffee market, the prevailing culture and politics in China potentially posed significant problems. In April 2000, Beijing city authorities ordered Kentucky Fried Chicken to close its store near the Forbidden City when its lease expired in 2002. Similarly, under pressure from local authorities, McDonald's removed its golden arches from outlets near Tiananmen Square. These incidents demonstrated China's ambiguous attitude toward a growing Western economic and cultural influence.

Another major concern with starting operations in China was recruiting the right staff. Uniformity of customer experience and coffee quality was the key driver behind the Starbucks brand; failure to recruit the staff to ensure these key criteria not only would mean failure for the Chinese retail outlets but also could harm the company's image globally.

Although these factors made licensing an attractive entry model, with growing experience in the Chinese market, Starbucks is steadily reducing its reliance on the licensing model and switching to its core company-operated business model to increase control and reap greater rewards.

Starbucks' globalization history shows that while it was a "first mover" in the United States, it was forced to push harder in international markets to compete with existing players. In Japan, Starbucks was initially a huge success and became profitable 2 years earlier than anticipated. However, just 2 years after Starbucks Japan had become profitable, the company announced a loss of $3.9 million in Japan, its second largest market at the time, reflecting a major increase in local competition. Additional international challenges were a result of Starbucks' chosen entry mode. Although joint ventures provided Starbucks with local knowledge about the market and a low-risk entry into unproven territory, joint ventures did not always reap the rewards that the partners had anticipated. One key factor was that it was often difficult for Starbucks to control the costs in a joint venture, resulting in lower profitability.

Points to Remember

1. Selecting global target markets, entry modes, and deciding how much to adapt the company's basic value proposition are intimately related. The choice of customers to serve in a particular country or region with a particular culture determines how and how much a company must adapt its basic value proposition. Conversely, the extent of a company's capabilities in tailoring its offerings around the globe limits or broadens its options to successfully enter new markets or cultures.

2. Few companies can afford to enter all markets open to them. The track record shows that picking the most attractive foreign markets, determining the best time to enter them, and selecting the right partners and level of investment has proven difficult for many companies, especially when it involves large emerging markets such as China.

3. Research shows there is a pervasive the-grass-is-always-greener effect that infects global strategic decision making in many, especially globally inexperienced, companies and causes them to overestimate the attractiveness of foreign markets.

4. Four key factors in selecting global markets are (a) a market's size and growth rate, (b) a particular country or region's institutional contexts, (c) a region's competitive environment, and (d) a market's cultural, administrative, geographic, and economic distance from other markets the company serves.

5. There is a wide menu of options regarding market entry, from conservative strategies such as first establishing an export base or licensing products to gain experience in a newly targeted country to more aggressive options such as entering an alliance, making an acquisition, or even starting a new subsidiary.

6. Selecting the right timing of entry is equally critical. And just as many companies have overestimated market potential abroad, and underestimated the time and effort needed to create a real market presence, so have they justified their overseas' expansion on the grounds of an urgent need to participate in the market early.

CHAPTER 6

Globalizing the Value Proposition

Managers sometimes assume that what works in their home country will work just as well in another part of the world. They take the same product, the same advertising campaign, even the same brand names and packaging, and expect instant success. The result in most cases is failure. Why? Because the assumption that one approach works everywhere fails to consider the complex mosaic of differences that exists between countries and cultures.

Of course, marketing a standardized product with the same positioning and communications strategy around the globe—the purest form of *aggregation*—has considerable attraction because of its cost-effectiveness and simplicity. It is also extremely dangerous, however. Simply assuming that foreign customers will respond positively to an existing product can lead to costly failure. Consider the following classic examples of failure:

- Coca-Cola had to withdraw its 2-liter bottle in Spain after discovering that few Spaniards owned refrigerators with large enough compartments to accommodate it.
- General Foods squandered millions trying to introduce packaged cake mixes to Japanese consumers. The company failed to note that only 3% of Japanese homes were equipped with ovens.
- General Foods' Tang initially failed in France because it was positioned as a substitute for orange juice at breakfast. The French drink little orange juice and almost none at breakfast.

With a few exceptions, the idea of an identical, fully standardized global value proposition is a myth, and few industries are truly global. How to adapt a value proposition in the most effective manner is therefore a key strategic issue.

Value Proposition Adaptation Decisions

Value proposition adaptation deals with a whole range of issues, ranging from the quality and appearance of products to materials, processing, production equipment, packaging, and style. A product may have to be adapted to meet the physical, social, or mandatory requirements of a new market. It may have to be modified to conform to government regulations or to operate effectively in country-specific geographic and climatic conditions. Or it may be redesigned or repackaged to meet the diverse buyer preferences or standard-of-living conditions. A product's size and packaging may also have to be modified to facilitate shipment or to conform to possible differences in engineering or design standards in a country or in regional markets. Other dimensions of value proposition adaptation include changes in brand name, color, size, taste, design, style, features, materials, warranties, after-sale service, technological sophistication, and performance.

The need for some changes, such as accommodating different electricity requirements, will be obvious. Others may require in-depth analysis of societal customs and cultures, the local economy, technological sophistication of people living in the country, customers' purchasing power, and purchasing behavior. Legal, economic, political, technological, and climatic requirements of a country market may all dictate some level of localization or adaptation.

As tariff barriers (tariffs, duties, and quotas) are gradually reduced around the world in accordance with World Trade Organization (WTO) rules, other *nontariff barriers*, such as *product standards*, are proliferating. For example, consider regulations for food additives. Many of the United States' "generally recognized as safe" (GRAS) additives are banned today in foreign countries. In marketing abroad, documentation is important not only for the amount of additive but also for its source, and often additives must be listed on the label of ingredients. As a result, product labeling and packaging must often be adapted to comply with another country's legal and environmental requirements.

Many kinds of equipment must be engineered in the *metric system* for integration with other pieces of equipment or for compliance with the standards of a given country. The United States is virtually alone in its adherence to a nonmetric system, and U.S. firms that compete successfully in the global market have found metric measurement to be an important detail in selling to overseas customers. Even instruction or maintenance manuals, for example, should be made available in centimeters, weights in grams or kilos, and temperatures in degrees Celsius.

Many products must be adapted to local *geographic and climatic* conditions. Factors such as topography, humidity, and energy costs can affect the performance of a product or even define its use in a foreign market. The cost of petroleum products, along with a country's infrastructure, for example, may mandate the need to develop products with a greater level of energy efficiency. Hot, dusty climates of countries in the Middle East and other emerging markets may force automakers to adapt automobiles with different types of filters and clutch systems than those used in North America, Japan, and European countries. Even shampoo and cosmetic product makers have to chemically reformulate their products to make them more suited for people living in hot, humid climates.

The availability, performance, and level of sophistication of a *commercial infrastructure* will also warrant a need for adaptation or localization of products. For example, a company may decide not to market its line of frozen food items in countries where retailers do not have adequate freezer space. Instead, it may choose to develop dehydrated products for such markets. Size of packaging, material used in packaging, before- and after-sale service, and warranties may have to be adapted in view of the scope and level of service provided by the distribution structure in the country markets targeted. In the event that postsale servicing facilities are conspicuous by their absence, companies may need to offer simpler, more robust products in overseas markets to reduce the need for maintenance and repairs.

Differences in *buyer preferences* are also major drivers behind value proposition adaptation. Local customs, such as religion or the use of leisure time, may affect market acceptance. The sensory impact of a product, such as taste or its visual impression, may also be a critical factor. The Japanese consumer's desire for beautiful packaging, for example, has led many U.S. companies to redesign cartons and packages specifically for this market. At the same time, to make purchasing mass-marketed consumer products more affordable in lesser developed countries, makers of products such as razor blades, cigarettes, chewing gum, ball-point pens, and candy bars repackage them in small, single units rather than multiple units prevalent in the developed and more advanced economies.

Expectations about *product guarantees* may also vary from country to country depending on the level of development, competitive practices, and degree of activism by consumer groups; local standards of production quality; and prevalent product usage patterns. Strong warranties may be required to break into a new market, especially if the company is an unknown supplier. In other cases, warranties similar to those in the home country market may not be expected.

As a general rule, *packaging design* should be based on customer needs. For industrial products, packaging is primarily functional and should reflect needs for storage, transportation, protection, preservation, reuse, and so on. For consumer products, packaging has additional functionality and should be protective, informative, appealing, conform to legal requirements, and reflect buying habits (e.g., Americans tend to shop less frequently than Europeans, so larger sizes are more popular in the United States).

In analyzing adaptation requirements, careful attention to *cultural differences* between the target customers in the home country (country of origin) and those in the host country is extremely important. The greater the cultural differences between the two target markets, the greater the need for adaptation. Cultural considerations and customs may influence branding, labeling, and package considerations. Certain colors used on labels and packages may be found unattractive or offensive. Red, for example, stands for good luck and fortune in China and parts of Africa; aggression, danger, or warning in Europe, America, Australia, and New Zealand; masculinity in parts of Europe; mourning (dark red) in the Ivory Coast; and death in Turkey. Blue denotes immortality in Iran, while purple denotes mourning in Brazil and is a symbol of expense in some Asian cultures. Green is associated with high tech in Japan, luck in the Middle East, connotes death in South America and countries with dense jungle areas, and is a forbidden color in Indonesia. Yellow is associated with femininity in the United States and many other countries but denotes mourning in Mexico and strength and reliability in Saudi Arabia. Finally, black is used to signal mourning, as well as style and elegance, in most Western nations, but it stands for trust and quality in China, while white—the symbol for cleanliness and purity in the West—denotes mourning in Japan and some other Far Eastern nations.

A country's *standard of living* and the *target market's purchasing power* can also determine whether a company needs to modify its value proposition. The level of income, the level of education, and the availability of energy are all factors that help predict the acceptance of a product in a foreign market. In countries with a lower level of purchasing power, a manufacturer may find a market for less-sophisticated product models or products that are obsolete in developed nations. Certain high-technology products are inappropriate in some countries, not only because of their cost but also because of their function. For example, a computerized, industrial washing machine might replace workers in a country where employment is a high priority. In addition, these products may need a level of servicing that is unavailable in some countries.

When potential customers have limited purchasing power, companies may need to develop an entirely new product designed to address the market opportunity at a price point that is within the reach of a potential target market. Conversely, companies in lesser-developed countries that have achieved local success may find it necessary to adopt an "up-market strategy" whereby the product may have to be designed to meet world-class standards.

Minicase 6.1. Kraft Reformulates Oreo Cookies in China[1]

Kraft's Oreo has long been the top-selling cookie in the U.S. market, but the company had to reinvent it to make it sell in China. Unlike their American counterparts, Oreo cookies sold in China are long, thin, four-layered, and coated in chocolate.

Oreos were first introduced in 1912 in the United States, but it was not until 1996 that Kraft introduced Oreos to Chinese consumers. After more than 5 years of flat sales, the company embarked on a complete makeover. Research had shown, among other findings, that traditional Oreos were too sweet for Chinese tastes and that packages of 14 Oreos priced at 72 cents were too expensive. In response, Kraft developed and tested 20 prototypes of reduced-sugar Oreos with Chinese consumers before settling on a new formula; it also introduced packages containing fewer Oreos for just 29 cents.

But Kraft did not stop there. The research team had also picked up on China's growing thirst for milk, which Kraft had not considered before. It noted that increased milk demand in China and other developing markets was a contributing factor to higher milk prices around the world. This put pressure on food manufacturers like Kraft, whose biggest business is cheese, but it also spelled opportunity.

Kraft began a grassroots marketing campaign to educate Chinese consumers about the American tradition of pairing milk with cookies. The company created an Oreo apprentice program at 30 Chinese universities that drew 6,000 student applications. Three hundred were accepted and trained as Oreo-brand ambassadors. Some of them rode around Beijing on bicycles, outfitted with wheel covers resembling Oreos, and handed out cookies to more than 300,000 consumers. Others organized Oreo-themed basketball games to reinforce the idea of dunking cookies in milk. Television commercials showed kids twisting apart Oreo cookies, licking the cream center, and dipping the chocolate cookie halves into glasses of milk.

Still, Kraft realized it needed to do more than just tweak its recipe to capture a bigger share of the Chinese biscuit market. China's cookie-wafer segment was growing faster than the traditional biscuit-like cookie segment, and Kraft needed to catch up to rival Nestlé SA, the world's largest food company, which had introduced chocolate-covered wafers there in 1998.

So Kraft decided this market opportunity was big enough to justify a complete remake of the Oreo itself and, departing from longstanding corporate policy for the first time, created an Oreo that looked almost nothing like the original. The new Chinese Oreo consisted of four layers of crispy wafer filled with vanilla and chocolate cream, coated in chocolate. To ensure that the chocolate product could be shipped across the country, could withstand the cold climate in the north and the hot, humid weather in the south, and would still melt in the mouth, the company had to develop a new proprietary handling process.

Kraft's adaptation efforts paid off. In 2006, Oreo wafer sticks became the best-selling biscuit in China, outpacing Hao-ChiDian, a biscuit brand made by the Chinese company Dali. The new Oreos also outsell traditional (round) Oreos in China. They also have created opportunities for further aggregation and product innovation. Kraft now sells the wafers elsewhere in Asia, as well as in Australia and Canada, and the company has introduced another new product in China: wafer rolls, a tube-shaped wafer lined with cream. The hollow cookie can be used as a straw through which to drink milk.

This success encouraged Kraft to empower managers in other businesses around the globe. For example, to take advantage of the European preference for dark chocolate, Kraft introduced dark chocolate in Germany under its Milka brand. Research showed that Russian consumers like premium instant coffee, so Kraft positioned its Carte Noire freeze-dried coffee as an upscale brand. And in the Philippines, where iced tea is popular, Kraft launched iced-tea-flavored Tang.

As Kraft's experience shows, successful global marketing and branding is rooted in a careful blend of aggregation, adaptation, and arbitrage strategies that is tailored to the specific needs and preferences of a particular region or country.

Adaptation or Aggregation: The Value Proposition Globalization Matrix

A useful construct for analyzing the need to adapt the offer and message (positioning) dimensions is the *value proposition globalization matrix* shown in Figure 6.1, which illustrates four generic global strategies:

1. A pure aggregation approach (also sometimes referred to as a "global marketing mix" strategy) under which both the offer and the message are the same

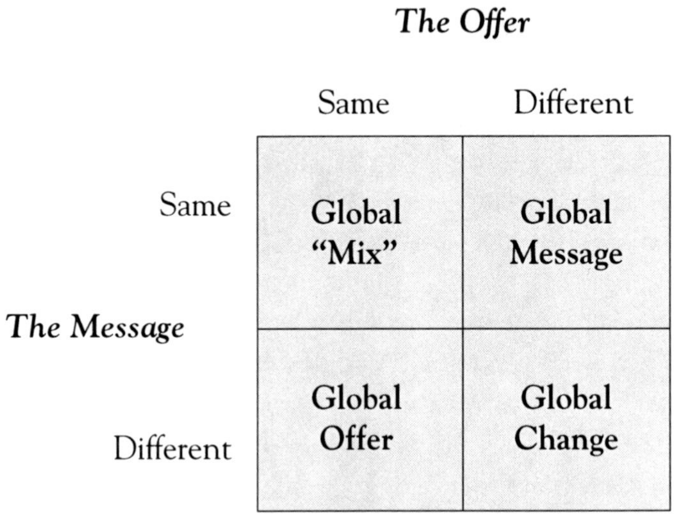

The Offer

	Same	Different
Same	Global "Mix"	Global Message
Different	Global Offer	Global Change

The Message (row label, left of table)

Figure 6.1. *The value proposition globalization matrix.*

2. An approach characterized by an identical offer (product/service aggregation) but different positioning (message adaptation) around the world (also called a "global offer" strategy)
3. An approach under which the offer might be different in various parts of the world (product adaptation) but where the message is the same (message aggregation; also referred to as a "global message" strategy)
4. A "global change" strategy under which both the offer and the message are adapted to local market circumstances

Global mix or pure aggregation strategies are relatively rare because only a few industries are truly global in all respects. They apply (a) when a product's usage patterns and brand potential are homogeneous on a global scale, (b) when scale and scope cost advantages substantially outweigh the benefits of partial or full adaptation, and (c) when competitive circumstances are such that a long-term, sustainable advantage can be secured using a standardized approach. The best examples are found in industrial product categories such as basic electronic components or certain commodity markets.

Global offer strategies are feasible when the same offer can be advantageously positioned differently in different parts of the world. There are several reasons for considering differential positioning. When fixed costs associated with the offer are high, when key core benefits offered are identical, and when there are natural market boundaries, adapting the message for stronger local advantage is tempting. Although such strategies increase local promotional budgets, they give country managers a degree of flexibility in positioning the product or service for maximum local advantage. The primary disadvantage associated with this type of strategy is that it could be difficult to sustain or even dangerous in the long term as customers become increasingly global in their outlook and confused by the different messages in different parts of the world.

Minicase 6.2. Starwood's Branding in China[2]

Check into a Four Points Hotel by Sheraton in Shanghai and you will get all the perks of a quality international hotel: a free Internet connection, several in-house restaurants, a mah-jongg parlor, and an assortment of moon cakes, a Chinese delicacy. All this for $80 a night, about 20% less than the average cost of a room in Shanghai.

For travelers who associate the Sheraton brand with plastic ice buckets and polyester bedspreads in the United States, this may come as a surprise. Like Buick, Kentucky Fried Chicken (KFC), and Pizza Hut, Sheraton is one of those American names that, to some, seems past its prime at home, but it is still popular and growing abroad. The hotel brand has particular cachet in China, going back to 1985, when it opened the Great Wall Sheraton Hotel Beijing. Local developers still compete to partner with Sheraton's parent company—Starwood Hotels & Resorts Worldwide—to develop new properties. In the near future, the company will have more rooms in Shanghai than it does in New York.

Like many other U.S. companies experiencing pressure at home, Starwood sees China as one of its best hopes for growth. The company, which also owns the upscale St. Regis, Westin, W, and Le Meridien brands, expects much of this growth will come from outlying regions. Big cities such as Beijing now have plenty of rooms, thanks in part to the Olympics, but there is growing demand for business-class accommodation in second- and third-tier cities such as Jiangyin and Dalian. Lower construction costs and inexpensive labor mean the company's Chinese hotel owners can offer guests a lot more than comparably priced U.S. properties.

In recent years, the focus in China has shifted from international travelers to Chinese consumers. Starwood now asks its hotel staff to greet guests in Mandarin instead of English, which was long used to convey a sense of prestige. Many of its hotels do not label their fourth floors as such because four is considered an unlucky number.

Starwood is not alone in recognizing the potential of the Chinese market. Marriott International hopes to increase its China presence by 50%, to 61 hotels by 2014. And InterContinental Hotels Group, parent of Holiday Inn, plans to double the 118 hotels it has in China over the next 3 years.

One major perk Starwood can offer over local competitors is its extensive global network and loyalty perks. More than 40% of its Chinese business comes through its preferred-guest program, and Chinese membership in the program is increasing rapidly. But local customers are not particularly focused on accruing points to earn a free stay. They are more interested in "status," using points to get room upgrades, a free breakfast, or anything that accords them conspicuous VIP treatment. Among other things, the preferred guest system allows staffers to see people's titles immediately. That makes it easier to give better rooms to managers than the subordinates they are traveling with and to greet them first when a party arrives.

After a long period in which Starwood paid more attention to its hipper W and Westin brands, the company has recently been remodeling its U.S. Sheratons. Among mainland Chinese travelers, the Sheraton name has continued to exude an aura of international class. While that is helpful for Sheraton's domestic Chinese business, the real potential will only be realized when they start to travel. The company's goal is to lock in the loyalty of mainland customers so they will stay at a Sheraton when they travel abroad. Indeed, if the experience with Japanese tourists in the mid-1980s is any guide, Starwood could be looking at 100 million or more outbound trips from China.

Global message strategies use the same message worldwide but allow for local adaptation of the offer. McDonald's, for example, is positioned virtually identical worldwide, but it serves vegetarian food in India and wine in France. The primary motivation behind this type of strategy is the enormous power behind a global brand. In industries in which customers increasingly develop similar expectations, aspirations, and values; in which customers are highly mobile; and in which the cost of product or service adaptation is fairly low, leveraging the global brand potential represented by one message worldwide often outweighs the possible disadvantages associated with factors such as higher local research and development (R&D) costs. As with global-offer strategies, however, global message strategies can be risky in the long run—global customers might not find elsewhere what they expect and regularly experience at home. This could lead to confusion or even alienation.

Minicase 6.3. KFC Abroad[3]

KFC is synonymous with chicken. It has to be because chicken is its flagship product. One of the more recent offers the company created—all around the world—is the marinated hot and crispy chicken that is "crrrrisp and crunchy on the outside, and soft and juicy on the inside." In India, KFC offers a regular Pepsi with this at just 39 rupees. But KFC also made sure not to alienate the vegetarian community—in Bangalore, you can be vegetarian and yet eat at KFC. Why? Thirty-five percent of the Indian population is vegetarian, and in metros such as Delhi and Mumbai, the number is almost 50%. Therefore, KFC offers a wide range of vegetarian products, such as the tangy, lip-smacking Paneer Tikka Wrap 'n Roll, Veg De-Lite Burger, Veg Crispy Burger. There are munchies such as the crisp golden veg fingers and crunchy golden fries served with tangy sauces. You can combine the veg fingers with steaming, peppery rice and a spice curry. The mayonnaise and sauces do not have egg in them.

While the vegetarian menu is unique to India because of the country's distinct tastes, KFC's "standard" chicken products are also adapted to suit local tastes. For example, chicken strips are served with a local sauce, or the sauce of the wrap is changed to local tastes. Thus, KFC tries to balance aggregation with adaptation: standardization of those parts of the value offering that travel easily (KFC's core products and positioning), tailoring of standard chicken products with a different topping or sauce, and offering a vegetarian menu.

This adaptation strategy is used in every country that KFC serves: the U.S. and European markets have a traditional KFC menu based on chicken burgers and wraps, while Asian offerings like those in India are more experimental and adventurous and include rice meals, wraps, and culture-appropriate sides.

Global change strategies define a "best fit" approach and are by far the most common. As we have seen, for most products, some form of adaptation of both the offer and the message is necessary. Differences in a product's usage patterns, benefits sought, brand image, competitive structures, distribution channels, and governmental and other regulations all dictate some form of local adaptation. Corporate factors also play a role. Companies that have achieved a global reach through acquisition, for example, often prefer to leverage local brand names, distribution systems, and suppliers rather than embark on a risky global one-size-fits-all approach. As the markets they serve and the company become more global, selective standardization of the message and the offer itself can become more attractive.

Minicase 6.4. Targeting Muslim Customers[4]

Muslims often experience culture shock while staying in Western hotels. Minibars, travelers in bikinis, and loud music, among other things, embarrass Muslim travelers.

That is no longer necessary. A growing number of hotels has started to cater to Muslim travelers. In one, the lobby—decorated in white leather, brick, and glass, with a small waterfall—is quiet. Men in *dishdashas* and veiled women mingle with Westerners who are sometimes discreetly reminded to respect local customs. Minibars are stocked not with alcohol but with Red Bull, Pepsi, and the malt drink Barbican.

"Buying Muslim" used to mean avoiding pork and alcohol and getting your meat from a halal butcher, who slaughtered in accordance with Islamic principles. But the halal food market has exploded in the past decade and is now worth an estimated $632 billion annually, according to the *Halal Journal*, a Kuala Lumpur–based magazine. That amounts to about 16% of the entire global food industry. Throw in the fast-growing Islam-friendly finance sector and the myriad of other products and services—cosmetics, real estate, hotels, fashion, insurance, for example—that comply with Islamic law and the teachings of the Koran, and the sector is worth well over $1 trillion a year.

Seeking to tap that huge market, multinationals like Tesco, McDonald's, and Nestlé have expanded their Muslim-friendly offerings and now control an estimated 90% of the global halal market. Governments in Asia and the Middle East are pouring millions into efforts to become regional "halal hubs," providing tailor-made manufacturing centers and "halal logistics"—systems to maintain product purity during shipping and storage. The intense competition has created some interesting partnerships in unusual places. Most of Saudi Arabia's chicken is raised in Brazil, which means Brazilian suppliers had to build elaborate halal slaughtering facilities. Abattoirs in New Zealand, the world's biggest exporter of halal lamb, have hosted delegations from Iran and Malaysia. And the Netherlands, keen to exploit Rotterdam's role as Europe's biggest port, has built halal warehouses so that imported halal goods are not stored next to pork or alcohol.

It is not just about food. Major drug companies now sell halal vitamins free of the gelatins and other animal derivatives that some

Islamic scholars say make mainstream products *haram*, or unlaw-ful. The Malaysia-based company Granulab produces synthetic bone-graft material to avoid using animal bone, while Malaysian and Cuban scientists are collaborating on a halal meningitis vac-cine. For Muslim women concerned about skin-care products containing alcohol or lipsticks that use animal fats, a few cosmet-ics firms are creating halal makeup lines.

The growing Islamic finance industry is trying to win non-Muslim customers. Investors are attracted by Islamic banking's more conservative approach: Islamic law forbids banks from charging interest (though customers pay fees), and many schol-ars discourage investment in excessively leveraged companies. Though it currently accounts for just 1% of the global market, the Islamic finance industry's value is growing at around 15% a year, and it could reach $4 trillion in 5 years, according to a 2008 report from Moody's Investors Service.

Combining Aggregation and Adaptation: Global Product Platforms

One way around the trade-off between creating global efficiencies and adapting to local requirements and preferences is to design a global prod-uct or communication platform that can be adapted efficiently to dif-ferent markets. This modularized approach to global product design has become particularly popular in the automobile industry. One of the first "world car platforms" was introduced by Ford in 1981. The Ford Escort was assembled simultaneously in three countries—the United States, Germany, and the United Kingdom—with parts produced in 10 coun-tries. The U.S. and European models were distinctly different but shared standardized engines, transmissions, and ancillary systems for heating, air conditioning, wheels, and seats, thereby saving the company millions of dollars in engineering and development costs.

Minicase 6.5. Creating the Perfect Fit: New Car-Seat Design[5]

Imagine the challenge of being an automotive-seat engineer these days, and picture one of the hugest men you know—a large, American male weighing about 275 lbs. Now consider a petite woman, and throw in someone with lower-back pain. Your challenge: design a single seat that comfortably accommodates each of these physically and physiologically diverse individuals, not just for a few minutes but for a 4-hour drive. Welcome to the global automotive design challenge.

While the economic pressures to standardize are becoming stronger, car buyers are getting more size-diverse, more ergonomically distressed, and more demanding of power adjustments and other amenities. Seat developers are responding: they are using more versatile materials, new engineering techniques, digital technologies, and novel designs to make sitting in a car as, or even more, comfortable as sitting in your living room.

This concern for comfort is relatively new; hard benches were the standard during the industry's earliest days. Even into the 1980s, most cars and trucks had simple bench seating in both the front and rear of the automobile. Automotive seat design only became a crucial discipline during the last generation as Americans began to spend more and more time in their vehicles and as interior comfort and appointments became a major competitive issue.

Federal regulations affect seat design only minimally, with the most important requirements focusing on headrests. And there are distance requirements between the driver's body and the steering wheel, an issue that can also be addressed with telescoping steering wheels and adjustable pedals. In the end, automakers must mainly make sure the seat design helps the car pass the government's crash-safety standards.

Consumers are far more demanding. Comfort and ergonomic functionality have become the focal points of seat design. Americans are getting bigger and heavier, and automakers try to design seats that can accommodate everyone from the smallest females to the largest males. This is not a simple feat, with the 95th-percentile American man now weighing about 24 lbs more than 2 decades ago. At the same time, while U.S. women in general also have gotten larger, the influx of immigrants from Asia actually kept the overall increase in the size of the 5th-percentile American woman down to under 5 lbs over the last 2 decades.

And just as airlines and home-furniture manufacturers have had to respond to wider girths by making seats bigger, auto companies are also faced with having to squeeze bigger people into cabins that are getting smaller as gas prices rise. At the same time, seats must secure tiny drivers and allow them to see clearly over the steering wheel and reach the accelerator and brake pedals.

The aging of the American population poses special difficulties. Younger demographics like their seats harder, but baby boomers and older customers are used to a soft seat. Whether this is best ergonomically is not important, despite the fact that more and more consumers are carrying specific maladies of aging into their cars, including back pain, aching knees, and a general decline in the basic nimbleness required to get in and out of an automobile.

It is one thing to design a single seat that can accommodate the frames of the smallest to the largest Americans. Now add the globalization challenge. As automakers seek to globalize vehicle platforms, their seats also have to be able to accommodate the diverse body proportions, size ranges, and consumer preferences of people around the world.

For example, while Europeans definitely prefer longer cushions, and Asians like shorter ones, Americans are somewhere in between. And in China, the second row must be as comfortable as the first because as many as 40% of car owners have a driver, and the owners tend to sit in the right rear seat.

Combining Adaptation and Arbitrage: Global Product Development

Globalization pressures have changed the practice of product development (PD) in many industries in recent years.[6] Rather than using a centralized or local cross-functional model, companies are moving to a mode of global collaboration in which skilled development teams dispersed around the world collaborate to develop new products. Today, a majority of global corporations have engineering and development operations outside of their home region. China and India offer particularly attractive opportunities: Microsoft, Cisco, and Intel all have made major investments there.

The old model was based on the premise that colocation of cross-functional teams to facilitate close collaboration among engineering, marketing, manufacturing, and supply-chain functions was critical to effective product development. Colocated PD teams were thought to be more effective at concurrently executing the full range of activities involved, from understanding market and customer needs through conceptual and detailed design, testing, analysis, prototyping, manufacturing engineering, and technical product support and engineering. Such colocated concurrent practices were thought to result in better product designs, faster time to market, and lower-cost production. They were generally located in corporate research and development centers, which maintained linkages to manufacturing sites and sales offices around the world.

Today, best practice emphasizes a highly distributed, networked, and digitally supported development process. The resulting global product development process combines centralized functions with regionally distributed engineering and other development functions. It often involves outsourced engineering work as well as captive offshore engineering. The benefits of this distributed model include greater engineering efficiency (through utilization of *lower-cost* resources), *access to technical expertise* internationally, more *global input to product design*, and greater *strategic flexibility*.

Combining Aggregation, Adaptation, and Arbitrage: Global Innovation

Many companies now have global supply chains and product development processes, but few have developed effective global innovation capabilities.[7] Increasingly, however, technology access and innovation are becoming key global strategic drivers. This move from cost to growth and innovation is likely to continue as the center of gravity of economic activity shifts further to the East.

To illustrate the significant advantages of a truly global innovation strategy, Santos and others cite the battle between Motorola, Inc. and Nokia Corporation in the cellular phone industry. Motorola was a pioneer in the technology, building on initial path-breaking research from Bell Laboratories. But by focusing primarily on U.S. customers and U.S. solutions, it missed the market shift toward digital mobile technology and the global system for mobile (GSM) communication, which became the standard in Europe. The company also failed to appreciate that consumers were rapidly developing different use patterns and preferences about product design, thereby rendering a one-size-fits-all strategy obsolete.

A core competency in global innovation—the ability to leverage new ideas all around the world—has become a major source of global competitive advantage, as companies such as Nokia, Airbus, SAP, and Starbucks demonstrate. They realize that the principal constraint on innovation "performance" is knowledge. Accessing a diverse set of sources of knowledge is therefore a key challenge and is critical to successful differentiation. Companies whose knowledge pool is the same as that of its competitors will likely develop uninspired "me, too" products; access to a diversity of knowledge allows a company to move beyond incremental innovation to attention-grabbing designs and breakthrough solutions.

There is an interesting relationship between *geography* and *knowledge* diversity. In Finland, for example, the high cost of installing and maintaining fixed telephone lines in isolated places has spurred advances in radiotelephony. In Germany, cultural and political factors have encouraged the growth of a strong "green movement," which in turn has generated a distinctive market and technical knowledge in recycling and renewable energy. Just-in-time production systems were pioneered in part because of high land costs there. Recognition of the role played by geography in innovation has prompted many companies to globalize their perspective on the innovation process. For example, pharmaceutical companies such as Novartis AG and GlaxoSmithKline plc now realize that the knowledge they need extends far beyond traditional chemistry and therapeutics to include biotechnology and genetics. What is more, much of this new knowledge comes from sources other than the companies' traditional R&D labs in Basel, Bristol, and in New Jersey, from places such as California, Tel Aviv, Cuba, or Singapore. For these companies, globalization of innovation processes is no longer optional—it has become imperative.

Companies that globalize their supply chains by accessing raw materials, components, or services from around the world are typically able to reduce the overall costs of their operations. Similarly, a side benefit of global innovation is cost reduction. Consider, for example, how companies are now leveraging software programmers in Bangalore, India, aerospace technologists in Russia, or chipset designers in China to cut the costs of their innovation processes.

To reap the benefits of global innovation, companies must do three things:

1. *Prospect* (find the relevant pockets of knowledge from around the world)
2. *Assess* (decide on the optimal "footprint" for a particular innovation)
3. *Mobilize* (use cost-effective mechanisms to move distant knowledge without degrading it)[8]

Prospecting—that is, finding valuable new pockets of knowledge to spur innovation—may well be the most challenging task. The process involves knowing what to look for, where to look for it, and how to tap into a promising source. Santos and colleagues cite the efforts of the cosmetics maker Shiseido Co., Ltd., in entering the market for fragrance products. Based in Japan, a country with a very limited tradition of perfume use, Shiseido was initially unsure of the precise knowledge it needed to enter the fragrance business. But the company did know where to look for it. So it bought two exclusive beauty boutique chains in Paris, mainly as a way to experience, firsthand, the personal care demands of the most sophisticated customers of such products. It also hired the marketing manager of Yves Saint Laurent Parfums and built a plant in Gien, a town located in the French perfume "cluster." France's leadership in that industry made the *where* fairly obvious to Shiseido. The *how* had also become painfully clear because the company had previously flopped in its efforts to develop perfumes in Japan. Those failures convinced Shiseido executives that to access such complex knowledge—deeply rooted in local culture and combining customer information, aesthetics, and technology—the company had to immerse itself in the French environment and learn by doing. Having figured out the *where* and *how*, Shiseido would gradually learn *what* knowledge it needed to succeed in the perfume business.

Assessing new sources of innovation, that is, incorporating new knowledge into and optimizing an existing innovation network, is the second important challenge companies face. If a semiconductor manufacturer is developing a new chip set for mobile phones, for example, should it access technical and market knowledge from Silicon Valley, Austin, Hinschu, Seoul, Bangalore, Haifa, Helsinki, and Grenoble? Or should it restrict itself to just some of those sites? At first glance, determining the best footprint for innovation does not seem fundamentally different from the trade-offs companies face in optimizing their global supply chains: adding a new source might reduce the price or improve the quality of a required component, but more locations may also mean additional complexity and cost. Similarly, every time a company adds a source of knowledge to the innovation process, it might improve its chances of developing a novel product, but it also increases costs. Determining an optimal innovation footprint is more complicated, however, because the direct and indirect cost relationships are far more imprecise.

Mobilizing the footprint, that is, integrating knowledge from different sources into a virtual melting pot from which new products or technologies can emerge, is the third challenge. To accomplish this, companies must bring the various pieces of (technical) knowledge that are scattered around the world together and provide a suitable organizational form for innovation efforts to flourish. More importantly, they would have to add the more complex, contextual (market) knowledge to integrate the different pieces into an overall innovation blueprint.

Minicase 6.6. P&G's Success in Trickle-Up Innovation: Vicks Cough Syrup With Honey[9]

A new over-the-counter medicine from Vicks that has recently become popular in Switzerland is not as new as it seems. The product, Vicks Cough Syrup with Honey, is really just the latest incarnation of a product that Vicks parent company, Procter & Gamble (P&G), initially created for lower-income consumers in Mexico and then "trickled up" to more affluent markets.

The term "trickle up" refers to a strategy of creating products for consumers in emerging markets and then repackaging them for developed-world customers. Until recently, affluent consumers in the United States and Western Europe could afford the latest and greatest in everything. Now, with purchasing power dramatically reduced because of the global recession, budget items once again make up a growing portion of total sales in many product categories.

P&G is not the only multinational company using this strategy. Other practitioners of trickle-up innovation include General Electric (GE), Nestlé, and Nokia. In early 2008, GE Healthcare launched the MAC 400, GE's first portable Electrocardiograph (ECG) that was designed in India for the fast-growing local market there. The company simplified elements of its earlier, 65-lb devices made for U.S. hospitals by shrinking its case to the size of a fax machine and removing features such as the keyboard and screen. The smaller MAC 400 costs only $1,500, versus $15,000 for its U.S. predecessor. This trickle-down innovation trickled back up again when GE Healthcare decided to sell the unit in Germany as well.

Nestlé offers inexpensive instant noodles in India and Pakistan under its Maggi brand. The line includes dried noodles that are engineered to taste as if they were fried, while they have a whole-wheat flavor that is popular in South Asia. And Nokia researches how people in emerging nations share phones, such as the best-selling 1100 series of devices created for developing-world consumers. The company then uses the information as inspiration for new features for developed-world users.

But what is unique about P&G's Honey Cough, as it is also called, is that it has moved around the globe in more than one direction. Honey Cough originated in 2003 in P&G's labs in Caracas, Venezuela, which creates products for all of Latin America. Market research revealed that Latin American shoppers tended to prefer homeopathic remedies for coughs and colds, so P&G set out to create a medicine using natural honey rather than the artificial flavors typically used. The company first introduced the syrup in Mexico, under the label VickMiel, and then in other Latin American markets, including Brazil.

P&G deduced that the product would appeal to parts of the United States that have large Hispanic populations. In 2005, the company rebranded it as Vicks Casero for sale in California and Texas, at a price slightly less than Vicks' mainstay product, Vicks Formula 44. Within the first year of its release, the company boosted distribution to 27% more outlets.

Figuring that natural ingredients could appeal to even wider groups, P&G took the product to other markets where research indicated that homeopathic cold medicines are popular. In the past 2 years, the company has been marketing the product in Britain, France, Germany, and Italy, as well as Switzerland, and plans to add other Western European countries to the roster.

And Western Europe is not the last destination for iterations of Honey Cough. If P&G's current market research in the greater United States shows that mainstream American shoppers will buy Honey Cough, P&G will repackage it and market it nationwide, not just as Vicks Casero in Latino markets.

Developing and marketing a new product for each nation or ethnic group can take half a decade. Trickle-up innovation can reduce this time by several years, which explains its appeal. In each rollout, P&G has needed to do little more than make adjustments for each nation's health regulations.

At a time when companies are looking to speed product offerings while dealing with shrinking budgets and cash-strapped consumers, P&G's experience with its Honey Cough line shows how an international product portfolio can be tapped quickly and cheaply—that is, if American companies learn how to go against the flow.

Points to Remember

1. Managers sometimes assume that what works in their home country will work just as well in another part of the world. The result in most cases is failure. Why? Because the assumption that one approach works everywhere fails to consider the complex mosaic of differences that exists between countries and cultures.

2. With a few exceptions, the idea of an identical, fully standardized global value proposition is a myth, and few industries are truly global. How to adapt a value proposition in the most effective manner is therefore a key strategic issue.

3. Value proposition adaptation deals with a whole range of issues, ranging from the quality and appearance of products to materials, processing, production equipment, packaging, and style.

4. A useful construct for analyzing the need to adapt the product or service and message (positioning) dimensions is the *value proposition globalization matrix.*

5. One way around the trade-off between creating global efficiencies and adapting to local requirements and preferences is to design a global product or communication platform that can be adapted efficiently to different markets.

6. Globalization pressures have changed the practice of product development in many industries in recent years. Today, a majority of global corporations have engineering and development operations outside of their home region.

7. Many companies now have global supply chains and product development processes but few have developed effective global innovation capabilities. Increasingly, however, technology access and innovation are becoming key global strategic drivers.

8. A core competency in global innovation—the ability to leverage new ideas all around the world—has become a major source of global competitive advantage.

CHAPTER 7

Global Branding

As companies expand globally, a brand like Coke or Nike can be the greatest asset a firm has, but it also can quickly lose its power if it comes to signify something different in every market. Successfully leveraging a brand's power globally requires companies to consider aggregation, adaptation, and arbitrage strategies all at the same time, beginning with defining the universal "heart and soul" of every one of a company's brands (aggregation) and then expressing that in suitable words, images, and music (adaptation and arbitrage). In doing so, allowance must be made for flexibility in execution because even the smallest differences in different markets' consumer preferences, habits, or underlying cultures can make or break a brand's global success. In allowing such flexibility, a key consideration is how a product's current positioning in a particular market might affect the company's future offerings. If a product's positioning varies significantly in different markets, any "follow-on products" will likely have to be positioned differently as well, and this raises costs and can create operational problems.

Global Branding Versus Global Positioning

Johnson & Johnson (J&J) will not sacrifice premium pricing for its well-known brands. It believes that its popular Band-Aid adhesive bandages are superior to competitors' products, and a premium price is a way to signal that. But even in this dimension of its marketing strategy, J&J must allow for some improvisation as it expands around the world and pushes deeper into less-developed countries. Specifically, the company accepts lower margins in a developing market and sometimes delivers a smaller quantity of a product to make it more affordable. For instance, it might sell a four-pack of Band-Aids instead of the larger box it markets in the developed world or a sample-sized bottle of baby shampoo instead of a full-sized one.

Carefully adhering to a particular positioning is both aggregation and adaptation; this creates uniformity in different world markets, but it also serves to define target segments as the company enters new countries or regions. Consider the decision by Diageo, the British beer-and-spirits company, to stick to premium pricing wherever it does business, even when it enters a new market. By projecting a premium positioning for brands such as Johnnie Walker Black, Smirnoff vodka, Captain Morgan rum, Tanqueray gin, and Guinness stout, and foregoing price cutting to grow volume, it identifies loyal consumers who will pay for its well-known products. Rather than sell its products' functional benefits, Diageo successfully markets its drinks as either sophisticated, as it does with Tanqueray, or cool, as it does with Captain Morgan in its recent "Got a Little Captain in You?" ad campaign.[1]

Minicase 7.1. Global Positioning of MasterCard[2]

Back in 1997, the MasterCard "brand" did not stand for any one thing. The parent company—MasterCard International—had run through five different advertising campaigns in 10 years and was losing market share at home and abroad. Fixing the brand was a key element of the turnaround. Working with McCann-Erikson, the company developed the highly successful "priceless" campaign. The positioning created by "priceless" allowed MasterCard to integrate all its other campaigns and marketing practices within the United States, and this became a marketing platform that formed the basis for many globalization decisions.

Up until that time, every country used a different agency, a different campaign, and a different strategy. The success of "priceless" as a platform in the United States helped the company persuade other countries to adopt one, single approach, which, over time, produced a consistent global positioning. The "priceless" campaign now appears in more than 100 countries and more than 50 languages and informs all brand communications.

Starting with a locally developed positioning and then success-fully expanding it globally is one way to approach the global brand-ing and positioning challenge. More typically, companies start by identifying a unique consumer insight that is globally appli-cable in order to create a global positioning platform. No matter which route is selected, successful global branding and position-ing requires (a) identifying a globally "robust" positioning plat-form—MasterCard's new positioning was readily accepted across all markets because of the quality of the insight and its instant recognition across cultural boundaries—and (b) clarity about roles and responsibilities for decision making locally and globally. There was a shared understanding of how the primary customer insight should be used at every stage in the process and which aspects of the branding platform were nonnegotiable; expectations for performance were clearly defined and communicated on a global basis; and a strategic partnership with a single advertising agency allowed for consistent, seamless execution around the world.

By providing a single, unifying consumer insight that "defines" the brand's positioning, MasterCard has created economies of scale and scope and, hence, benefited from aggregation principles. The company uses adaptation and arbitrage strategies in its approach to implementation. It empowers local teams by inviting them to create content for their own markets within a proven, globally robust positioning framework. Additional, ongoing research gen-erates insights that allow local marketers to create a campaign that they truly feel has local resonance while at the same time main-taining the core brand positioning.

Global Brand Structures

Multinational companies typically operate with one of three brand struc-tures: (a) a corporate-dominant, (b) a product-dominant, or (c) a hybrid structure. A corporate-dominant brand structure is most common among firms with relatively limited product or market diversity, such as Shell, Toyota, or Nike. Product-dominant structures, in contrast, are often used by (mostly industrial) companies, such as Akzo Nobel, that have multiple national or local brands or by firms such as Procter & Gamble (P&G) that have expanded internationally by leveraging their "power" brands. The most commonly used structure is a hybrid (think of Toyota Corolla cars or Cadbury Dairy Milk chocolate) consisting of a mix of global (corporate), regional, and national product-level brands or different structures for different product divisions.

In many companies, "global" branding evolves as the company enters new countries or expands product offerings within an existing country. Typically, expansion decisions are made incrementally, and often on a country-by-country, product-division, or product-line basis, without considering their implications on the overall balance or coherence of the global brand portfolio. As their global market presence evolves and becomes more closely interlinked, however, companies must pay closer attention to the coherence of their branding decisions across national markets and formulate an effective global brand strategy that transcends national boundaries. In addition, they must decide how to manage brands that span different geographic markets and product lines, who should have custody of international brands and who is responsible for coordinating their positioning in different national or regional markets, as well as making decisions about use of a given brand name on other products or services.

To make such decisions, companies must formulate a coherent set of principles to guide the effective use of brands in the global marketplace. These principles must define the company's "brand architecture," that is, provide a guide for deciding which brands should be emphasized at what levels in the organization, how brands are used and extended across product lines and countries, and the extent of brand coordination across national boundaries.

Minicase 7.2. Henkel's "Fox" Brands: An Example of a Hybrid Strategy[3]

Like many European companies, Henkel, the German consumer-brands corporation, has globalized mostly via acquisitions, and, consequently, it has a portfolio of localized brands with a national heritage and good local market shares. As the portfolio grew, escalating media costs, increased communication and stronger linkages across markets, and the globalization of distribution created pressures for parsimony in the number of the firm's brands and the consolidation of architecture across countries and markets. Henkel executives understood very well that a focus on a limited number of global strategic brands can yield cost economies and potential synergies. At the same time, they also knew that they needed to develop procedures for managing the custody of these brands, and that these should be clearly understood and shared throughout all levels of the organization, thus promoting a culture focused on global growth. They knew that failing to do so would likely trigger territorial power struggles between corporate and local teams for control of the marketing agenda.

While many companies would have focused on deciding between sacrificing local brand equity to develop "global power brands" (aggregation) or continuing to sacrifice global marketing economies of scale by investing separately in its portfolio of local brands (adaptation), Henkel chose an ingenious middle path. Henkel's choice serves as a model for globalization of marketing concepts without loss of local brand equity through the grouping of all its "value-for-money" brands under the umbrella "Fox" brand. In each country, Henkel retained the local brand name but identifies it with the Fox umbrella brand. (In most cultures, the fox is seen as clever, selfish, and cunning—the sort of character who would buy a value-for-money brand but not a brand so cheap that its quality might be compromised.)

By using a fox to represent smart and cunning shoppers, Henkel has created a "global power brand concept" that can travel to almost any culture to enrich a local brand—especially local brands that individually could not have been globalized. But the scale economies Henkel gains from this program are more managerial than economic in nature. Programs and ideas to promote the Fox brands, and the concept of value-for-money detergents, are managed centrally and offered as a menu to all local markets in which these brands participate. Thus, a manager experienced in managing one of the Fox families of brands in one market can be transferred to another market and rapidly reach effective levels of performance. Because each brand still requires local investment, financial economies of scale are more modest.

Compare Henkel's success to the failures of its major competitors as they tried to fully globalize their brand portfolios. Years ago, P&G, for example, attempted to globalize its European laundry detergent operations. In 2000, the company renamed its popular "Fairy" laundry detergent in Germany "Dawn" to position the latter as a global brand. There was no change in the product's formulation. But by the end of 2001, P&G's market share of Dawn in Germany had fallen drastically. While Fairy had represented a familiar and trusted brand persona to German consumers, Dawn meant nothing. With the renaming, the bond between consumers and the brand was broken; not even changing the brand's name back to Fairy could restore it.

This experience suggests that attempting to achieve global brand positioning by deleting local brands can be problematic. In fact, a strategy of acquisition, and the subsequent shedding, of local brands by multinationals may actually create fragmentation in consumer demand rather than be a globalizing force. Such a scenario is particularly plausible if one or more of the local brands have reached "icon" status. Icon brands do not necessarily have distinctive features, deliver good service, or represent innovative technology. Rather, they resonate deeply with consumers because they possess cultural brand equity. Most of these brands fall into lifestyle categories: food, apparel, alcohol, and automobiles.

Determinants of Global Brand Structure

The kinds of issues a company must resolve as it tries to shape a coherent global branding strategy reflect its globalization history—how it has expanded internationally and how it has organized its international operations. At any given point, the structure of a brand portfolio reflects a company's past management decisions as well as the competitive realities the brand faces in the marketplace. Some companies, such as P&G and

Coca-Cola, expanded primarily by taking domestic "power" brands to international markets. As they seek to expand further, they must decide whether to further extend their power brands or to develop brands geared to specific regional or national preferences and how to integrate the latter into their overall brand strategy. Others, such as Nestlé and Unilever, grew primarily by acquisition. As a consequence, they relied mainly on country-centered strategies, building or acquiring a mix of national and international brands. Such companies must decide how far to move toward greater harmonization of brands across countries and how to do so. This issue is particularly relevant in markets outside the United States, which often are fragmented, have small-scale distribution, and lack the potential or size to warrant the use of heavy mass-media advertising needed to develop strong brands.

Specifically, a company's international brand structure is shaped by three sets of factors: (a) *firm-based characteristics*, (b) *product-market characteristics*, and (c) *underlying market dynamics*.[4]

Firm-Based Characteristics

Firm-based characteristics reflect the full array of past management decisions. First, a company's *administrative heritage*—in particular, its organizational structure—defines the template for its brand structure. Second, a firm's *international expansion strategy*—acquisition or organic growth—affects how its brand structure evolves over time. What is more, the use of strategic alliances to broaden the geographic scope of the firm's operations often results in a "melding" of the brand strategies of the partners. Third and fourth, the importance of *corporate identity* and the *diversity of the firm's product lines and product divisions* also determine the range and number of brands.

An appreciation of a company's *administrative heritage* is critical to understanding its global brand structure.[5] A firm that has historically operated on a highly decentralized basis, in which country managers have substantial autonomy and control over strategy as well as day-to-day operations, is likely to have a substantial number of local brands. In some cases, the same product may be sold under different brand names in different countries. In others, a product may be sold under the same brand name but have a different positioning or formulation in different countries.

Firms with a centralized organizational structure and global product divisions, such as Panasonic or Siemens, are more likely to have global brands. Both adopted a corporate branding strategy that emphasizes quality and reliability. Product lines are typically standardized worldwide, with minor variations in styling and features for local country markets.

Firms that *expand internationally* by acquiring local companies, even when the primary goal is to gain access to distribution channels, often acquire local brands. If these brands have high local recognition or a strong customer or distributor franchise, the company will normally retain the brand. This is particularly likely if the brand does not occupy a similar positioning to that of another brand currently owned by the firm. Nestlé and Unilever are examples of companies following this type of expansion strategy.

Expansion is often accompanied by diversification. Between 1960 and 1990, Nestlé expanded by acquiring a number of companies in a range of different product-markets, mostly in the food and beverage segment. These acquisitions included well-known global brands such as Perrier and San Pellegrino (mineral water), confectionery companies such as Rowntree and Perugina, pet food companies and brands such as Spillers and Alpo, and grocery companies such as Buitoni, Crosse & Blackwell, and Herta. The resulting proliferation of brands created the need to consolidate and integrate company-branding structures.[6]

Firms that have expanded predominantly by extending strong domestic, so-called power brands into international markets primarily use product-level brand strategies. P&G, for instance, has rolled out several of its personal products brands, such as Camay and Pampers, into international markets. This strategy appears most effective when customer interests and desired product attributes are similar worldwide and brand image is an important cue for the consumer.

The relative importance placed by the firm on its *corporate identity* also influences brand structure. Companies such as General Electric (GE) and Apple place considerable emphasis on corporate identity in the communications strategies. In the case of GE, "Imagination at Work" is associated with a corporate reputation dedicated to turning innovative ideas into leading products and services that help alleviate some of the world's toughest problems. Equally, Apple uses its apple logo to project the image of a vibrant innovator in the personal computer market. Increasingly, companies use their corporate identity as a means of reassuring customers and distributors that the company is reliable and stands behind its products. As a result, even companies with highly diverse product lines—such as Samsung—rely on the corporate brand name (and its logo) to project an image of reliability.

A fourth determinant of a company's brand structure is the *diversity, or, conversely, the interrelatedness of the product businesses* in which the firm is involved. Firms that are involved in closely related product lines or businesses that share a common technology or rely on similar core competencies often emphasize corporate brands. 3M Corporation, for example, is involved in a wide array of product businesses worldwide, ranging from displays and optics to health care products to cleaners to abrasives and adhesives. All rely heavily on engineering skills and have a reputation of being cutting-edge. The use of the 3M brand provides reassurance and reinforces the firm's reputation for competency and reliable products worldwide.

Minicase 7.3. Pharmaceutical Companies Try Global Branding

In Paris, stomach ulcers are treated with Mopral; in Chicago, it is called Prilosec. These two products are, in fact, exactly the same drug. Prilosec is the U.S. brand of AstraZeneca's omeprazole; Mopral is its French counterpart. Unlike manufacturers of consumer goods, the pharmaceutical industry traditionally has been wary of creating big, international brands. But that is about to change. Take a look at pharmacists' shelves. Viagra is there. So are Celebrex for arthritis pain, the antidiabetic agent Avandia, and the anticoagulant Plavix.

It is perhaps surprising that companies did not consider global branding sooner because a drug works for everybody in the same way in every country. While the industry has become global from a technological and geopolitical perspective, few companies have mastered globally integrated marketing practices. But change is coming—and fast. As more people travel internationally and the Internet makes information—including drug advice—readily available for doctors and patients, companies want to avoid any brand inconsistencies while maximizing exposure. Another globalizing force is growing standardization of the regulatory environment. With the establishment of the European Medical Evaluations Agency, for example, which approves drugs for all the members of the European Union, the borders are coming down. Japan has also adapted its approval system to facilitate the entry of Western products.

And then there is direct-to-consumer (DTC) advertising. While doctors and health care professionals remained the targets for pharmaceutical marketing, consumer-style branding was unnecessary. But companies are preparing for the spread of DTC beyond the shores of the United States. The introduction of global branding anticipates the transition to a more consumer-driven market.

Pressure to cut or contain costs is perhaps the most powerful driver behind the industry's move to global branding. Mega mergers were a way to contain the costs of research and development and find pipeline products, yet the big companies still need about five new blockbuster products each year to return the promised growth. Global branding promises reduced marketing costs and much faster and higher product rollout.

Local market conditions, such as reimbursement policies, however, may still override the benefits of global strategies and therefore inhibit the globalization of brands. Local flexibility will be key to success. Significant cost savings may therefore be slow in coming. Even with a centralized, global brand, most companies will still likely use local agencies for their marketing campaigns.

Product-Market Factors

Three product-market factors play an important role in brand architecture: the *nature and scope of the target market*, the product's *cultural associations*, and the *competitive market structure*.[7]

When companies target a *global market segment* with relatively homogeneous needs and preferences worldwide, global brands provide an effective means of establishing a distinctive global identity. Luxury brands such as Godiva, Moet and Chandon, and Louis Vuitton, as well as brands such as deBeers, Benetton, and L'Oreal are all targeted to the same market segment worldwide and benefit from the cachet provided by their appeal to a global consumer group. Sometimes it is more effective to segment international markets by region and target regional segments with similar interests and purchase behavior, such as Euro-consumers. This provides cost efficiencies when such segments are readily accessible through targeted regional media and distribution channels.

A critical factor influencing brand structure is the extent to which the *product is associated with a particular culture*, that is, the extent to which there are strong and deeply ingrained local preferences for specific products or product variants (think of beer) or the products are an integral part of a culture (think of bratwurst, soccer teams). The stronger the cultural association, the less likely it is that global product brands will thrive; instead, local branding may be called for.

A third product-market driver of a company's brand structure is the product's *competitive market structure*, defined as the relative strength of local (national) versus global competitors in a given product market. If markets are fully integrated and the same competitors compete in these markets worldwide, as in aerospace, the use of global brands helps provide competitive differentiation on a global basis. If strong local, national, or regional competitors, as well as global competitors, are present in a given national or regional market, the use of a multitier branding structure, including global corporate or product brands as well as local brands, is desirable. Coca-Cola, for example, beyond promoting its power brands, has introduced several local and regional brands that cater to specific market tastes around the world.

Minicase 7.4. Use of Country of Origin Effects in Global Branding[8]

Whether you prefer obscure imports or something mainstream, most beer brands like to invoke their country of origin. Guinness comes from Ireland, Corona is Mexican, Heineken and Amstel are Dutch, and Budweiser is a truly American brand.

The use of "country of origin effects" is an essential part of beer branding. Using the country of origin as part of the brand equity is free, so companies can avoid having to build an image from scratch over decades. For a long time, Foster's used a kangaroo in its advertisements, while Lapin Kulta, from Lapland in Finland, relies heavily on its unusual provenance in its marketing. Images of Finland's stark landscapes adorn communications material and bottle labels.

Swiss watchmakers certainly know the value of their "Swiss made" brand. The Federation of the Swiss Watch Industry actively polices all uses of the term and has strict guidelines on how it may be used on clocks and watches. In a similar vein, the French leverage their reputation for good wine, cooking, and fashion and the Italians view themselves as the masters of style.

German companies have been particularly effective in leveraging country effects. Of Interbrand's Top 100 Global Brands in 2008, 10 were German brands—five automobile brands (BMW, Porche, Mercedes-Benz, Volkswagen, and Audi), while brands in technology (SAP and Siemens), clothing (Adidas), financial services (Allianz), and cosmetics (Nivea) were also represented. Together, this group of German brands is valued at over $98 billion. Germany was second only to the United States in the number of brands making the Top 100 list.

It should come as no surprise, then, that Germany itself was ranked the best overall "country brand" in the 2008 Anholt-GfK Roper Nation Brands Index, which measures the world's perception of each nation as if it were a public brand. Fifty nations were measured in the study. The United States, the world's leading branding powerhouse, ranked seventh. So what is it about German brands, and the country that produces them, that is so special? Two words might be all the explanation that's required: discipline and quality.

German companies are highly disciplined in their approach to creating, introducing, and selling brands. They have the ability to consistently produce exceptional-quality products that are of lasting value. "German engineering" is a term closely associated with the country's automobile industry, which has seen a level of global success second only to the Japanese automakers. In fact, between 1990 and 2000, Mercedes-Benz and BMW more than doubled their sales in the United States alone.

Why do customers like German brands? German companies are widely admired for their intense focus on product quality and service, thought to be less interested in competing on price and strict about adhering to safety and other government standards.

BMW, a maker of premium automobiles, is one such revered brand. Founded in 1917 in Munich, Germany, as "Bavarian Motor Works," BMW produced aircraft engines during World War I, then built motorcycles in 1923 and went on to make cars in 1928. In recent years, BMW has been recognized as much for its innovative, quality marketing as for its high-performance cars.

But Germany's branding power extends well beyond automobiles. NIVEA, whose name comes from the Latin for "snow white," was created in late 1911. From its origins as a simple cream, NIVEA has now grown into a global manufacturer of a broad range of cosmetic and personal care products. NIVEA was voted the most trusted skin-care brand in 15 countries in the *Reader's Digest* survey of European Trusted Brands 2007.

Adidas, named after its founder Adolf (Adi) Dassler (Das), is an 80-year-old company that today is a global leader in sports footwear, apparel, and accessories. In 1996, Adidas equipped 6,000 Olympic athletes from 33 countries with its athletic gear. "Adidas athletes" won 220 medals, including 70 gold, and apparel sales increased 50%.

SAP, founded in 1972, is the world's largest business software company and the third-largest software supplier overall. The company employs almost 52,000 people and serves more than 76,000 customers in over 120 countries.

Other well-known global brands, from Bayer (pharmaceuticals) to Becks (beer) to Boss (clothing) to Braun (consumer products), are a testament to the fact that Germany is, and will continue to be, a prolific producer of some of the world's finest products. It is Germany's disciplined approach to quality that inspires consumer loyalty to German brands.

Market Dynamics

Finally, while the firm's history and the product markets in which it operates shape its brand structure, market dynamics—including *ongoing political and economic integration, the emergence of a global market infra-structure, and consumer mobility*—shape and continually change the context in which this evolves.[9]

Increasing *political and economic integration* in many parts of the world has been a key factor behind the growth of international branding. As governments remove tariff and nontariff barriers to business transactions and trade with other countries, and as people and information move easily across borders, the business climate has become more favorable to the marketing of international brands. Firms are less frequently required to modify products to meet local requirements or to develop specific variants for local markets and increasingly can market standardized products with the same brand name in multiple country markets. In many cases, harmonization of product regulation across borders has further facilitated this trend.

The growth of a global *market infrastructure* is also a major catalyst to the spread of international brands. Global and regional media provide economical and effective vehicles for advertising international brands. At the same time, global media help lay the groundwork for consumer acceptance of, and interest in, international brands by developing awareness of these brands and the lifestyles with which they are associated in other countries. In many cases, this stimulates a desire for the brands that consumers perceive as symbolic of a coveted lifestyle.

The globalization of retailing has further facilitated and stimulated the development of international manufacturer brands. As retailers move across borders, they provide an effective channel for international brands and, at the same time, increase their power. This forces manufacturers to develop strong brands with an international appeal so that they can negotiate their shelf position more effectively and ensure placement of new products.

A final factor shaping the context for international branding is increased *consumer mobility*. While global media provide passive exposure to brands, increasing international travel and movement of customers across national boundaries provides active exposure to brands in different countries. Awareness of the availability and high visibility of an international brand in multiple countries enhances its value to consumers and provides reassurance of its strength and reliability. Increased exposure to, and familiarity with, new and diverse products and the lifestyles and cultures in which they are embedded also generate greater receptivity to products of foreign origin or those perceived as international rather than domestic. All these factors help create a climate more favorable to international brands.

Formulating a Global Brand Strategy

To create an effective global brand structure capable of spanning operations in different countries and product lines, companies must clearly define the importance and role of each level of branding (corporate, product division, or product brand level), as well as the interrelation or overlap of branding at each level. They should also determine the appropriate geographic scope for each level relative to the firm's current organizational structure. To be effective, such "architecture" should satisfy three key principles: *parsimony, consistency, and connectivity.*

Parsimony requires that the brand architecture should incorporate all existing brands, whether developed internally or acquired, and provide a framework for consolidation to reduce the number of brands and strengthen the role of individual brands. Brands that are acquired need to be melded into the existing structure, especially when these brands occupy similar market positions to those of existing brands. When the same or similar products are sold under different brand names or are positioned differently in each country, ways to harmonize these should be examined.

A second important element of brand architecture is its *consistency* relative to the number and diversity of products and product lines within the company. A balance needs to be struck between the extent to which brand names differentiate product lines or establish a common identity across different products. Development of strong and distinctive brand images for different product lines helps establish their separate identities. Conversely, use of a common brand name consolidates effort and can produce synergies.

The value of corporate brand endorsement across different products and product lines and at lower levels of the brand hierarchy—a brand's *connectivity*—also needs to be assessed. The use of corporate brand endorsement as either a name identifier or logo connects the different product brands to the company and helps provide reassurance to customers, distributors, and other value-chain partners. Implemented well, corporate brand endorsement can integrate and unify different brand identities across national boundaries. At the same time, corporate endorsement of a highly diverse range of product lines can result in dilution of image. Worse, if one product brand is "damaged," corporate endorsement can spread the resulting negative effects or associations to other brands in the portfolio and create lasting effects across multiple product lines. Thus, both aspects need to be weighed in determining the role of corporate brand endorsement in brand architecture.

Managing Key Strategic Brands

Companies must also think about how to globally manage and monitor key strategic brands to ensure that they build and retain their integrity, visibility, and value. This entails assigning brand custody or appointing a brand champion responsible for approving brand extensions and monitoring brand positioning.

One option is to negotiate the harmonization of specific brand positions between corporate headquarters and country managers. This is appropriate for firms with strong country management that operate in product markets where brands were historically tailored to local market characteristics.

A more proactive and increasingly popular solution is to appoint a brand champion responsibility for building and managing a brand worldwide. This includes monitoring the consistency of the brand positioning in international markets as well as authorizing use of the brand (brand extensions) on other products or other product businesses. The brand champion can be a senior manager at corporate headquarters, a country manager, or a product development group. It is critical that the brand champion report directly to top management and have clear authority to sanction or refuse brand extensions to other product lines and product businesses so as to maintain the integrity of the brand and avoid brand dilution.

A third option is to centralize control of brands within a global product division. This approach is likely to be most effective when the business is targeted to a specific global market segment, with new products or brands, when there is greater consistency in market characteristics across countries, and when the company's administrative heritage has only a limited history of strong country management.

Benefits of Corporate Branding

Corporations around the world are increasingly becoming aware of the enhanced value that corporate branding strategies can provide.[10] A strong corporate branding strategy can add significant value in terms of helping the entire corporation and the management team with implementing its long-term vision, creating unique positions in the marketplace for the company and its brands, and signaling a commitment to a broader set of stakeholder issues. An effective corporate branding strategy therefore enables the company to leverage its tangible and nontangible assets and promote excellence throughout the corporation. To be effective and meet such objectives, corporate branding requires a high level of personal attention and commitment from the CEO and the senior management. Examples of effective corporate brands include Microsoft, Intel, Singapore Airlines, Disney, CNN, Samsung, and Mercedes. In recent years, the global financial powerhouses HSBC and Citibank have both acquired a vast number of companies across the globe and have fully adopted them under their international corporate brands with great success and within a relatively short time frame. All these companies understand that a well-executed corporate branding strategy can confer significant benefits.

Corporate Brand as the "Face of the Company"

A strong corporate brand acts as the face of the company, portraying what it wants to do and what it wants to be known for in the marketplace. In other words, the corporate brand is the umbrella for the corporation's activities and encapsulates its vision, values, personality, positioning, and image, among many other dimensions. Think of HSBC. It employs the same slogan—"The world's local bank"—around the world. This creative platform enables the corporation to portray itself as a bridge between cultures.

Simplicity

An effective corporate branding strategy creates simplicity by making the top of the brand portfolio the ultimate identifier of the corporation. P&G is widely known for its multibrand strategy. Yet, the corporate name P&G encapsulates all of its activities. Depending on the business strategy and the potential need for multiple brands, a corporate brand can assist management focus on the company's core vision and values. Once established, it facilitates revisiting the definition of other brands in the corporations' portfolio and the creation of new brand identities.

Cost Savings

A corporate branding strategy is often more cost-efficient than a multi-brand architecture. Specifically, corporate branding produces efficiencies in terms of marketing and advertising spending as the corporate brand replaces budgets for individual product marketing efforts. Even a combined corporate and product branding strategy can often enable management to reduce costs and exploit synergies from a new and more focused brand architecture. The Apple brand has established a very strong position of being a design-driven and innovative company offering many types of products and services. Their corporate brand encapsulates the body and soul of the company, and the main messages from the company use the corporate Apple brand. Various sub-brands then help to identify the individual product lines.

Corporate Brands as Assets

In recent years, corporate brands themselves have become valuable assets on the company balance sheet, with market values very often much beyond book value.

Minicase 7.5. The Best Global Brands[11]

Interbrand, a leading international brand consultancy specializing in brand services and activities, has developed a method for valuing (global) brands. It examines brands through the lens of financial strength, the importance of the brand in driving consumer selection, and the likelihood of ongoing revenue generated by the brand.

Each year, Interbrand compiles a list of global brands for analysis based on five criteria:

1. There must be substantial publicly available financial data for the brand.
2. One-third of the brand's revenues must come from outside its country of origin.
3. The brand must be positioned to play a significant role in the consumers' purchase decision.
4. The Economic Value Added (EVA) must be positive, showing that there is revenue above the company's operating and financing costs.
5. The brand must have a broad public profile and awareness.

The use of these criteria excludes a number of brands one might expect to be included. The Mars and BBC brands, for example, are privately held and do not have financial data publicly available. Wal-Mart, although it does business in international markets, does not do so under the Wal-Mart brand and is therefore not sufficiently global. Certain industry sectors are also not included in Interbrand's study. An example is provided by telecommunication brands, which tend to have strong national roots and have faced awareness challenges due to numerous mergers and acquisitions. The major pharmaceutical companies, while very valuable businesses, are also excluded since their consumers tend to build a relationship with the product brands rather than the corporate brand.

For brands that meet the Interbrand criteria, the company next looks at the current financial health of the business and brand, the brand's role in creating demand, and the future strength of the brand as an asset to the business.

Financial Analysis

Interbrand's model first forecasts the current and future revenue specifically attributable to the branded products. It subtracts operating costs from this revenue to calculate branded operating profit. Next, a charge is applied to the branded profit that is based on the capital a business spends versus the money it makes. This yields an estimate of a business's economic earnings. All financial analysis is based on publicly available company information.

Role of Brand Analysis

Brand analysis involves a measurement of how a brand influences customer demand at the point of purchase. It is applied to the economic earnings in order to arrive at the revenue that the brand alone generates (branded earnings). Interbrand uses in-house market research to establish individual brand scores against industry benchmarks to define the role a brand plays within the category. For example, *role of brand* is traditionally much higher in the luxury category than in the energy and utilities sector. The brand, not the business, is the principal reason consumers choose these goods and services.

Brand Strength Score

As brands are assets, valuing them requires an assessment of their ability to secure future earnings on behalf of the businesses that own them. Brand strength is a measure of the brand's ability to secure demand, and therefore earnings, over time. Securing customer demand typically means achieving loyalty, advocacy, and favorable levels of customer trial, as well as maintaining a price premium. Interbrand's methodology generates a discount factor that adjusts the forecasted brand earnings for their riskiness based on the level of demand the brand is able to secure. Brand strength is calculated by assessing the brand's performance against a set of seven critical factors, including measures of relevance, leadership, market position, customer franchise, diversification, and brand support.

Brand Value

A brand's value is a financial representation of a business's earnings due to the superior demand created for its products and services through the strength of its brand. Brand value is the absolute financial worth of the brand as it stands today. Accordingly, the brand's value can be compared to the total value of the business as it would be assessed on the stock exchange.

The winner and number 1 global brand on Interbrand's 2009 list, once again, is *Coca-Cola*, which has topped the list for more than 20 years. *IBM* is number 2, *Microsoft* ranks third, *GE* comes in fourth, and *Nokia* has moved up to fifth position. Rounding out the top 10 are *McDonald's* (6), *Google* (7), *Toyota* (8), *Intel* (9), and *Disney* (10).

Interestingly, not one of the 100 Best Global Brands emanates from the developing world, at least for now. But Interbrand's research suggests this may soon change. With their huge populations, there is a decided shift in economic power to countries like China, India, Russia, Brazil, and Africa, and former global giants are making way for new leaders from fast developing markets.

The following brands are strong leaders in their home markets and already show some early signs of globalization:

- China: *Lenovo* (PCs), *Haier* (refrigerators), *Tsingtao* (beer)
- India: *Tata* (communications and information technology, engineering, materials, services, energy, consumer products, and chemicals), *Reliance* (energy and materials), *ArcelorMittal* (steel)
- Russia: *Kaspersky Lab* (information security to computer users), *Aeroflot* (airline), *Gazprom* (gas)

- South Africa: *MTN* (communications), *Anglo American* (mining), *SABMiller* (beer and soft drinks).
- Brazil: *Banco Itaú* (finance), *Vale* (mining), *Natura Cosmético* (cosmetics)

Points to Remember

1. As companies expand globally, a brand like Coke or Nike can be the greatest asset a firm has, but it can also quickly lose its power if it comes to signify something different in every market.
2. Successfully leveraging a brand's power globally requires that marketers consider aggregation, adaptation, and arbitrage strategies all at the same time.
3. Multinational companies typically operate with one of three brand structures: a *corporate-dominant*, a *product-dominant*, or a *hybrid* structure.
4. A company's international brand structure is shaped by three sets of factors: *firm-based characteristics*, *product-market characteristics*, and *underlying market dynamics*.
5. An effective global brand structure reflects *parsimony, consistency*, and *connectivity*.
6. Companies must also think about how to globally manage and monitor key strategic brands to ensure that they build and retain their integrity, visibility, and value.
7. A strong corporate branding strategy can add significant value in terms of helping the entire corporation and the management team with implementing its long-term vision, creating unique positions in the marketplace for the company and its brands, and signaling a commitment to a broader set of stakeholder issues.
8. The number 1 global brand on Interbrand's 2009 list is *Coca-Cola*, which has topped the list for more than 20 years. Next on the list are *IBM, Microsoft, GE*, and *Nokia*. *McDonald's, Google, Toyota, Intel*, and *Disney round out the top 10.*

CHAPTER 8

Globalizing the Value Chain Infrastructure

Globalizing a company's value creation infrastructure—from the sourcing of raw materials and components, to manufacturing and research and development (R&D), to distribution and customer service—has three primary dimensions: (a) deciding which activities to perform in-house and which ones to outsource, and to whom and where; (b) developing the right partnerships to support a company's globalization efforts; and (c) implementing a suitable supply-chain management model for integrating them into a cost-effective, seamless value-creating network. This chapter looks at the first two dimensions; the third—supply-chain management—is the subject of the next chapter.

Core Competencies

Core competencies represent unique capabilities that allow a company to build a competitive advantage. 3M has developed a core competency in coatings. Canon has core competencies in optics, imaging, and microprocessor controls. Procter & Gamble's marketing prowess allows it to adapt more quickly than its rivals to changing opportunities. The development of core competencies has become a key element in building a long-term strategic advantage. An evaluation of strategic resources and capabilities must therefore include assessments of the core competencies a company has or is developing, how they are nurtured, and how they can be leveraged.

Core competencies evolve as a firm develops its business model and incorporates its intellectual assets. Core competencies are not just things a company does particularly well; rather, they are sets of skills or systems that create a uniquely high value for customers at best-in-class levels. To qualify, such skills or systems should contribute to perceived customer benefits, be difficult for competitors to imitate, and allow for leverage across markets. Honda's use of small engine technology in a variety of products—including motorcycles, jet skis, and lawn mowers—is a good example.

Core competencies should be focused on creating value and should be adapted as customer requirements change. Targeting a carefully selected set of core competencies also benefits innovation. Charles Schwab, for example, successfully leveraged its core competency in brokerage services by expanding its client communication methods to include Internet, telephone, offices, and financial advisors.

Hamel and Prahalad suggest three tests for identifying core competencies. First, core competencies should provide access to a broad array of markets. Second, they should help differentiate core products and services. Third, core competencies should be hard to imitate because they represent multiple skills, technologies, and organizational elements.[1]

Experience shows that only a few companies have the resources to develop more than a handful of core competencies. Picking the right ones, therefore, is the key. A key question to ask is, which resources or capabilities should be kept in-house and developed into core competencies and which ones should be outsourced? Pharmaceutical companies, for example, increasingly outsource clinical testing in an effort to focus their resource base on drug development. Generally, the development of core competencies should focus on long-term platforms capable of adapting to new market circumstances; on unique sources of leverage in the value chain in which the firm thinks it can dominate; on elements that are important to customers in the long run; and on key skills and knowledge, not on products.

To Outsource or Not to Outsource

Few companies, especially ones with a global presence, are self-sufficient in all of the activities that make up their value chain. Growing global competitive pressures force companies to focus on those activities they judge as critical to their success and excel at—core capabilities in which they have a distinct competitive advantage—and that can be leveraged across geographies and lines of business. Which activities should be kept in house and which ones can effectively be outsourced depends on a host of factors, most prominently the nature of the company's core strategy and dominant value discipline.[2]

In principle, every functional or value-adding activity, from research to manufacturing to customer service, is a candidate for outsourcing. It is hard to imagine, however, that operationally excellent companies would consider outsourcing activities that are critical to the efficacy of their supply chain. Similarly, companies operating with a customer-intimate business model should be reluctant to outsource customer-service-related functions, while product leaders should nurture their capacity to innovate. That is why Toyota made continuous investments in its production system as it globalized its operations, Procter & Gamble focused on strengthening its world-class innovation and marketing capabilities as it expanded abroad, and Wal-Mart continued to refine its supply-chain management capabilities.

Firms tend to concentrate their investments in global value chain activities that contribute directly to their competitive advantage and, at the same time, help the company retain the right amount of strategic flexibility. Making such decisions is a formidable challenge—capabilities that may seem unrelated at first glance can turn out to be critical for creating an essential advantage when they are combined. As an example, consider the case of a leading consumer packaged-goods company that created strong embedded capabilities in sales. Its smaller brands showed up on retailers' shelves far more regularly than comparable brands from competitors. It was also known for the efficacy of its short-term R&D in rapidly bringing product variations to market. These capabilities are worth investing in separately, but, together, they add up to a substantial advantage over competitors, especially in introducing new products.

Outsourcing and offshoring of component manufacturing and support services can offer compelling strategic and financial advantages including *lower costs, greater flexibility, enhanced expertise, greater discipline*, and *the freedom to focus on core business activities*.

Lower Costs

Savings may result from lower inherent, structural, systemic, or realized costs. A detailed analysis of each of these cost categories can identify the potential sources of advantage. For example, larger suppliers may capture greater scale benefits than the internal organization. The risk is that efficiency gains lead to lower quality or reliability. Offshoring typically offers significant infrastructure and labor cost advantages over traditional outsourcing. In addition, many offshoring providers have established very large-scale operations that are not economically possible for domestic providers.

Greater Flexibility

Using an outside supplier can sometimes add flexibility to a company such that it can rapidly adjust the scale and scope of production at low cost. As we have learned from the Japanese *keiretsu* and Korean *chaebol* conglomerates, networks of organizations can often adjust to demand more easily than fully integrated organizations.

Enhanced Expertise

Some suppliers may have proprietary access to technology or other intellectual property advantages that a firm cannot access by itself. This technology may improve operational reliability, productivity, efficiency, or long-term total costs and production. The significant scale of today's offshore manufacturers, in particular, allows them to invest in technology that may be cost prohibitive for domestic providers.

Greater Discipline

Separation of purchasers and providers can assist with transparency and accountability in identifying true costs and benefits of certain activities. This can enable transactions under market-based contracts where the focus is on output rather than input. At the same time, competition among suppliers creates choice for purchasers and encourages the adoption of innovative work practices.

Focus on Core Activities

The ability to focus frees up resources internally to concentrate on those activities at which the company has distinctive capability and scale, experience, or differentiation to yield economic benefits. In other words, focus allows a company to concentrate on creating *relative* advantage to maximize total value and allows others to produce supportive goods and services.

While outsourcing is largely about scale and the ability to provide services at a more competitive cost, offshoring is primarily driven by the dramatic wage-cost differentials that exist between developed and developing nations. However, cost should not be the only consideration in making offshoring decisions; other relevant factors include the quality and reliability of labor continuous process improvements, environment, and infrastructure. Political stability and broad economic and legal frameworks should also be taken into account. In reality, even very significant labor cost differentials between countries cannot be the sole driver of offshoring decisions. Companies need to be assured of quality and reliability in the services they are outsourcing. This is the same whether services are outsourced domestically or offshore.

The Growth in Knowledge-Based Outsourcing

In the last 20 years companies have outsourced many activities, including manufacturing, back-office functions, information technology (IT) services, and customer support. Now the focus is shifting to more knowledge-intensive areas, such as product development, R&D, engineering, and analytical services.[3] For example, as noted above, pharmaceutical companies depend on a steady pipeline of new products from R&D. The competitive pressures on these firms to bring out new products at an ever rapid pace to meet market needs are increasing. With it, the pressures on the R&D function are increasing. In order to alleviate the pressure, firms have to either increase R&D budgets or find ways to utilize the resources in a more productive way. There are situations when a firm should consider outsourcing some of its R&D work to contract research organizations or universities, for example, when (a) in-house new product design is ineffective or too slow, (b) the company is plagued by consistent project time and cost overruns, (c) loss of key talent has slowed new product development, (d) there is a need for an immediate competitive response, or (e) when problems of quality or yield reduce R&D effectiveness.

The growth in knowledge-based outsourcing is mainly driven by cost imperatives, but, increasingly, shortages of talent in home markets and the growing availability of skills in nations such as India, China, and Russia play a role. A second driver behind the growth in knowledge-based outsourcing is the increasing "commoditization" of standard business processes and IT services, depressing margins on such activities for outsourcers. This has further encouraged service providers to switch to other activities for which profits are potentially greater—including "innovation services" such as new product development (NPD), R&D, and engineering. According to Booz & Company, there has been 95% growth in the provision of such capabilities since the millennium.[4] At the same time, providers of standardized services have come to recognize that they need to focus on efficiency and more seamless client integration if they are to continue making sufficient returns. By contrast, innovation services, including everything from prototype design to credit analysis, are more complex and client-specific, and therefore are more likely to command a premium.

For companies considering knowledge-based outsourcing, the lack of standardization means that partner vetting is critical and that outsourcers need to consider investing in captive or near-captive operations that can be sufficiently customized. That may mean turning to smaller providers—that is, those with fewer than 500 employees—that are better able to meet exacting requirements. The process of contracting with multiple, small service providers in different parts of the world is challenging. Many companies are still struggling to integrate more standardized processes with their existing core operations. Outsourcing knowledge-intensive activities will involve a whole new level of managerial complexity, potentially upending fundamental notions of how companies see themselves and what they do. Outsourcing vital activities such as prototype design and engineering support will be fraught with risk, with potentially significant downsides. However, organizations will have little choice: the need to identify talent outside the home territory will force them to work with partners overseas, whatever the pitfalls.

Companies that successfully manage knowledge-based outsourcing are looking to create collaborative management models that share responsibilities, risks, and rewards, enabling both sides to reach their objectives. This "comanagement" approach involves outsourcers treating contractors as valued collaborators even in cases where competitors are employing the same company. It will also necessitate joint investment in offshore staff development, helping providers to retain talent and maintain their revenue margins.

Increased use of knowledge-based offshoring could have significant ramifications on how companies are organized. Rather than multinational organizations with business units staffed by expatriate managers and orchestrated from a central headquarters, the organization of the future will be more globally distributed, with managers seeking out talent wherever it is located and plugging in capabilities when needed. Unlike the outsourcing of the past, knowledge-based offshoring is not simply about labor arbitrage; it is about transforming companies into more nimble, flexible entities.

Minicase 8.1. Outsourcing of R&D in the Pharmaceutical Industry[5]

To cut costs and speed development, Eli Lilly outsources a substantial portion of its R&D—including clinical trials—to countries such as India and China. Lilly is not the only pharmaceutical company that has relocated R&D operations to the developing world; Pfizer tests drugs in Russia, and AstraZeneca conducts clinical trials in China. The main driver is rising development costs, estimated at some $1.1 billion per drug—including expenses on all the products that do not make it to the market—and expected to increase to $1.5 billion by 2010.

More recently, Lilly and other drug makers have begun to expand their R&D efforts in India and China to include clinical trials. These are the late-stage experiments to prove a drug can be used on humans. These tests are enormously expensive; Lilly estimates that each Phase III test costs at least $50 million a year. To reduce costs, Lilly plans to move 20% to 30% of this testing in the next few years. While cost reduction is the main reason for the migration, this migration is made possible by the investments these nations have made in the necessary research labs, hospitals, and professional staffs to conduct studies that meet the stringent regulations of the U.S. Food & Drug Administration or drug regulators in the European Union.

While these outsourcing initiatives are extremely successful, it is unlikely that Lilly will move its entire R&D portfolio abroad. It will likely keep a number of centers of excellence in the United States, renowned for their path-breaking research in cancer and heart disease, to maintain its leadership in these areas and to keep a research presence in the country. Another reason that prevents pharmaceutical companies from outsourcing all of its research is that they may not be able to sell their newest products in countries like India and China because patients cannot afford them or because of worries about patent protection.

Risks Associated With Outsourcing

Outsourcing can have significant benefits but is not without risk.[6] Some risks, such as potentially higher offshoring costs due to the eroding value of the U.S. dollar, can be anticipated and addressed through contracts by employing financial-hedging strategies. Others, however, are harder to anticipate or deal with.

As a general principle, functions that have the potential to "interrupt" the flow of product or service between a company and its customers are the riskiest to outsource. For example, delegating control of the distribution process to an online retailer can result in customers not receiving goods promptly; outsourcing call-center responsibilities can result in customers being dissatisfied with the product or service and, thus, in higher product returns, lower repurchases, or complaints that could endanger the company's reputation.

The second riskiest type of activity to outsource is one that affects the relationship between a company and its employees. Outsourcing the human resources function, for example, can affect employee-hiring quality; outsourcing payroll and benefits processing can result in information breaches that generate identity theft issues and resultant legal issues; or outsourcing software design can generate a decline in organizational innovation. By contrast, support functions such as accounts payable and maintenance are less risky to outsource because they have few direct links to customers or internal organizational processes.

More formally, risks associated with outsourcing typically fall into four general categories: *loss of control, loss of innovation, loss of organizational trust,* and *higher-than-expected transaction costs.*

Loss of Control

Managers often complain about loss of control over their own process technologies and quality standards when specific processes or services are outsourced. The consequences can be severe. When tasks previously performed by company personnel are given to outsiders, over whom the firm has little or no control, quality may suffer, production schedules may be disrupted, or contractual disagreements may develop. If outsourcing contracts inappropriately or incorrectly detail work specifications, outsourcers may be tempted to behave opportunistically—for example, by using subcontractors or by charging unforeseen or unwarranted price increases to exploit the company's dependency. Control issues can also be exacerbated by geographic distance, particularly when the vendor is offshore. Monitoring performance and productivity can be challenging, and coordination and communication maybe difficult with offshore vendors. The inability to engage in face-to-face discussions, brainstorm, or explore nuances of obstacles could cripple a project's flow. Distance, too, can increase the likelihood of outages disabling the communication infrastructure between the vendor and the outsourcing firm. Depending on where the outsourced work is performed, there can be critical cultural or language-related differences between the outsourcing company and the vendor. Such differences can have important customer implications. For example, if customer call centers are outsourced, the manner in which an agent answers, interprets, and reacts to customer telephone calls (especially complaints) may be affected by local culture and language.

Loss of Innovation

Companies pursuing innovation strategies recognize the need to recruit and hire highly qualified individuals, provide them with a long-term focus and minimal control, and appraise their performance for positive long-run impact. When certain support services—such as IT, software development, or materials management—are outsourced, innovation may be impaired. Moreover, when external providers are hired for the purposes of cutting costs, gaining labor pool flexibility, or adjusting to market fluctuations, long-standing cooperative work patterns are interrupted, which may adversely affect the company's corporate culture.

Loss of Organizational Trust

For many firms, a significant nonquantifiable risk occurs because outsourcing, especially of services, can be perceived as a breach in the employer-employee relationship. Employees may wonder which group or what function will be the next to be outsourced. Workers displaced into an outsourced organization often feel conflicted as to who their "real" boss is: the new external service contractor or the client company by which they were previously employed?

Higher-Than-Expected Transaction Costs

Some outsourcing costs and benefits are easily identified and quantified because they are captured by the accounting system. Other costs and benefits are decision-relevant but not part of the accounting system. Such factors cannot be ignored simply because they are difficult to obtain or because they require the use of estimates. One of the most important and least understood considerations in the make-or-buy decision is the cost of outsourcing risk.

There are many other factors to consider in selecting the right level of participation in the value chain and the location for key value-added activities. Factor conditions, the presence of supporting industrial activity, the nature and location of the demand for the product, and industry rivalry should all be considered. In addition, such issues as tax consequences, the ability to repatriate profits, currency and political risk, the ability to manage and coordinate in different locations, and synergies with other elements of the company's overall strategy should be factored in.

Minicase 8.2. Nokia's Global Brain Trust: Encouraging the Mobility of Ideas[7]

Nokia likes to team up with leading international universities in search of the next great communications technology ideas. The Finnish company's research center in the United Kingdom works with the University of Cambridge to develop nanotechnologies for mobile communication and what is being called "ambient intelligence"—electronic environments that are sensitive and responsive to the presence of people. In Beijing, Nokia's research hub was set up to take advantage of China's top-level universities and to gather valuable local perspectives on communications trends and market potential.

But the other aspect of Nokia's open innovation model—its abundant use of the Internet to harvest new ideas—is far less conventional. The progress of current projects is posted on company wikis. The Nokia Beta Labs website plays host to a legion of testers who provide feedback on new and potential applications. And Forum Nokia, a portal available in English, Chinese, and Japanese, gives outside developers access to resources to help them design, test, certify, market, and sell their own applications, content, services, or websites to mobile users via Nokia devices.

By encouraging the mobility of ideas across its network and then exploiting them commercially, Nokia is able to succeed with an innovation strategy that represents the best of global and local approaches. But Nokia's open-innovation thrust is by itself only part of a long-term innovation strategy aimed at supporting sustained expansion into markets outside the company's traditional European markets.

Venture capital investment is the other thrust. The company's Nokia Growth Partners, with offices in China, Finland, India, and the United States, manages $350 million for direct investments and fund-of-fund investments in other venture capital players, primarily in the United States, Europe, and Asia. One recent fund investment was in Madhouse, China's leading mobile advertisement network—a crucial driver for continued growth in mobile communications markets.

Locating Value-Added Activities

The search for *growth* is a primary driver of manufacturing relocation.[8] Emerging economies have significantly higher trend rates of growth than mature economies. This is the inevitable result of the arrival of large-scale capital investment in low-wage and low-cost economies.

This phenomenon is clearly evident in the automotive industry—an industry challenged by low sales growth and declining margins in mature markets. The world's automotive assemblers want to capture market share in the fastest growing markets of the near future, and they want their chosen suppliers to be with them. Suppliers, for their part, also want to be part of the growth story, serving not only their traditional global Original Equipment Manufacturer OEM customers but also the emerging local automakers that are capturing new markets with low cost and often innovative products, such as China's Chery Auto and India's Tata Motors.

Reducing cost is a second powerful driver of manufacturing relocation. A recent survey by KPMG Peat Marwick showed that among companies that are primarily motivated by costs to invest in new markets, the opportunity to lower *material costs is considered marginally more important than labor or capital costs*.[9] This somewhat surprising result reflects the fact that companies still find that the costs of internationally traded raw materials and partially processed commodities, such as automotive steel, remain cheaper in some lower-cost economies. The same survey showed that even if costs can be reduced, companies remain concerned about the cost of complexity that may be introduced when operations become distributed over several locations that may be separated by large distances and may be in numerous jurisdictions. The companies interviewed also cited a wide range of other cost drivers of relocation. These include government incentives, regional interest rates, wages, and trade agreements.

The relative importance of a third driver—*innovation*—is increasing as the center of gravity of global business activity continues to shift eastward. In the automobile industry, for example, a vehicle manufactured today has, on average, 10 times the number of electronic functions of a vehicle manufactured 10 years ago. But while innovation has intensified, the sales volume to support the costs of this product innovation has failed to materialize. Price and income trends mean that sales volumes are unlikely to be rebuilt in the developed industrial markets; on the contrary, they are likely to fall further. In these markets, the average price of a new car has doubled over the last 20 years, but average incomes have only risen by 50%, and this price-income gap continues to widen, implying further falls in sales volumes if costs cannot be cut.

These trends are driving a multidirectional globalization of innovation in the supplier industry. Established companies in the automotive triad need both to cut the costs of innovation and find new sources of technology and process innovation. Suppliers in emerging economies need to acquire, rather than just develop, technologies and R&D skills in order to gain the innovation critical mass that will allow them to compete as global suppliers.

Companies participating in the KPMG's Supplier Survey divide roughly equally between those who believe that R&D should be located close to production and those who are happy with geographically separated R&D and production. These responses suggest that a minority of companies plan to relocate R&D to emerging markets, despite cost pressures.

Companies who believe that R&D should be located close to production tend not to be planning R&D relocations. They believe that R&D for process improvement is more important than R&D for application engineering, and their R&D centers are most likely to be located in Western Europe and Asia, followed by North America. In contrast, companies willing to operate R&D centers remote from production are predisposed to relocating production facilities, although most of these companies say that innovation is a less important criterion than cost, growth, or risk.

These primary drivers—the need to find growth, to reduce costs, and to facilitate innovation—must be balanced by a company's capacity to manage risks. Yet, in many cases, the upside and downside of all these factors may be more subtle or less clear than companies commonly suppose. Where markets offer the promise of *growth*, companies should consider how consistent that growth would be over the term of the investment. They might consider whether it is necessary to locate in a given economy, or even region, to access the expected growth. Where companies seek to reduce *costs*, they should also consider whether direct cost reductions in areas like labor and raw materials are accompanied by indirect cost increases in areas like logistics and quality assurance. Where companies seek to facilitate *innovation*, they should consider whether risks and costs are best balanced by a conservative strategy of centralized R&D or a radical strategy of globally distributed R&D. And, in seeking to manage *risks*, companies need to understand that globalized operations may offer risk mitigation opportunities through the hedging of production, currency exposure and raw materials sourcing, as well as the increased risk challenges inherent in global operations.

Minicase 8.3. Nestlé Adapts Its Business Model to Target the Global Halal Food Market[10]

In 2006, the Malaysian operations of the world's biggest food company played a leading role as Nestlé began to target the fast-growing halal food business. Its annual turnover of $73 billion (in 2005) dwarfed that of its nearest rivals, notably Kraft Foods, PepsiCo, Unilever, and Coca-Cola, whose sales ranged from $20 billion to $35 billion. Nevertheless, Nestlé was positioning itself to grow its food business even further.

With a market share of only 2% of the global food industry, Nestlé had ample room for growth. The halal segment, where it was well ahead of its major competitors in terms of market share and preparation, looked particularly promising. Worth $150 billion and with Muslims forming about 25% of the world's population and having higher per capita income growth, Nestlé estimated that the halal food business would grow to $500 billion by 2010. Nestlé's 2006 sales of halal products were in the region of $6 billion.

The strategic importance of this segment of the market was clearly highlighted at Nestlé's product exhibition center on the sixth floor of its headquarters in Vevey, Switzerland. In a special corner for halal food exhibits, posters displayed such messages as "As disposable incomes of Muslim countries increase, global halal food sales will skyrocket"; "In Europe, many supermarkets are selling halal products"; and "Worldwide, halal food sales exceed $150 billion."

Growth was expected to come from not only large, populated Muslim countries like Indonesia, Bangladesh, Pakistan, and the

Middle East but also non-Muslim countries with a large number of Muslims, like India and the Muslim belt of North Africa, and in cities such as London.

There were a number of factors Nestlé believed would drive growth. One was an increasing demand for products that follow Islamic law. Another was the growing divide between the West and the Islamic world. One implication of the latter was an expected increase in trade between Muslim countries—halal food products would be strong beneficiaries. Third, Muslim governments were widely expected to launch initiatives to encourage private-sector participation in expanding the halal food business. In the case of Malaysia, for example, the government had initiated an ambitious plan to turn the country into the world's premier halal hub. Finally, the international Muslim community was getting closer to standardizing and harmonizing matters pertaining to halal food manufacturing practices, certification, and product labeling.

To capitalize on these opportunities, Nestlé was prepared to make significant changes to its business model. First, it designated its Malaysian operations to take the lead. Nestlé had begun producing halal food in Malaysia in the 1970s. That was the decade when the company established a halal committee comprising Muslim senior executives of various disciplines from the operational-factory side and the corporate level. In the 1990s, the committee became more structured, and a halal policy was established. In 1995, Nestlé Malaysia took the halal initiative to the global platform within the Nestlé Group. Two years later, Nestlé Malaysia, in collaboration with the Nestlé Group, established internal guidelines with input from Jakim (the Department of Islamic Development in Malaysia) to define what constituted halal food and how to manage its production and supply.

Second, working with the international Muslim community and governments, it had 75 of its 487 factories in 84 countries certified halal. Sixty-six were in Asia and the Middle East, seven were in Europe, and two were in the Americas. All eight of Nestlé's Malaysian factories were halal-certified, producing more than 300 products. The big items were powdered Milo beverage, Nescafé, Maggi noodles, sauces, and culinary mixes. The Malaysian operation was also the regional producer for Milo, Kit Kat chocolate, and infant cereals.

Third, at the retail level, Nestlé worked with the United Kingdom's largest supermarket chain, Tesco, to promote halal food products as a specialty category. Tesco had agreed to create halal corners in 40 stores in the United Kingdom, with the potential for expanding that number to 500 stores. Nestlé was finalizing a list of products, including those made by its Malaysian factories, to be featured in this section of the supermarket.

Finally, to help the Malaysian government reach its target, Nestlé conducted a mentoring program for small- and medium-scale enterprises in the food industry to improve their standards with regard to hygiene and food safety. All these preparations were about to pay a dividend.

Partnering

Formulating cooperative strategies—*joint ventures, strategic alliances,* and *other partnering* arrangements—is the complement of outsourcing. For many corporations, cooperative strategies capture the benefits of internal development and acquisition while avoiding the drawbacks of both.

Globalization is an important factor in the rise of cooperative ventures. In a global competitive environment, going it alone often means taking extraordinary risks. Escalating fixed costs associated with achieving global market coverage, keeping up with the latest technology, and increased exposure to currency and political risk all make risk-sharing a necessity in many industries. For many companies, a global strategic posture without alliances would be untenable.

Cooperative strategies take many forms and are considered for many different reasons. However, the fundamental motivation in every case is the corporation's ability to spread its investments over a range of options, each with a different risk profile. Essentially, the corporation is trading off the likelihood of a major payoff against the ability to optimize its investments by betting on multiple options. The key drivers that attract executives to cooperative strategies include the need for *risk sharing*, the corporation's *funding limitations*, and the *desire to gain market* and *technology access*.[11]

Risk Sharing

Most companies cannot afford "bet-the-company" moves to participate in all product markets of strategic interest. Whether a corporation is considering entry into a global market or investments in new technologies, the dominant logic dictates that companies prioritize their strategic interests and balance them according to risk.

Funding Limitations

Historically, many companies focused on building sustainable advantage by establishing dominance in *all* the business's value-creating activities. Through cumulative investment and vertical integration, they attempted to build barriers to entry that were hard to penetrate. However, as the globalization of the business environment accelerated and the technology race intensified, such a strategic posture became increasingly difficult to sustain. Going it alone is no longer practical in many industries. To compete in the global arena, companies must incur immense fixed costs with a shorter payback period and at a higher level of risk.

Market Access

Companies usually recognize their lack of prerequisite knowledge, infrastructure, or critical relationships necessary for the distribution of their products to new customers. Cooperative strategies can help them fill the gaps. For example, Hitachi has an alliance with Deere & Company in North America and with Fiat Allis in Europe to distribute its hydraulic excavators. This arrangement makes sense because Hitachi's product line is too narrow to justify a separate distribution network. What is more, customers benefit because the gaps in its product line are filled with quality products such as bulldozers and wheel loaders from its alliance partners.

Technology Access

A large number of products rely on so many different technologies that few companies can afford to remain at the forefront of all of them. Carmakers increasingly rely on advances in electronics, application software developers depend on new features delivered by Microsoft in its next-generation operating platform, and advertising agencies need more and more sophisticated tracking data to formulate schedules for clients. At the same time, the pace at which technology is spreading globally is increasing, making time an even more critical variable in developing and sustaining competitive advantage. It is usually beyond the capabilities, resources, and good luck in R&D of any corporation to garner the technological advantage needed to independently create disruption in the marketplace. Therefore, partnering with technologically compatible companies to achieve the prerequisite level of excellence is often essential. The implementation of such strategies, in turn, increases the speed at which technology diffuses around the world.

Other Factors

Other reasons to pursue a cooperative strategy are a lack of particular *management skills;* an *inability to add* value in-house; and a *lack of acquisition opportunities* because of size, geographical, or ownership restrictions.

The airline industry provides a good example of some of the drivers and issues involved in forging strategic alliances. Although the U.S. industry has been deregulated for some time, international aviation remains controlled by a host of bilateral agreements that smack of protectionism. Outdated limits on foreign ownership further distort natural market forces toward a more global industry posture. As a consequence, airline companies have been forced to confront the challenges of global competition in other ways. With takeovers and mergers blocked, they have formed all kinds of alliances—from code sharing to aircraft maintenance to frequent flyer plans.

Cooperative strategies cover a wide spectrum of nonequity, cross-equity, and shared-equity arrangements. Selecting the most appropriate arrangement involves analyzing the nature of the opportunity, the mutual strategic interests in the cooperative venture, and prior experience with joint ventures of both partners. The essential question is, how can this opportunity be structured in order to maximize benefit(s) to both parties?

The Boston Consulting Group (BSC) divides alliances into four groups on the basis of whether the participants are competitors or not and on the relative depth and breadth of the alliance itself: *expertise alliances, new business alliances, cooperative alliances*, and *merger and acquisition M&A-like alliances*.

Expertise alliances typically bring together noncompeting firms to share expertise and specific capabilities. Outsourcing of IT services provides a good example. *New business alliances* are partnerships focused on entering a new business or market. Many companies, for example, have partnered when venturing into new parts of the world, such as China. *Cooperative alliances* are joint efforts by competing firms, formed to attain critical mass or economies of scale. Competitors combining to seek cheaper health insurance for employees, for example, or combined purchasing arrangements, illustrate this kind of alliance. *M&A-like alliances*—as the name implies—focus on near-complete integration but may be prevented from doing so, either because of legal regulatory constraints (e.g., airline industry) or because of unfavorable stock market conditions.

BCG found that while *new-business* alliances compose a clear majority (over 50%), *expertise-based* alliances are most favored by the stock market, and *M&A-like* alliances are least favored. The latter is not surprising since such alliances are created in response to unfavorable regulatory or market conditions.[12]

Minicase 8.4. May 2009: The Air France/KLM Group and Delta Air Lines Launch New Transatlantic Global Joint Venture[13]

The Air France KLM Group and Delta Air Lines announced a new, long-term joint venture whereby the partners will jointly operate their transatlantic business by coordinating operations and sharing revenues and costs of their transatlantic-route network. The airlines will cooperate on routes between North America and Africa, the Middle East and India, as well as on flights between Europe and several countries in Latin America.

For customers, this joint venture will result in more choices, frequencies, convenient flight schedules, competitive fares, and harmonized services on all transatlantic flights operated by the partners. The joint venture represents approximately 25% of total transatlantic capacity, with annual revenues estimated at more than $12 billion (approximately 9.3 billion euros, reference year 2008–2009).

Global passengers will be able to access a vast network offering over 200 flights and approximately 50,000 seats daily. That network is structured around six main hubs: Amsterdam, Atlanta, Detroit, Minneapolis, New York-JFK, and Paris-CDG, together with Cincinnati, Lyon, Memphis, and Salt Lake City. The airline partners will provide their corporate clients with a broad global offering that best meets their expectations for the most convenient airline system, while providing efficient account management as well as ease of travel for their clients. Going forward, this structure will represent a major strength for the SkyTeam alliance, of which all three airlines are members.

The joint venture's geographic scope includes all flights between North America and Europe, between Amsterdam and India, and between North America and Tahiti. On these routes, the business will be jointly operated, with the strategy and economics equally shared among the Air France-KLM Group and Delta.

Air France and KLM have been working with their respective American partners for many years. KLM signed a joint venture agreement with Northwest in 1997, while Air France and Delta signed a joint-venture agreement in 2007. Following the merger of Delta and Northwest, the next logical business strategy was to establish a single transatlantic joint venture. The agreement is the result of that collaboration.

Governance of the joint venture will be equally shared between the Air France KLM Group and Delta. An executive committee comprising the three CEOs and a management committee comprising representatives from marketing, network, sales, alliances, finance, and operations will define strategy. Ten working groups will be responsible for implementing and managing the agreement in the sectors of network, revenue management, sales, product, frequent flyer, advertising and brand, cargo, operations, IT, and finance. The joint venture will not lead to the creation of a subsidiary.

The venture is a long-term, evergreen arrangement that can only be canceled with a three-year notice and after an initial term of 10 years.

Minicase 8.5. GE Money Announces Joint Venture With One of Colombia's Largest Banking Groups[14]

Stamford, Connecticut, February 28, 2007: Furthering its growth strategy in Latin America, GE Money, the consumer lending unit of General Electric Company, today announced that it would acquire a minority position in Banco Colpatria—Red Multibanca Colpatria S.A.—a consumer and commercial bank based in Bogota, Colombia. GE Money will acquire a 39.3% stake in Red Multibanca Colpatria in two installments, with options to acquire up to an additional 25% stake from Mercantil Colpatria S.A. by 2012. The initial purchase, subject to regulatory approvals, is expected to close within the next few months. "We are excited to be entering Colombia to partner with Banco Colpatria and its customers," said the president and CEO of GE Money, Americas. "Colombia is an important growth market for GE as we continue to expand our business in Latin America. The Banco Colpatria team has built an exciting bank in Colombia. We look forward to partnering with them to help accelerate their growth."

Banco Colpatria, a member of the Mercantil Colpatria S.A. group, had over $2.4 billion in assets and was the second-largest credit card issuer in Colombia. With 139 branches, the bank served more than 1 million customers. The new partnership positioned the two companies to deliver enhanced consumer credit products to the growing Colombian financial services market.

"This partnership will enable Banco Colpatria to expand its product offerings and to further accelerate the bank's strong growth in the Colombian market," said the chairman of the board of Banco Colpatria. "This is part of the vision that we share with our new partner. GE Money is the perfect partner to help us broaden our business in Colombia."

GE Money, Latin America, began operations in 2000, offering consumer loans and private-label credit cards. The business now operates in Mexico, Argentina, and Brazil, as well as in Costa Rica, El Salvador, Guatemala, Honduras, Nicaragua, and Panama, through a joint venture with BAC-Credomatic Holding Co., Ltd. (BAC). With approximately $7 billion in assets, GE Money, Latin America, offers a wide range of financial products, including mortgages, auto loans, credit cards, insurance products, and personal loans in more than 430 branches and locations.

Points to Remember

1. Globalizing a company's value creation infrastructure—from the sourcing of raw materials and components to manufacturing and R&D to distribution and customer service—has three primary dimensions: (a) deciding which activities to perform in house and which ones to outsource, to whom and where; (b) developing the right partnerships to support a company's globalization efforts, and (c) implementing a suitable supply-chain management model for integrating them into a cost-effective, seamless, value-creating network.

2. *Core competencies* represent unique capabilities that allow a company to build a competitive advantage. Experience shows that only a few companies have the resources to develop more than a handful of core competencies. Picking the right ones, therefore, is the key.

3. Few companies, especially ones with a global presence, are self-sufficient in all the activities that make up their value chain. Growing global competitive pressures force companies to focus on those activities that they judge critical to their success and excel at—core capabilities in which they have a distinct competitive

advantage—and that can be leveraged across geographies and lines of business. Which activities should be kept in house and which ones can effectively be outsourced depends on a host of factors, most prominently the nature of the company's core strategy and dominant value discipline.

4. Outsourcing and offshoring of component manufacturing and support services can offer compelling strategic and financial advantages including *lower costs, greater flexibility, enhanced expertise, greater discipline*, and *the freedom to focus on core business activities.*

5. In the last 20 years, companies have outsourced many activities, including manufacturing, back-office functions, IT services, and customer support. Now the focus is shifting to more knowledge-intensive areas, such as product development, research and development, engineering, and analytical services.

6. Outsourcing can have significant benefits but is not without risk. Some risks, such as potentially higher offshoring costs due to the eroding value of the U.S. dollar, can be anticipated and addressed through contracts by employing financial hedging strategies. Others, however, are harder to anticipate or deal with. Risks associated with outsourcing typically fall into four general categories: *loss of control, loss of innovation, loss of organizational trust,* and *higher-than-expected transaction costs.*

7. The search for *growth* is a primary driver of manufacturing relocation. Others include *cutting costs and innovation.*

8. Formulating cooperative strategies—*joint ventures, strategic alliances, and other partnering* arrangements—is the complement of outsourcing. For many corporations, cooperative strategies capture the benefits of internal development and acquisition while avoiding the drawbacks of both.

9. The key drivers that attract executives to cooperative strategies include the need for *risk sharing*, the corporation's *funding limitations*, and the *desire to gain market* and *technology access.*

10. The Boston Consulting Group divides alliances into four groups on the basis of whether the participants are competitors or not and on the relative depth and breadth of the alliance itself: *expertise alliances, new business alliances, cooperative alliances,* and *M&A-like alliances.*

11. BCG found that while *new-business* alliances compose a clear majority (over 50%), *expertise-based* alliances are most favored by the stock market, and *M&A-like* alliances are least favored. The latter is not surprising since such alliances are created in response to unfavorable regulatory or market conditions.

CHAPTER 9

Global Supply-Chain Management

In today's global competitive environment, individual companies no longer compete as autonomous entities but as supply-chain networks. Instead of brand versus brand or company versus company, it is increasingly suppliers-brand-company versus suppliers-brand-company. In this new competitive world, the success of a single business increasingly depends on management's ability to integrate the company's intricate network of business relationships. Supply-chain management (SCM) offers the opportunity to capture the synergy of intra- and intercompany integration and management. SCM deals with total business-process excellence and represents a new way of managing business and relationships with other members of the supply chain.

Top-performing supply chains have three distinct qualities.[1] First, they are *agile* enough to readily react to sudden changes in demand or supply. Second, they *adapt* over time as market structures and environmental conditions change. And, third, they *align* the interests of all members of the supply-chain network in order to optimize performance. These characteristics—agility, adaptability, and alignment—are possible only when partners promote knowledge-flow between supply-chain nodes. In other words, the flow of knowledge is what enables a supply chain to come together in a way that creates a true value chain for all stakeholders. Knowledge-flow creates value by making the supply chain more transparent and by giving everyone a better look at customer needs and value propositions. Broad knowledge about customers and the overall market, as opposed to just information from order points, can provide other benefits, including a better understanding of market trends, resulting in better planning and product development.[2]

Supply Chains: From Push to Pull

A supply chain refers to the flow of physical goods and associated information from the source to the consumer. Key supply-chain activities include production planning, purchasing, materials management, distribution, customer service, and sales forecasting. These processes are critical to the success manufacturers, wholesalers, or service providers alike.

Electronic commerce and the Internet have fundamentally changed the nature of supply chains and have redefined how consumers learn about, select, purchase, and use products and services. The result has been the emergence of new business-to-business supply chains that are consumer-focused rather than product-focused. They also provide customized products and services.

In the traditional supply-chain model, raw material suppliers define one end of the supply chain. They were connected to manufacturers and distributors, which, in turn, were connected to a retailer and the end customer. Although the customer is the source of the profits, they were only part of the equation in this *"push"* model. The order and promotion process, which involves customers, retailers, distributors, and manufacturers, occurred through time-consuming paperwork. By the time customers' needs were filtered through the agendas of all the members of the supply chain, the production cycle ended up serving suppliers every bit as much as customers.

Driven by e-commerce's capabilities to empower clients, most companies have moved from the traditional *"push"* business model, where manufacturers, suppliers, distributors, and marketers have most of the power, to a customer-driven *"pull"* model. This new business model is less product-centric and more directly focused on the individual consumer. As a result, the new model also indicates a shift in the balance of power from suppliers to customers.

Whereas in the old "push" model, many members of the supply chain remained relatively isolated from end users, the new "pull" model has each participant scrambling to establish direct electronic connections to the end customer. The result is that electronic supply-chain connectivity gives end customers the opportunity to become better informed through the ability to research and give direction to suppliers. The net result is that customers now have a direct voice in the functioning of the supply chain, and companies can better serve customer needs, carry less inventory, and send products to market more quickly.

Minicase 9.1. Zara's Global Business Model[3]

Inditex, the parent company of cheap, chic-fashion chain Zara, has transformed itself into Europe's leading apparel retailer over the past 10 years and has racked up impressive results in Asia and the United States. Since 2000, Inditex has more than quintupled its sales and profits as it has tripled the number of stores of its eight brands. (Zara is the biggest, accounting for two-thirds of total revenues.) More recently, Inditex increased its year-on-year net sales by 6% in the first nine months of its 2009 fiscal year to 7,759 million euros. Net income grew to 831 million euros. The retailer launched 266 new stores in the first nine months, bringing the group's total number of stores to 4,530 by the end of October 2009.

Key highlights for the period included openings in Asian markets, with 90 new establishments inaugurated by October 31, 2009. These store openings reflect the strategic importance of Asian markets for the group and underscore a year of robust growth in China, Japan, and South Korea. High points of store launches so far this year include flagship locations in Japan and Mainland China.

In Japan, Zara now has a total of 50 stores, including a second flagship location in Tokyo's Shibuya district, which is a must-see global fashion destination. Prior to this opening, Zara had already welcomed shoppers at another upscale store in Shibuya. Zara thus enhances its excellent retail presence in Tokyo's four key shopping areas: the two aforementioned flagship stores in Shibuya, two each in Ginza and Shinjuku, and one in Harajuku.

Meanwhile, in Beijing, the group celebrated the opening of a flagship location in one of the Chinese capital's busiest shopping hubs. The store, which opened its doors on the pedestrian Wangfujing Street, brings the group's number of stores in China to more than 60. The company's firm commitment to expansion in the Chinese fashion market is reflected in its decision to locate shops not only in Beijing and Shanghai but also in emerging cities such as Harbin, Dalian, Qingdao, Changchun, and Kunming.

To get where it is today, Zara has turned globalization on its head, distributing all of its merchandise, regardless of origin, from Spain. With more outlets in Asia and the United States, replenishing stores twice a week—as Zara does now—will become increasingly complex and expensive. The strain is already starting to show. Costs are climbing and growth in same-store sales is slowing: at outlets open for 2 years or more, revenues were up by 5% last year, compared with a 9% increase in 2004. So far, the company has managed to offset that problem by charging more for its goods as it gets farther from headquarters. For instance, Zara's prices in the United States are some 65% higher than in Spain, brokerage Lehman Brothers, Inc., estimates.

Zara has succeeded by breaking every rule in retailing. For most clothing stores, running out of best-selling items is a disaster, but Zara encourages occasional shortages to give its products an air of exclusivity. With new merchandise arriving at stores twice a week, the company trains its customers to shop and shop often. And forget about setting trends—Zara prefers to follow them. Its aim is to give customers plenty of variety at a price they can afford. Zara made 30,000 different items last year, about triple what the Gap did.

Zara does not collaborate with big-name designers and or use multimillion-dollar advertising campaigns. Instead, it uses its spacious, minimalist outlets—more Gucci than Target—and catwalk-inspired clothing to build its brand. Their advertising is their stores. To get shoppers' attention, Zara is located on some of the world's priciest streets: New York's Fifth Avenue, Tokyo's Ginza, Rome's Via Condotti, and the Champs-Elysees in Paris.

Keeping those locations flush with an ever-changing supply of new clothing means striking the right balance between flexibility and cost. So while rivals outsource to Asia, Zara makes its most fashionable items—half of all its merchandise—at a dozen company-owned factories in Spain. Clothes with a longer shelf life, such as basic T-shirts, are outsourced to low-cost suppliers, mainly in Asia and Turkey.

The tight control makes Zara more fleet-footed than its competitors. While rivals push their suppliers to churn out goods in bulk, Zara intentionally leaves extra capacity in the system. That results in fewer fashion mistakes, which means Zara sells more at full price, and when it discounts, it does not have to go as deep. The chain books 85% of the full ticket price for its merchandise, while the industry average is 60%.

Zara's nerve center is an 11,000-square-foot hall at its headquarters in Arteixo, a town of 25,000 in Galicia. That is where hundreds of twenty-something designers, buyers, and production planners work in tightly synchronized teams. It is there that the company does all of its design and distribution and half of its production. The concentrated activity enables it to move a dress, blouse, or coat from drawing board to shop floor in just 2 weeks, less than a quarter of the industry average.

Consider how Zara managed to latch onto one of hottest trends in just 4 weeks in 2006. The process started when trend-spotters spread the word back to headquarters: white eyelet—cotton with tiny holes in it—was set to become white-hot. A quick telephone survey of Zara store managers confirmed that the fabric could be a winner, so in-house designers got down to work. They zapped patterns electronically to Zara's factory across the street, and the fabric was cut. Local subcontractors stitched white-eyelet v-neck belted dresses and finished them in less than a week. The $129 dresses were inspected, tagged, and transported through a tunnel under the street to a distribution center. From there, they were quickly dispatched to Zara stores from New York to Tokyo, where they were flying off the racks just 2 days later.

Supply-Chain Management

Supply-chain management (SCM) has three principal components: (a) creating the *supply-chain network structure*, (b) developing *supply-chain business processes*, and (c) *managing the supply-chain activities*.[4]

The *supply-chain network structure* consists of the member firms and the links between these firms. Primary *members* of a supply chain include all autonomous companies or strategic business units that carry out value-adding activities in the business processes designed to produce a specific output for a particular customer or market. Supporting members are companies that simply provide resources, knowledge, utilities, or assets for the primary members of the supply chain. For example, supporting companies include those that lease trucks to a manufacturer, banks that lend money to a retailer, or companies that supply production equipment, print marketing brochures, or provide administrative assistance.

Supply chains have three *structural dimensions*: horizontal, vertical, and the horizontal position of the focal company within the end points of the supply chain. The first dimension, *horizontal structure*, refers to the number of tiers across the supply chain. The supply chain may be long, with numerous tiers, or short, with few tiers. As an example, the network structure for bulk cement is relatively short. Raw materials are taken from the ground, combined with other materials, moved a short distance, and used to construct buildings. The second dimension, *vertical structure*, refers to the number of suppliers or customers represented within each tier. A company can have a narrow vertical structure, with few companies at each tier level, or a wide vertical structure with many suppliers or customers at each tier level. The third structural dimension is the company's *horizontal position* within the supply chain. A company can be positioned at or near the initial source of supply, be at or near to the ultimate customer, or be somewhere between these end points of the supply chain.

Business processes are the activities that produce a specific output of value to the customer. The *management function* integrates the business processes across the supply chain. Traditionally, in many companies, upstream and downstream portions of the supply chain were not effectively integrated. Today, competitive advantage increasingly depends on integrating eight key supply-chain processes—customer relationship management, customer service management, demand management, order fulfillment, manufacturing flow management, procurement, product development and commercialization, and managing returns—into an effective value delivery network.[5]

Regarding the supply-chain management function itself, in some companies, management emphasizes a functional structure, others a process structure, and yet others a combined structure of processes and functions. The number of business processes that it is critical or beneficial to integrate and manage between companies will likely vary. In some cases, it may be appropriate to link just one key process, and, in other cases, it may be appropriate to link multiple or all the key business processes. However, in each specific case, it is important that executives thoroughly analyze and discuss which key business processes to integrate and manage. With the shift from the traditional "push" to the modern "pull" model, supply-chain management has changed—the integration of e-commerce has produced (a) greater cost efficiency, (b) distribution flexibility, (c) better customer service, and (d) the ability to track and monitor shipments.

Supply-Chain Agility and Resiliency

The best companies create supply chains that can respond to sudden and unexpected changes in markets. Agility—the ability to respond *quickly* and *cost-effectively* to unexpected change—is critical because in most industries, both demand and supply fluctuate more rapidly and widely than they used to. In fact, the best companies use agile supply chains to differentiate themselves from rivals. For instance, Zara has become Europe's most profitable apparel brands by building agility into every link of their supply chains. At one end of the product pipeline, Zara has created an agile design process. As soon as designers spot possible trends, they create sketches and order fabrics. That gives them a head start over competitors because fabric suppliers require the longest lead times. However, the company approves designs and initiates manufacturing only after it gets feedback from its stores. This allows Zara to make products that meet consumer tastes and reduces the number of items they must sell at a discount. At the other end of supply chain, the company has created a superefficient distribution system. In part because of these decisions,

Zara has grown at more than 20% annually since the late 1990s, and its double-digit net profit margins are the envy of the industry.

Agility and resiliency have become more critical in recent years because sudden shocks to supply chains have become more frequent. The terrorist attack in New York in 2001, the dockworkers' strike in California in 2002, and the SARS epidemic in Asia in 2003, for instance, disrupted many companies' supply chains.

Agility and resiliency help supply chains recover more quickly from such sudden setbacks. When, in September 1999, an earthquake hit Taiwan, shipments of computer components to the United States were delayed by weeks and, in some cases, by months. Most computer manufacturers, such as Compaq, Apple, and Gateway, could not deliver products to customers on time and incurred losses. One exception was Dell. The company changed the prices of PC configurations overnight to steer consumer demand away from hardware built with components that were not available to machines that did not require those parts. Dell could do this because it had contingency plans in place. Not surprisingly, Dell gained market share in the earthquake's aftermath.[6]

Supply-chain agility and resilience no longer imply merely the ability to manage risk. It now assumes that the ability to manage risk means being better positioned than competitors to deal with—and even gain advantage from—disruptions. Key to increasing agility and resilience is building *flexibility* into the supply-chain structure, processes, and management.[7]

Making Supply Chains Adaptable

Global companies must be able to adapt their supply networks when markets or strategies change. The best companies tailor their supply chains to the nature of the markets they serve. They often end up with more than one supply chain, which can be expensive, but, in return, they secure the best manufacturing and distribution capabilities for each offering. Cisco, for example, uses contract manufacturers in low-cost countries such as China for standard, high-volume networking products. For its broad line of midvalue items, the company uses vendors in low-cost countries to build core products, but it customizes those products itself in major markets such as the United States and Europe. And for highly customized, low-volume products, Cisco uses vendors close to main markets, such as Mexico for the United States and Eastern European countries for Europe. Despite the fact that it uses three different supply chains at the same time, the company is careful not to become less agile. Because it uses flexible designs and standardized processes, Cisco can switch the manufacture of products from one supply network to another, when necessary.[8]

Companies that compete primarily on the basis of operational excellence typically focus on creating supply chains that deliver goods and services to consumers as quickly and inexpensively as possible. They invest in state-of-the art technologies and employ metrics and reward systems aimed at boosting supply-chain performance.

For companies competing on the basis of customer intimacy or product leadership, a focus on efficiency is not enough—agility is a key factor. Customer-intimate companies must be able to add and delete products and services as customer needs change; product leadership companies must be able to adapt their supply chains to changes in technology and to capitalize on new ideas.

All companies must align their supply-chain infrastructure and management with their underlying value proposition to achieve a sustainable competitive advantage. That is, they must align the interests of all the firms in the supply network so that companies optimize the chain's performance when they maximize their interests.

Minicase 9.2. Nikon, With the Help of UPS, Focuses on Supply-Chain Innovation[9]

To support the launch of its new digital cameras, Nikon, with the help of UPS Supply Chain Solutions, reengineered its distribution network to keep retailers well supplied. Nikon knew that customer service capabilities needed to be completely up to speed from the start and that distributors and retailers would require up-to-the-minute information about product availability. While the company had previously handled new product distribution in-house, this time Nikon realized that burdening its existing infrastructure with a new, demanding, high-profile product line could impact customer service performance adversely. So Nikon applied its well-known talent for innovation to creating an entirely new distribution strategy, and it took the rare step of outsourcing distribution of an entire consumer-electronics product line. With UPS Supply Chain Solutions on board, Nikon was able to quickly execute a synchronized supply-chain strategy that moves products to retail stores throughout the United States, Latin America, and the Caribbean, and allows Nikon to stay focused on the business of developing and marketing precision optics.

Starting at Nikon's manufacturing centers in Korea, Japan, and Indonesia, UPS Supply Chain Solutions now manages air and ocean freight and related customs brokerage. Nikon's freight is directed to Louisville, Kentucky, which not only serves as the all-points connection for UPS's global operations but is also home to the UPS Supply Chain Solutions Logistics Center main campus. Here, merchandise can be either "kitted" with accessories such as batteries and chargers or repackaged to in-store display specifications. Finally, the packages are distributed to literally thousands of retailers across the United States or shipped for export to Latin American or Caribbean retail outlets and distributors, using any of UPS's worldwide transportation services to provide the final delivery.

With the UPS Supply Chain Solutions system in place, the process calibrates the movement of goods and information by providing SKU-level visibility within complex distribution and information technology (IT) systems. UPS also provides Nikon advance shipment notifications throughout the U.S., Caribbean, and Latin American markets. The result: a "snap shot" of the supply chain that rivals the performance of a Nikon camera.

Nikon has already seen the results of its innovation in both digital technology and product distribution. The consumer digital-camera sector is one of Nikon's fastest-growing product lines. In addition, supply-chain performance and customer service have measurably improved. Products leaving Nikon manufacturing facilities in Asia can now be on a retailer's shelf in as few as 2 days. While products are en route, Nikon also has the ability to keep retailers informed of delivery times and to adjust them as needed so that no retailer needs to miss sales opportunities due to lack of product availability.

Creating Supply-Chain Alignment

Leading companies take care to align the interests of all the firms in their supply chain with their own. This is important, because every supply-chain partner firm—whether a supplier, an assembler, a distributor, or a retailer—will focus on its own interests. If any company's interests differ from those of the other organizations in the supply chain, its actions will not maximize the chain's performance.

One way companies align their partners' interests with their own is by redefining the terms of their relationships so that firms share risks, costs, and rewards equitably. Another involves the use of intermediaries, for example, when financial institutions buy components from suppliers at hubs and resell them to manufacturers. Everyone benefits because the intermediaries' financing costs are lower than the vendors' costs. Although such an arrangement requires trust and commitment on the part of suppliers, financial intermediaries, and manufacturers, it is a powerful way to align the interests of companies in supply chains.

A prerequisite to creating alignment is the availability of information so that all the companies in a supply chain have equal access to forecasts, sales data, and plans. Next, partner roles and responsibilities must be carefully defined so that there is no scope for conflict. Finally, companies must align incentives so that when companies try to maximize returns, they also maximize the supply chain's performance.

Minicase 9.3. Nestlé Pieces Together Its Global Supply Chain[10]

A few years ago, Nestlé, the world's largest food company, set out to standardize how it operates around the world. It launched GLOBE (Global Business Excellence), a comprehensive program aimed at implementing a single set of procurement, distribution, and sales management systems. The logic behind the $2.4-billion project was impeccable: implementing a standardized approach to demand forecasting and purchasing would save millions and was critical to Nestlé's operating efficiency in 200 countries around the world.

Nestlé's goal was simple: to replace its 14 different SAP enterprise-planning systems—in place in different countries—with a common set of processes, in factory and in administration, backed by a single way of formatting and storing data and a single set of information systems for all of Nestlé's businesses.

For Nestlé, this was not an everyday project. When it built a factory to make coffee, infant formula, water, or noodles, it would spend $30 to $40 million; committing billions in up-front capital to a backroom initiative was unheard of, or, as someone noted, "Nestlé makes chocolate chips, not electronic ones."

The GLOBE project also stood as the largest-ever deployment of mySAP.com. But whether the software got rolled out to 230,000 Nestlé employees or 200 was not the point. The point was to make Nestlé the first company to operate in hundreds of countries in the same manner as if it operated in one. And that had not been achieved by any company—not even the British East India Company at the peak of its tea-trading power—in the history of global trade.

Consider the complexities. Nestlé was the world's largest food company, with almost $70 billion in annual sales. By comparison, the largest food company based in the United States, Kraft Foods, was less than half that size. Nestlé's biggest Europe-based competitor, Unilever, had about $54 billion in sales. In addition, Nestlé grew to its huge size by selling lots of small-ticket items—Kit Kat, now the world's largest-selling candy bar; Buitoni spaghetti; Maggi packet soups; Lactogen dried milk for infants; and Perrier sparkling water.

The company operated in some 200 nations, including places that were not yet members of the United Nations. It ran 511 factories and employed 247,000 executives, managers, staff, and production workers worldwide.

What is more, for Nestlé, nothing was simple. The closest product to a global brand it had was Nescafé; more than 100 billion cups were consumed each year. But there were more than 200 formulations, made to suit local tastes. All told, the company produced 127,000 different types and sizes of products. Keeping control of its thousands of supply chains, scores of methods of predicting demand, and its uncountable variety of ways of invoicing customers and collecting payments was becoming evermore difficult and eating into the company's bottom line.

The three baseline edicts for project GLOBE were: harmonize processes, standardize data, and standardize systems. This included how sales commitments were made, factory production schedules established, bills to customers created, management reports pulled together, and financial results reported. Gone would be local customs, except where legal requirements and exceptional circumstances mandated an alternative manner of, say, finding a way to pay the suppliers of perishable products like dairy or produce in a week rather than 30 days. And when was this all to be done? In just 3 and a half years. The original GLOBE timeline, announced by Nestlé's executive board, called for 70% of the company's $50 billion business to operate under the new unified processes by the end of 2003.

Mission impossible? The good news was that in one part of the world, Asia, market managers had shown they could work together and create a common system for doing business with their customers. They had used a set of applications from a Chicago supplier, SSA Global, that allowed manufacturers operating worldwide to manage the flow of goods into their factories, the factories themselves, and the delivery of goods to customers while making sure the operations met all local and regional legal reporting requirements. The system was adopted in Indonesia, Malaysia, the Philippines, Thailand, even South Africa, and was dubbed the "Business Excellence Common Application."

But this project was orders of magnitude more involved and more complex. Instead of just a few countries, it would affect 200 of them. Change would have to come in big, not small, steps. Using benchmarks they could glean from competitors such as Unilever and Danone, and assistance from PricewaterhouseCoopers consultants and SAP's own deployment experts, the executives in charge of the GLOBE project soon came to a conclusion they had largely expected going in: this project would take more people, more money, and more time than the board had anticipated. Instead of measuring workers in the hundreds, and Swiss francs in the hundreds of millions, as originally expected, the team projected that 3,500 people would be involved in GLOBE at its peak. The new cost estimate was 3 billion Swiss francs, about $2.4 billion. And the deadline was pushed back as well. The new target: putting the "majority of the company's key markets" onto the GLOBE system by the end of 2005, not 2003.

To lead this massive undertaking, GLOBE's project manager chose a group of business managers, not technology managers, from all of Nestlé's key functions—manufacturing, finance, marketing, and human resources—and from all across the world—Europe, Asia, the Americas, Africa, and Australia.

These were people who knew how things actually worked or should work. They knew how the company estimated the demand for each of its products, how supplies were kept in the pipeline, even mundane things like how to generate an invoice, the best way to process an order, how to maintain a copier or other office equipment, and how to classify all the various retail outlets, from stores to vending machines, that could take its candy bars and noodles. The system would allow managers to manage it all from the web.

The process for the team of 400 executives started with finding, and then documenting, the four or five best ways of doing a particular task, such as generating an invoice. Then, the GLOBE team brought in experts with specific abilities, such as controlling financial operations, and used them as "challengers." They helped eliminate weaknesses, leaving the best practices standing.

At the end of that first year, the project teams had built up the basic catalog of practices that would become what they would consider the "greatest asset of GLOBE": its "Best Practices Library." This was an online repository of step-by-step guides to the 1,000 financial, manufacturing, and other processes that applied across all Nestlé businesses. Grouped into 45 "solution sets," like demand planning or closing out financial reports, the practices could now be made available online throughout the company, updated as necessary, and commented on at any time.

It was not always possible to choose one best practice. Perhaps the hardest process to document was "generating demand." With so many thousands of products, hundreds of countries, and local tastes to deal with, there were "many different ways of going to market," many of which were quite valid. This made it hard to create a single software template that would serve all market managers.

So GLOBE executives had to practice a bit more tolerance on that score. The final GLOBE template included a half-dozen or so different ways of taking products to market around the world. But no such tolerance was shown for financial reporting. The 400 executives were determined to come up with a rigorous step-by-step process that would not change.

Experts were brought in along the way to challenge each process. But in the end, one standard would, in this case, have to stand. Financial terms would be consistent. The scheme for recording dates and amounts would be the same. The timing of inputting data would be uniform; only the output could change. In Thailand, there would have to be a deviation so that invoices could be printed out in Thai characters so that they could be legal and readable. In the Philippines, dates would have to follow months, as in the United States. Most of the rest of the world would follow the European practice of the day preceding the month.

Progress was slow, however. Nestlé managers had always conducted their businesses as they saw fit. As a consequence, even standardizing on behind-the-scenes practices, like how to record information for creating bills to customers met, with resistance. As country managers saw it, decision making was being taken out of local markets and being centralized. Beyond that, someone had to pay the bill for the project itself. That would be the countries, too.

By the fall of 2005, almost 25% of Nestlé was running on the GLOBE templates. And GLOBE's project manager was confident that 80% of the company would operate on the new standardized processes by the end of 2006. The greatest challenge was getting managers and workers to understand that their jobs would change—in practical ways. In many instances, workers would be entering data on raw materials as they came into or through a factory. Keeping track of that would be a new responsibility. Doing it on a computer would be a wholly new experience. And figuring out what was happening on the screen could be a challenge. Minutia? Maybe. Considerable change? Definitely.

But the templates got installed and business went on—in Switzerland, Malaysia-Singapore, and the Andean region. In each successive rollout, the managers of a given market had 9 months or more to document their processes and methodically adjust them to the templated practices. In 2003, Thailand, Indonesia, and Poland went live. In 2004, Canada, the Philippines, and the Purina pet food business in the United Kingdom joined the network. But, by then, the system was bumping up against some technical limits. In particular, the mySAP system was not built for the unusual circumstances of the Canadian food retailing market. Food manufacturers have lots of local and regional grocery chains to sell to, and promotional campaigns are rife. MySAP was not built to track the huge amount of trade promotions engaged in by Nestlé's Canadian market managers: there were too many customers, too many products, and too many *data points*.

In India, changing over in mid-2005 was complicated by the fact that not only was Nestlé overhauling all of its business processes, but it also did not know what some of the key financial processes would have to be. At the same time it was converting to the GLOBE system, India was changing its tax structure in all 29 states and six territories. Each would get to choose whether, and how, to implement a fee on the production and sale of products, known as a value-added tax. Meeting the scheduled go-live date proved difficult.

And all over the world, managers learned that the smallest problem in standardized systems means that product can get stopped in its tracks. In Indochina, for instance, pallets get loaded with 48 cases of liquids or powders, and are then moved out. If a worker fails to manually check that the right cases have been loaded on a particular pallet, all dispatching stops are held up until the pallet is checked.

These setbacks notwithstanding, GLOBE taught Nestlé how to operate as a truly global company. For example, managers from the water businesses initially rejected the idea of collecting, managing, and disseminating data in the same way as their counterparts in chocolate and coffee. Some managers figured that if they were able to produce all the water or all the chocolate they needed for their market locally, that should be enough. But the idea was to get Nestlé's vast empire to think, order, and execute as one rather than as a collection of disparate companies. This meant that a particular manufacturing plant in a particular manager's region might be asked to produce double or triple the amount of coffee it had in the past. Or it might mean that a particular plant would be closed.

So, while the company did away with data centers for individual countries, each one does now have a data manager. The task is to make sure that the information that goes into GLOBE's data centers is accurate and complete. That means that country managers can concentrate more on what really matters: serving customers.

Points to Remember

1. In today's global competitive environment, individual companies no longer compete as autonomous entities but as supply-chain networks. Instead of brand versus brand or company versus company, then network is increasingly suppliers-brand-company versus suppliers-brand-company.

2. Top-performing supply chains have three distinct qualities. First, they are *agile* enough to react readily to sudden changes in demand or supply. Second, they *adapt* over time as market structures and environmental conditions change. And third, they *align* the interests of all members of the supply-chain network in order to optimize performance.

3. Driven by e-commerce's capabilities to empower clients, most companies have moved from the traditional *"push"* business model—where manufacturers, suppliers, distributors, and marketers have most of the power—to a customer-driven *"pull"* model.

4. Supply-chain management (SCM) has three principal components: (a) creating the *supply-chain network structure*, (b) developing *supply-chain business processes*, and (c) *managing the supply-chain activities*. The *supply-chain network structure* consists of the member firms and the links between these firms. *Business processes* are the activities that produce a specific output of value to the customer. The *management function* integrates the business processes across the supply chain.

5. The best companies create supply chains that can respond to sudden and unexpected changes in markets. Agility—the ability to respond *quickly* and *cost-effectively* to unexpected change—is critical because in most industries, both demand and supply fluctuate more rapidly and widely than they used to. Key to increasing agility and resilience is building *flexibility* into the supply-chain structure, processes, and management.

6. Global companies must be able to adapt their supply networks when markets or strategies change. Companies that compete primarily on the basis of operational effectiveness typically focus on creating supply chains that deliver goods and services to consumers as quickly and inexpensively as possible. They invest in state-of-the-art technologies and employ metrics and reward systems aimed at boosting supply-chain performance. For companies competing on the basis of customer intimacy or product leadership, a focus on efficiency is not enough; agility is a key factor. Customer-intimate companies must be able to add and delete products and services as customer needs change; product leadership companies must be able to adapt their supply chains to changes in technology and to capitalize on new ideas.

7. Leading companies take care to align the interests of all the firms in their supply chain with their own. This is important because every supply-chain partner firm—whether a supplier, an assembler, a distributor, or a retailer—will focus on its own interests. If any company's interests differ from those of the other organizations in the supply chain, its actions will not maximize the chain's performance.

CHAPTER 10

Globalizing the Management Model

Previous chapters focused on the challenges associated with globalizing the first three components of the business model framework—the value proposition, market choices, and the value-chain infrastructure. This chapter looks at globalizing the fourth component—the company's *management model*—which summarizes its choices about a suitable global organizational structure and decision-making framework.

The judicious globalization of a company's management model is critical to unlocking the potential for global competitive advantage. But globalizing a company's management model can be ruinous if conditions are not right or the process for doing so is flawed. So key questions include when, and to what extent, should a company globalize its decision-making processes and its organizational and control structure; what are some of the key implementation challenges; and how does a company get started?

This chapter is organized in two parts. The first discusses a key "soft" dimension of globalizing a company's management model—creating and embedding *a global mind-set*—a prerequisite for global success. The second part deals with the "hard" dimensions of creating a global architecture: choosing a suitable *organizational structure* and streamlining *global decision-making* processes.

Pitfalls in Globalizing a Management Model

Globalizing a company's management model is hard. As firms increase their revenue by expanding into more countries and by extending the lives of existing products by bringing them into emerging markets, costs can often be reduced through global sourcing and better asset utilization.

But capitalizing on such profit opportunities is hard because every opportunity for increased globalization has a cost and carries a danger of actually reducing profit. For example, the company's customer focus may blur as excessive standardization makes products appeal to the lowest common denominator, alienating key customer segments and causing market share to fall. Or a wrong globalization move makes innovation slow down and causes price competition to sharpen.

The best executives in a worldwide firm are often country managers who are protective of "their" markets and value delivery networks. Globalization shrinks their power. Some rise to new heights within the organization by taking extra global responsibilities; some leave. Many fight globalization, making it tough for the CEO. Sometimes they win and the CEO loses. Overcoming organizational resistance is therefore key to success.

Minicase 10.1. When Global Strategy Goes Wrong[1]

In April of 2002, Japan's leading mobile operator, NTT DoCoMo, Inc., announced it would write down the reduced value of its investment in AT&T Wireless Services, Inc., a move expected to contribute to an extraordinary loss of about 1 trillion yen ($7.53 billion) for the fiscal year. And when the full extent of the write-downs of all its recent European, U.S., and Asian investments was realized, the bill for the ambitious globalization strategy pursued by Japan's—and Asia's—most valuable company exceeded $10 billion.

NTT DoCoMo clearly had the cash flow from its domestic business to avoid, by a long way, the high-profile fate of now bankrupt Swissair. However, the two companies' approaches to global strategy provide interesting parallels and lessons for other international players in all industries. NTT DoCoMo and the former Swiss flag carrier enjoyed strong economic success built around a former monopoly and highly protected incumbent positions in their home markets. NTT DoCoMo was the clear leader in the Japanese mobile market, with a 60% market share that drove an annual operating cash flow of more than $10 billion. Swissair's dominant carrier position delivered financial performance that was similarly blue chip.

But a strong domestic market position and excess cash flow do not guarantee success abroad. In fact, without a quite sophisticated understanding of the uniqueness of its domestic situation, a strong domestic position could conceal some of the risks of a global strategy. The first lesson is one of microeconomics: understand what drives superior economic performance in a particular business and do not take domestic success for granted. Both the airline and the telecommunications businesses are highly regulated, technology-driven, and capital-intensive industries with high fixed and very low marginal costs (per airline seat or per mobile-call minute). Rapid changes in regulation and technology are changing some of the rules of the game but not the basic economics of either of these businesses.

In the airline industry, cost advantages are driven by an airline's dominance in airport hubs and on specific routes. The airline with the most flights in and out of a specific airport generates lower unit costs per flight and per passenger than competitors. The airline with the highest market share and flight frequency on a given route typically has lower costs per seat, higher utilization, and superior pricing power. In the mobile industry, the significant fixed-cost components of the business (networks, product development, and brand advertising and promotion) provide unit cost advantages to the national market leader compared with its followers.

The second lesson from NTT DoCoMo and Swissair's experience is to have a clear view of the real economic boundaries of your business—is it a global business or, rather, a multilocal or regional one? Sitting on increasing cash balances, both DoCoMo and Swissair saw a high volume of merger and acquisition activity. They concluded a wave of "globalization" was underway in their industries and that they could not afford to be left out. The result: they developed growth aspirations beyond their national boundaries.

But while regulatory changes allowed increased foreign share-holdings in telecommunications and airlines opened up new international investment opportunities, they have not changed the laws of economics. Despite regulatory changes, the economics of the mobile-phone industry remain primarily national or regional in nature. This implies that it is better to be a market leader in one country than a follower in two countries. Similarly, regulatory changes in traditional, bilateral air-transport agreements have shifted barriers to entry and hence increased competition and reduced pricing power in the airline industry, but they have not changed its fundamental economics. All successful airline mergers have been driven around building or expanding hub or route dominance, not around building sheer, absolute scale in terms of either aircraft or destinations served

When both NTT DoCoMo and Swissair convinced themselves they needed to expand beyond domestic boundaries to survive, the race to fulfill their global aspirations seems to have resulted in a set of investments more focused on the number of flags on a boardroom map rather than on these basic economics driving superior profitability in their industries. The risks of these two aggressive expansion strategies were further compounded by not having control over most of their international investments. This suggests a third lesson: move to management control if you are serious about capturing acquisition synergies.

During the mid to late 1990s, Swissair kept its investment bankers busy with a nonstop string of deals. The company adopted an explicit "hunter strategy," which led to acquisitions of noncontrolling minority stakes in a string of strategically challenged nonincumbent carriers: German charter carrier LTU, the French airlines AOM-Air Liberte and Air Littoral, and Italy's Volare Airlines and Air Europe. In addition, Swissair acquired stakes in Polish flag carrier LOT, Belgium's Sabena, and South African Airways.

Without majority control, there was very limited scope for Swissair management to drive the economic benefits from these airline shareholdings through route consolidation, aircraft fleet rationalization and purchasing benefits. In addition, there was no ability to take corrective action when operational or financial performance deteriorated.

Similarly, in short order, DoCoMo accumulated direct or indirect stakes in nine mobile operators—most for cash—at the peak of the telecom bubble. But this acquisition spree resulted in equity stakes in only two market leaders, and these were in relatively minor geographic markets: KPN Mobile domestically in the Netherlands and Hutchison in Hong Kong. All the others were lesser players. DoCoMo acquired stakes in the No. 3 U.S. player, AT&T Wireless; Taiwan's No. 4 player, KG Telecom; the United Kingdom's No. 5 player, Hutchison U.K., and distant followers KPN Orange in Belgium and E-Plus in Germany. Worse still, all these investments were minority stakes and so gave DoCoMo limited ability to exert control over critical strategic and operational issues at these operators.

The Importance of a Global Mind-Set

A common challenge that many corporations encounter as they move to globalize their operations can be summed up in one word: mind-set. Successful global expansion requires corporate leaders who think proactively, who sense and foresee emerging trends, and who act upon them in a deliberate, timely manner. To accomplish this, they need a global mind-set and an enthusiasm to embrace new challenges, diversity, and a measure of ambiguity. Simply having the right product and technology is not sufficient; it is the caliber of a company's global leadership that that makes the difference.

Herbert Paul defines a mind-set as "a set of deeply held internal mental images and assumptions, which individuals develop through a continuous process of learning from experience."[2] These images exist in the subconscious and determine how an individual perceives a specific situation and his or her reaction to it. In a global context, a global mind-set is "the ability to avoid the simplicity of assuming all cultures are the same, and at the same time, not being paralyzed by the complexity of the differences."[3] Thus, rather than being frustrated and intimidated by cultural differences, an individual with a global mind-set enjoys them and seeks them out because they are fascinated by them and understand they present unique business opportunities.

The concept of a mind-set does not just apply to individuals: it can be logically extended to organizations as the aggregated mind-set of all of its members. Naturally, at the organizational level, mind-set also reflects how its members interact as well as such issues as the distribution of power within the organization. Certain individuals, depending on their position in the organizational hierarchy, will have a stronger impact on the company's mind-set than others. In fact, the personal mind-set of the CEO is sometimes the single most important factor in shaping the organization's mind-set.

A corporate mind-set shapes the perceptions of individual and corporate challenges, opportunities, capabilities, and limitations. It also frames how goals and expectations are set and therefore has a significant impact on what strategies are considered and ultimately selected and how they are implemented. Recognizing the diversity of local markets and seeing them as a source of opportunity and strength, while at the same time pushing for strategic consistency across countries, lies at the heart of global strategy development. To become truly global, therefore, requires a company to develop two key capabilities. First, the company must have the capability to enter any market in the world it wishes to compete in. This requires that the company constantly looks for market opportunities worldwide, processes information on a global basis, and is respected as a real or potential threat by competitors, even in countries or markets it has not yet entered. Second, the company must have the capability to leverage its worldwide resources. Making a switch to a lower cost position by globalizing the supply chain is a good example. Leveraging a company's global know-how is another.

To understand the importance of a corporate mind-set to the development of these capabilities, consider two often quoted corporate mantras: "think global and act local" and its opposite, "think local and act global." The "think global and act local" mind-set is indicative of a global approach in which management operates under the assumption that a powerful brand name with a standard product, package, and advertising concept serves as a platform to conquer global markets. The starting point is a globalization strategy focused on standard products, optimal global sourcing, and the ability to react globally to competitors' moves. While sometimes effective, this approach can discourage diversity, and it puts a lot of emphasis on uniformity. Contrast this with a "think local and act global" mind-set, which is based on the assumption that global expansion is best served by adaptation to local needs and preferences. In this mind-set, diversity is looked upon as a source of opportunity, whereas strategic cohesion plays a secondary role. Such a "bottom-up" approach can offer greater possibilities for revenue generation, particularly for companies wanting to rapidly grow abroad. However, it may require greater investment in infrastructure necessary to serve each market and can produce global strategic inconsistency and inefficiencies.

C. K. Prahalad and Kenneth Lieberthal first exposed the Western (which they refer to as "imperialist") bias that many multinationals have brought to their global strategies, particularly in developing countries. They note that they would perform better—and learn more—if they more effectively tailored their operations to the unique conditions of emerging markets. Arguing that literally hundreds of millions of people in China, India, Indonesia, and Brazil are ready to enter the marketplace, they observe that multinational companies typically target only a tiny segment of affluent buyers in these emerging markets: those who most resemble Westerners. This kind of myopia—thinking of developing countries simply as new places to sell old products—is not only shortsighted and the direct result of a Western "imperialist" mind-set; it causes these companies to miss out on much larger market opportunities further down the socioeconomic pyramid that are often seized by local competitors.[4]

Companies with a genuine global mind-set do not assume that they can be successful by simply exporting their current business models around the globe. Citicorp, for example, knew it could not profitably serve a client in Beijing or Delhi whose net wealth is less than $5,000 with its U.S. business model and attendant cost structure. It therefore had to create a new business model—which meant rethinking every element of its cost structure—to serve average citizens in China and India.

What is more, as we have seen, the innovation required to serve the large tier-two and tier-three segments in emerging markets has the potential to make them more competitive in their traditional markets and therefore in all markets. The same business model that Citicorp developed for emerging markets, for example, was found to have application to inner-city markets in the United States and elsewhere in the developed world.

To become truly global, multinational companies will also increasingly have to look to emerging markets for talent. India is already recognized as a source of technical talent in engineering, sciences, and software, as well as in some aspects of management. High-tech companies recruit in India not only for the Indian market but also for the global market. China, Brazil, and Russia will surely be next. Philips, the Dutch electronics giant, is downsizing in Europe and already employs more Chinese than Dutch workers. Nearly half of the revenues for companies such as Coca-Cola, Procter & Gamble (P&G), Lucent, Boeing, and GE come from Asia, or will in the near future.

As corporate globalization advances, the composition of senior management will also begin to reflect the importance of the BRIC (Brazil, Russia, India, and China) countries and other emerging markets. At present, with a few exceptions, such as Citicorp and Unilever, executive suites are still filled with nationals from the company's home country. As the senior managements for multinationals become more diverse, however, decision-making criteria and processes, attitudes toward ethics, and corporate responsibility, risk taking, and team building all will likely change, reflecting the slow but persistent shift in the center of gravity in many multinational companies toward Asia. This will make the clear articulation of a company's core values and expected behaviors even more important than it is today. It will also increase the need for a single company culture as more and more people from different cultures have to work together.

Determinants of a Corporate Global Mind-Set

What factors shape a corporation's mind-set? Can they be managed? Given the importance of mind-set to a company's global outlook and prospects, these are important questions. Paul cites four primary factors: (1) *top management's view of the world*; (2) *the company's strategic and administrative heritage*; (3) *the company's dominant organizational dimension*; and (4) *industry-specific forces driving or limiting globalization*.[5]

Top Management's View of the World

The composition of a company's top management and the way it exercises power both have an important influence on the corporate mind-set. The emergence of a visionary leader can be a major catalyst in breaking down existing geographic and competitive boundaries. Good examples are Jack Welch at General Electric or Louis Gerstner at IBM, who both played a dominant role in propelling their companies to positions of global leadership. In contrast, leaders with a parochial, predominantly ethnocentric vision are more likely to concentrate on the home market and not be very interested in international growth.

Administrative Heritage

The second factor is a company's "administrative heritage"—a company's strategic and organizational history, including the configuration of assets the company has acquired over the years, the evolution of its organizational structure, the strategies and management philosophies the company has pursued, its core competencies, and its corporate culture. In most companies, these elements evolve over a number of years and increasingly "define" the organization. As a consequence, changing one or more of these key tangible and intangible elements of a company is an enormous challenge and therefore a constraint on its global strategic options. For example, many traditional multinationals such as Philips and Unilever created freestanding subsidiaries with a high degree of autonomy and limited strategic coordination in many of the countries and markets where they chose to compete. Companies with such a history may encounter greater resistance in introducing a more global mind-set and related strategies than companies such as Coca-Cola, which have predominantly operated with a more centralized approach.

Organizational Structure

The type of *organizational structure* a company has chosen—discussed more fully in the next section—is also a key determinant of a corporate mind-set. In a strongly product-oriented structure, management is more likely to think globally as the entire information infrastructure is geared toward collecting and processing product data on a worldwide basis. Compare this to an organization with a focus on countries, areas, or regions—the mind-set of managers tends to be more local. Here, the information infrastructure is primarily oriented toward local and regional needs. It follows that in a matrix structure based on product as well as geographic dimensions, the mind-set of management is expected to reflect both global and local perspectives.

Industry Forces

Industry factors such as opportunities for economies of scale and scope, global sourcing, and lower transportation and communication costs push companies toward a global efficiency mind-set. Stronger global competition, the need to enter new markets, and the globalization of important customers pull in the same direction. Similarly, the trend toward a more homogeneous demand, particularly for products in fast-moving consumer goods industries, and more uniform technical standards for many industrial products, encourage a more global outlook. Another set of industry drivers, however, works in the opposite direction and calls for strategies with a high degree of local responsiveness. Such drivers include strong local competition in important markets and the existence of cultural differences, making the transfer of globally standardized concepts less attractive. Issues such as protectionism, trade barriers, and volatile exchange rates may also force a national business approach. All these forces work together and help create the conditions that shape the global mind-set of a company.

Creating the Right Global Mind-Set

Thus, to create the right global mind-set, management must understand the different, often opposite, environmental forces that shape it. At the corporate level, managers focusing on global competitive strategies tend to emphasize increased cross-country or cross-region coordination and more centralized, standardized approaches to strategy. Country managers, on the other hand, frequently favor greater autonomy for their local units because they feel they have a better understanding of local market and customer needs. Thus, different groups of managers can be expected to analyze data and facts in a different way and favor different strategic concepts and solutions depending on their individual mind-sets.

In practice, two different scenarios can develop. In the first scenario, one perspective consistently wins at the expense of the other. Under this scenario, the company may be successful for a certain period of time but will most likely run into trouble at a later time because its ability to learn and innovate will be seriously impaired as it opts for "short-sighted" solutions within a given framework. In the second scenario, a deliberate effort is made to maintain a "creative tension" between both perspectives. This scenario recognizes the importance of such a tension to the company's ability to break away from established patterns of thinking and look for completely new solutions. This ability to move beyond the existing paradigm and, in that sense, further develop the mind-set is probably one of the most important success factors for many of the established successful global players. Utilizing creative tension in a constructive manner requires the development of a corporate vision as well as a fair decision-making process. The corporate vision is expected to provide general direction for all managers and employees in terms of where the company wishes to be in the future. Equally important is setting up a generally understood and accepted fair decision process, which must allow for sufficient opportunities to analyze and discuss both global and local perspectives, and their merits, in view of specific strategic situations.

P&G has been particularly innovative in designing its global operations around the tension between local and global concerns. Four pillars—global business units, market development organizations, global business services, and corporate functions—form the heart of P&G's organizational structure. Global business units build major global brands with robust business strategies; market development organizations build local understanding as a foundation for marketing campaigns; global business services provide business technology and services that drive business success; and corporate functions work to maintain our place as a leader of our industries.

Organization as Strategy[6]

Organizational design should be about developing and implementing corporate strategy. In a global context, the balance between local and central authority for key decisions is one of the most important parameters in a company's organizational design. Companies that have partially or fully globalized their operations have typically migrated to one of four organizational structures: (a) an international, (b) a multidomestic, (c) a global, or (d) a so-called transnational structure. Each occupies a well-defined position in the global aggregation or local adaptation matrix first developed by Bartlett and Ghoshal and usefully describes the most salient characteristics of each of these different organizational structures (Figure 10.1).[7]

The *international* model characterizes companies that are strongly dependent on their domestic sales and that export opportunistically. International companies typically have a well-developed domestic infrastructure and additional capacity to sell internationally. As their globalization develops further, they are destined to evolving into multidomestic, global, or transnational companies. The international model is fairly unsophisticated, unsustainable if the company further globalizes, and is therefore usually transitory in nature. In the short term, this organizational form may be viable in certain situations where the need for

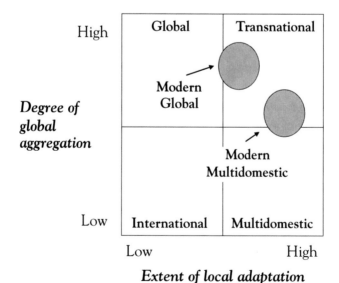

Figure 10.1. Global aggregation/local adaptation matrix.

localization and local responsiveness is very low (i.e., the domestic value proposition can be marketed internationally with very minor adaptations) and the economies of aggregation (i.e., global standardization) are also low.

The *multidomestic* organizational model describes companies with a portfolio of independent subsidiaries operating in different countries as a decentralized federation of assets and responsibilities under a common corporate name.[8] Companies operating with a multidomestic model typically employ country-specific strategies with little international coordination or knowledge transfer from the center headquarters. Key decisions about strategy, resource allocation, decision making, knowledge generation and transfer, and procurement reside with each country subsidiary, with little value added from the center (headquarters). The pure multidomestic organizational structure is positioned as high on local adaptation and low on global aggregation (integration). Like the international model, the traditional multidomestic organizational structure is not well suited to a global competitive environment in which standardization, global integration, and economies of scale and scope are critical. However, this model is still viable in situations where local responsiveness, local differentiation, and local adaptation are critical, while the opportunities for efficient production, global knowledge transfer, economies of scale, and economies of scope are minimal. As with the international model, the pure multidomestic company often represents a transitory organizational structure. An example of this structure and its limitations is provided by Philips during the last 25 years of the last century. In head-to-head competition with its principal rival, Matsushita, Philips' multidomestic organizational model became a competitive disadvantage against Matsushita's centralized (global) organizational structure.

The traditional *global* company is the antithesis of the traditional multidomestic company. It describes companies with globally integrated operations designed to take maximum advantage of economies of scale and scope by following a strategy of standardization and efficient production.[9] By globalizing operations and competing in global markets, these companies seek to reduce cost of research and development (R&D), manufacturing, production, procurement, and inventory; improve quality by reducing variance; enhance customer preference through global products and brands; and obtain competitive leverage. Most, if not all, key strategic decisions—about corporate strategy, resource allocation, and knowledge generation and transfer—are made at corporate headquarters. In the global aggregation-local adaptation matrix, the pure global company occupies the position of extreme global aggregation (integration) and low local adaptation (localization). An example of a pure global structure is provided by the aforementioned Japanese company Matsushita in the latter half of the last century. Since a pure global structure also represents an (extreme) ideal, it frequently is also transitory.

The *transnational* model is used to characterize companies that attempt to simultaneously achieve high global integration and high local responsiveness. It was conceived as a theoretical construct to mitigate the limitations of the pure multidomestic and global structures and occupies the fourth cell in the aggregation-adaptation matrix. This organizational structure focuses on integration, combination, multiplication of resources and capabilities, and managing assets and core competencies as a network of alliances as opposed to relying on functional or geographical division. Its essence, therefore, is matrix management. The ultimate objective is to have access and make effective and efficient use of all the resources the company has at its disposal globally, including both global and local knowledge. As a consequence, it requires management-intensive processes and is extremely hard to implement in its pure form. It is as much a mind-set, idea, or ideal rather than an organization structure found in many global corporations.[10]

Given the limitations of each of the above structures in terms of either their global competitiveness or their implementability, many companies have settled on matrix-like organizational structures that are more easily managed than the pure transnational model but that still target the simultaneous pursuit of global integration and local responsiveness. Two of these have been labeled the *modern multidomestic* and *modern global* models of global organization.[11]

The *modern multidomestic* model is an updated version of the traditional (pure) multidomestic model that includes a more significant role for the corporate headquarters. Accordingly, its essence no longer consists of a loose confederation of assets, but rather a matrix structure with a strong culture of operational decentralization, local adaptation, product differentiation, and local responsiveness. The resulting model, with national subsidiaries with significant autonomy, a strong geographical dimension, and empowered country managers allows companies to maintain their local responsiveness and their ability to differentiate and adapt to local environments. At the same time, in the modern multidomestic model, the center is critical to enhancing competitive strength. Whereas the primary role of the subsidiary is to be locally responsive, the role of the center is multidimensional; it must foster global integration by (a) developing global corporate and competitive strategies, and (b) playing a significant role in resource allocation, selection of markets, developing strategic analysis, mergers and acquisitions, decisions regarding R&D and technology matters, eliminating duplication of capital intensive assets, and knowledge transfer. An example of a modern multidomestic company is Nestlé.

The *modern global* company is rooted in the tradition of the traditional (pure) global form but gives a more significant role in decision making to the country subsidiaries. Headquarters targets a high level of global integration by creating low-cost sourcing opportunities, factor cost efficiencies, opportunities for global scale and scope, product standardization, global technology sharing and information technology (IT) services, global branding, and an overarching global corporate strategy. But unlike the traditional (pure) global model, the modern global structure makes more effective use of the subsidiaries in order to encourage local responsiveness. As traditional global firms evolve into modern global enterprises, they tend to focus more on strategic coordination and integration of core competencies worldwide, and protecting home country control becomes less important. Modern global corporations may disperse R&D, manufacture and production, and marketing around the globe. This helps ensure flexibility in the face of changing factor costs for labor, raw materials, exchange rates, as well as hiring talent worldwide. P&G is an example of a modern global company.

Realigning and Restructuring for Global Competitive Advantage

Creating the right environment for a global mind-set to develop and realigning and restructuring a company's global operations, at a minimum, requires (a) *a strong commitment by the right top management,* (b) *a clear statement of vision and a delineation of a well-defined set of global decision-making processes,* (c) *anticipating and overcoming organizational resistance to change,* (d) *developing and coordinating networks,* (e) *a global perspective on employee selection and career planning.*

A strong commitment by the right top management. Shaping a global mind-set starts at the top. The composition of the senior management team and the board of directors should reflect the diversity of markets in which the company wants to compete. In terms of mind-set, a multicultural board can help operating managers by providing a broader perspective and specific knowledge about new trends and changes in the environment. A good example of a company with a truly global top management team is the Adidas Group, the German-based sportswear company. Its executive board consists of two Germans, an American, and a New Zealander; the CEO is German. The company's supervisory board includes German nationals, a Frenchman, and Russians. Adidas is still an exception. Many other companies operating on a global scale still have a long way to go to make the composition of their top management and boards reflects the importance and diversity of their worldwide operations.

A clear statement of vision and a delineation of a well-defined set of global decision-making processes. For decades, it has been general management's primary role to determine corporate strategy and the organization's structure. In many global companies, however, top management's role has changed from its historical focus strategy, structure, and systems to one of developing purpose and vision, processes, and people. This new philosophy reflects the growing importance of developing and nurturing a strong corporate purpose and vision in a diverse, competitive global environment. Under this new model, middle and upper-middle managers are expected to behave more like business leaders and entrepreneurs rather than administrators and controllers. To facilitate this role change, companies must spend more time and effort engaging middle management in developing strategy. This process gives middle and upper-middle managers an opportunity to make a contribution to the (global) corporate agenda and, at the same time, helps create a shared understanding and commitment of how to approach global business issues. Instead of traditional strategic planning in a separate corporate planning department, Nestlé, for example, focuses on a combination of bottom-up and top-down planning approaches involving markets, regions, and strategic product groups. That process ensures that local managers play an important part in decisions to pursue a certain plan and the related vision. In line with this approach, headquarters does not generally force local units to do something they do not believe in. The new philosophy calls for development of the organization less through formal structure and more through effective management processes.

Anticipating and overcoming organizational resistance to change. The globalization of key business processes such as IT, purchasing, product design, and R&D is critical to global competitiveness. Decentralized, siloed local business processes simply are ineffective and unsustainable in today's intense, competitive global environment. In this regard, creating the right "metrics" is important. When all of a company's metrics are focused locally or regionally, locally or regionally inspired behaviors can be expected. Until a consistent set of global metrics is adopted, designed to encourage global behaviors, globalization is unlikely to take hold, much less succeed. Resistance to such global process initiatives runs deep, however. As many companies have learned, country managers will likely invoke everything from the "not invented here" syndrome to respect for local culture and business heritage to defend the status quo.

Developing and coordinating networks. Globalization has also brought greater emphasis on collaboration, not only with units inside the company but also with outside partners such as suppliers and customers. Global managers must now develop and coordinate networks, which give them access to key resources on a worldwide basis. Network building helps to replace nationally held views with a collective global mind-set. Established global companies, such as Unilever or GE, have developed a networking culture in which middle managers from various parts of the organization are constantly put together in working, training, or social situations. They range from staffing multicultural project teams, to sophisticated career path systems encouraging international mobility, to various training courses and internal conferences.

A global perspective on employee selection and career planning. Recruiting from diverse sources worldwide supports the development of a global mind-set. A multicultural top management, as described previously, might improve the company's chances of recruiting and motivating high-potential candidates from various countries. Many companies now hire local managers and put them through intensive training programs.

Microsoft, for example, routinely brings foreign talent to the United States for intensive training. P&G runs local courses in a number of countries and then sends trainees to its headquarters in Cincinnati or to large foreign subsidiaries for a significant period of time. After completion of their training, they are expected to take over local management positions.

Similarly, a career path in a global company must provide for recurring local and global assignments. Typically, a high-potential candidate will start in a specific local function, for example, marketing or finance. A successful track record in the chosen functional area provides the candidate with sufficient credibility in the company and, equally important, self-confidence to take on more complex and demanding global tasks, usually as a team member where he or she gets hands-on knowledge of the workings of a global team. With each new assignment, managers should broaden their perspectives and establish informal networks of contact and relationships. Whereas international assignments in the past were primarily demand-driven to transfer know-how and solve specific problems, they are now much more learning-oriented and focus on giving the expatriate the opportunity to understand and benefit from cultural differences as well as to develop long-lasting networks and relationships. Exposure to all major functions, rotation through several businesses, and different postings in various countries are critical in creating a global mind-set, both for the individual manager and for the entire management group. In that sense, global human resource management is probably one of the most powerful medium- and long-term tools for global success.

Minicase 10.2. March 31, 2008: Citi Announces New Corporate Organizational Structure[12]

Vikram Pandit, Citi's chief executive officer, recently announced a comprehensive reorganization of Citi's structure to achieve greater client focus and connectivity, global product excellence, and clear accountability. The new organizational structure is designed to let Citi focus its resources toward growth in emerging and developed markets and improve efficiencies throughout the company.

Specifically, Citi has established a regional structure to bring decision making closer to clients. The new structure gives the leaders of the geographic regions authority to make decisions on the ground. The geographic regions are each led by a single chief executive officer who reports to Mr. Pandit.

In addition, Citi reorganized its consumer group into two global businesses: Consumer Banking and Global Cards. This brings Citi's number of global businesses to four: Institutional Clients Group and Global Wealth Management are already organized as global businesses. The four global businesses will allow Citi to deliver on product excellence in close partnership with the regions. The product leaders also will report to Mr. Pandit.

"Our new organizational model marks a further important step along the path we are pursuing to make Citi a simpler, leaner and more efficient organization that works collaboratively across the businesses and throughout the world to benefit clients and shareholders," said Mr. Pandit. "With this new structure, we reinforce our focus on clients by moving the decision-making process as close to clients as possible and assigning some of our strongest talent to lead the regional areas and global product groups."

As part of the reorganization, in order to drive efficiency and reduce costs, Citi will further centralize global functions, including finance, IT, legal, human resources, and branding. By centralizing these global functions, particularly IT, Citi will reduce unnecessary complexity, leverage its global scale, and accelerate innovation. Risk is already centralized.

The business reorganization reflects priorities outlined by Mr. Pandit, who has been conducting intensive business reviews, since being named CEO, to drive greater cross-business collaboration; eliminate bureaucracy and create a nimbler, more client-focused organization; ensure strong risk management and capital resources; and drive cost and operational efficiencies to generate additional shareholder value.

Points to Remember

Developing a global mind-set requires companies to accomplish the following:

1. Integrate the global aspects of strategy into their overall corporate strategy and change thinking patterns from a single domestic focus to a broad global focus.
2. Manage uncertainty while constantly adapting to change and accepting it as part of a process.
3. Get the right people in place with the skills necessary to focus on international expansion.
4. Combine the various cultures and values of the corporate work force into a unique global organizational culture.
5. Invest in people so they can help the company to succeed globally.
6. Embrace diversity and differences.
7. Learn how to cooperate with partners worldwide by successfully managing global supply chains, teams, and alliances,

On the subject of creating a global organization, the following factors are important:

8. Globalization is driving a wholesale reinvention of organizational structure and management. The need for global scale and process efficiency is challenging corporate leaders to replace old paradigms of centralized control and decentralized autonomy with new models.
9. Achieving the potential of global operations requires a mix of "soft" and "hard" approaches. Optimizing global processes requires cultural change management, proactive team- and relationship-building, and also more traditional budgetary and accountability mechanisms and metrics.
10. Long-term vision, planning, and goal alignment can greatly increase chances of success. Corporations should start with a clear vision of their global objectives and values, and consciously develop shared language and identity, with participation from all global regions, not just headquarters.

11. Identifying and replicating successes quickly and continuously is crucial to global competitiveness. Today's complex global markets require multifaceted, not monolithic, approaches and capabilities. Global collaboration with face-to-face feedback loops, and a focus on identifying local successes and building them into the global process portfolio, can maximize the value of a corporation's global assets.

APPENDIX A

Global Trade: Doctrines and Regulation

Doctrines

Free Trade. Throughout history, *free trade* has been an important factor behind the prosperity of different civilizations. Adam Smith pointed to increased trade as the primary reason for the flourishing of the Mediterranean cultures, such as Egypt, Greece, and Rome, but also of Bengal (East India) and China. The great prosperity of the Netherlands, after it threw off Spanish imperial rule and came out in favor of free trade and freedom of thought, made the free trade versus mercantilist dispute the most important question in economics for centuries.[1] Ever since then, the "free-trade doctrine" has battled with mercantilist, protectionist, isolationist, and other trade doctrines and policies.

One of the strongest arguments for free trade was made by classical economist David Ricardo in his analysis of *comparative advantage*. Comparative advantage occurs when different parties (countries, regions, or individuals) have different opportunity costs of production. The theory is that free trade will induce countries to specialize in making the products that they are best at and that this will maximize the total wealth produced.

Adopting the free-trade doctrine means supporting and protecting (a) the trade of goods without taxes (including tariffs) or other trade barriers (e.g., quotas on imports or subsidies for producers); (b) trade in services without taxes or other trade barriers; (c) the absence of "trade-distorting" policies (such as taxes, subsidies, regulations, or laws) that give some firms, households, or factors of production an advantage over others; (d) free access to markets; (e) free access to market information; (f) efforts against firms trying to distort markets through monopoly or oligopoly power; (g) the free movement of labor between and within countries; and (h) the free movement of capital between and within nations.

Protectionism. Opposition to free trade, generally known as *protectionism*, is based on the notion that free trade is unrealistic or that the advantages are outweighed by considerations of national security, the importance of nurturing infant industries, preventing the exploitation of economically weak countries by stronger ones or of furthering various social goals.

Free trade is sometimes also opposed by domestic industries threatened by lower-priced imported goods. If U.S. tariffs on imported sugar were reduced, for example, U.S. sugar producers would have to lower their prices (and sacrifice profits). Of course, U.S. consumers would benefit from those lower prices. In fact, economics tells us that, collectively, consumers would gain more than the (domestic) producers would lose. However, since there are only a few domestic sugar producers, each one could lose a significant amount. This explains why domestic producers may be inclined to mobilize against the lifting of tariffs or, more generally, why they often favor domestic subsidies and tariffs on imports in their home countries, while objecting to subsidies and tariffs in their export markets.

Antiglobalization groups that maintain that, in reality, "free-trade agreements" often do not increase the economic freedom of the poor but rather make them poorer. These groups are another source of opposition to free trade. An example is the argument that letting subsidized corn from the United States into Mexico freely under NAFTA at prices well below production cost is ruinous to Mexican farmers. The real issue here, of course, is that such subsidies violate the principles of free trade and that this therefore exemplifies a flawed agreement rather than a valid argument against free trade.

As economic policy, protectionism is about restraining trade between nations, through methods such as tariffs on imported goods, restrictive quotas, and a variety of other restrictive government regulations designed to discourage imports and prevent foreign takeover of local markets and companies. This policy is closely aligned with antiglobalization and contrasts with free trade, where government barriers to trade are kept to a minimum. The term is mostly used in the context of economics, where protectionism refers to policies or doctrines that "protect" businesses and workers within a country by restricting or regulating trade between foreign nations.

Historically, protectionism was associated with economic theories such as mercantilism and import substitution. During that time, Adam Smith famously warned against the "interested sophistry" of industry, seeking to gain advantage at the cost of the consumers.[2] Virtually all modern-day economists agree that protectionism is harmful in that its costs outweigh the benefits and that it impedes economic growth. Economics Nobel Prize winner and trade theorist Paul Krugman once stated, "If there were an Economist's Creed, it would surely contain the affirmations 'I believe in the Principle of Comparative Advantage' and 'I believe in Free Trade.'"[3]

A variety of policies can be used to achieve protectionist goals, including the enactment of the following items:

1. *Tariffs*. Typically, tariffs (or taxes) are imposed on imported goods. Tariff rates vary according to the type of goods imported. Import tariffs will increase the cost to importers and increase the price of imported goods in the local markets, thus lowering the quantity of goods imported. Tariffs may also be imposed on exports, and in an economy with floating exchange rates, export tariffs have similar effects as import tariffs. However, for political reasons, such a policy is seldom implemented.

2. *Import quotas*. Import quotas reduce the quantity, and therefore increase the market price, of imported goods. Their economic effect is therefore similar to that of tariffs, except that the tax revenue gain from a tariff will instead be distributed to those who receive import licenses. This explains why economists often suggest that import licenses be auctioned to the highest bidder or that import quotas be replaced by an equivalent tariff.

3. *Administrative barriers*. Countries are sometimes accused of using their various administrative rules (e.g., regarding food safety, environmental standards, electrical safety) as a way to introduce barriers to imports.

4. *Antidumping legislation*. Dumping is the act of charging a lower price for a good in a foreign market than is charged for the same good in the domestic market (i.e., selling at less than "fair value").

Under the World Trade Organization (WTO) agreement, dumping is condemned (but not prohibited) if it causes or threatens to cause material injury to a domestic industry in the importing country. Supporters of antidumping laws argue that they prevent "dumping" of cheaper foreign goods that would cause local firms to close down. In practice, however, antidumping laws are often used to impose trade tariffs on foreign exporters.

5. *Direct subsidies.* Government subsidies (in the form of lump-sum payments or cheap loans) are sometimes given to local firms that cannot compete well against foreign imports. These subsidies are purported to "protect" local jobs and to help local firms adjust to the world markets.

6. *Export subsidies.* Under export subsidies, exporters are paid a percentage of the value of their exports. Export subsidies increase the amount of trade, and, in a country with floating exchange rates, have effects similar to import subsidies.

7. *Exchange rate manipulation.* A government may intervene in the foreign exchange market to lower the value of its currency by selling its currency in the foreign exchange market. Doing so will raise the cost of imports and lower the cost of exports, leading to an improvement in its trade balance. However, such a policy is only effective in the short run, as it will lead to higher price inflation in the country, which will in turn raise the cost of exports and reduce the relative price of imports.

In the modern trade arena, many other initiatives besides tariffs, quotas, and subsidies have been called protectionist. For example, some scholars, such as Jagdish Bhagwati, see developed countries' efforts in imposing their own labor or environmental standards as forms of protectionism.[4] The imposition of restrictive certification procedures on imports can also be seen in this light. Others point out that free-trade agreements often have protectionist provisions such as intellectual property, copyright, and patent restrictions that benefit large corporations. These provisions restrict trade in music, movies, drugs, software, and other manufactured items to high-cost producers with quotas from low-cost producers set to zero.

Arguments for protectionism. Opponents of free trade include those who argue that the comparative advantage argument for free trade has lost its legitimacy in a globally integrated world in which capital is free to move internationally. Herman Daly, a leading voice in the discipline of ecological economics, has stated that although Ricardo's theory of comparative advantage is one of the most elegant theories in economics, its application to the present day is illogical: "Free capital mobility totally undercuts Ricardo's comparative advantage argument for free trade in goods, because that argument is explicitly and essentially premised on capital (and other factors) being immobile between nations. Under the new globalization regime, capital tends simply to flow to wherever costs are lowest—that is, to pursue absolute advantage."[5]

Others criticize free trade as being "reverse protectionism in disguise," that is, of using tax policy to protect foreign manufacturers from domestic competition. By ruling out revenue tariffs on foreign products, government must fully rely on domestic taxation to provide its revenue, which falls disproportionately on domestic manufacturing. Or, in the words of Paul Craig Roberts, "[Foreign discrimination of U.S. products] is reinforced by the U.S. tax system, which imposes no appreciable tax burden on foreign goods and services sold in the U.S. but imposes a heavy tax burden on U.S. producers of goods and services regardless of whether they are sold within the U.S. or exported to other countries."[6]

Other defenses of protectionism include the idea that protecting newly founded, strategically important infant industries by imposing tariffs allows those domestic industries to grow and become self-sufficient within the international economy once they reach a reasonable size.

Arguments against protectionism. Most economists fundamentally believe in free trade and agree that protectionism reduces welfare. Nobel laureates Milton Friedman and Paul Krugman, for example, have argued that free trade helps third-world workers even though they may not be subject to the stringent health and labor standards of developed countries. This is because the growth of the manufacturing sector and the other jobs that a new export sector creates competition among producers, thereby lifting wages and living conditions.

Protectionism has also been accused of being one of the major causes of war. Proponents of this theory point to the constant warfare in the 17th and 18th centuries among European countries whose governments were predominantly mercantilist and protectionist; the American Revolution, which came about primarily due to British tariffs and taxes; as well as the protective policies preceding World War I and World War II.

Regulation of International Trade

Traditionally, trade was regulated through bilateral treaties between two nations. After World War II, as free trade emerged as the dominant doctrine, multilateral treaties like the GATT and *World Trade Organization* (WTO) became the principal regime for regulating global trade.

The WTO, created in 1995 as the successor to the General Agreement on Tariffs and Trade (GATT), is an international organization charged with overseeing and adjudicating international trade. The WTO deals with the rules of trade between nations at a near-global level; is responsible for negotiating and implementing new trade agreements; and is in charge of policing member countries' adherence to all the WTO agreements, signed by the majority of the world's trading nations and ratified in their parliaments. Additionally, it is the WTO's duty to review the national trade policies and to ensure the coherence and transparency of trade policies through surveillance in global economic policy making.

Headquartered in Geneva, Switzerland, the WTO has more than 150 members, which represent more than 95% of total world trade. It is governed by a ministerial conference, which meets every 2 years; a general council, which implements the conference's policy decisions and is responsible for day-to-day administration; and a director-general, who is appointed by the ministerial conference.

Five basic principles guide the WTO's role in overseeing the global trading system:

1. *Nondiscrimination.* This principle inspired two major policies—the most favored nation (MFN) rule and the national treatment policy—embedded in the main WTO rules on goods, services, and intellectual property. The MFN rule requires that a WTO member must apply the same conditions on all trade with other WTO members, that is, a WTO member has to grant the most favorable conditions under which it allows trade in a certain product type to all other WTO

members. The national treatment policy, adopted to address non-tariff barriers to trade (e.g., technical standards, security standards) dictates that imported and locally produced goods should be treated equally (at least after the foreign goods have entered the market).

2. *Reciprocity.* This principle reflects both a desire to limit the scope of free riding that that may arise because of the MFN rule and a desire to obtain better access to foreign markets.

3. *Binding and enforceable commitments.* The tariff commitments made by WTO members in a multilateral trade negotiation and on accession are enumerated in a list of concessions. A country can change its commitments but only after negotiating with its trading partners, which could mean compensating them for loss of trade. If satisfaction is not obtained, the complaining country may invoke the WTO dispute settlement procedures.

4. *Transparency.* WTO members are required to publish their trade regulations, to maintain institutions charged with review of administrative decisions affecting trade, to respond to requests for information by other members, and to notify changes in trade policies to the WTO.

5. *Safety valves.* Under specific circumstances, governments can (within limits) restrict trade to attain noneconomic objectives, to ensure "fair competition," and under special economic circumstances.

The WTO operates on a *"one country, one vote"* system, but actual votes have never been taken. Ostensibly, decisions are made by consensus, with relative market size as the primary source of bargaining power. In reality, most WTO decisions are made through a process of informal negotiations between small groups of countries, often referred to as the "green room" negotiations (after the color of the WTO director-general's office in Geneva) or "miniministerials" when they occur in other countries. These processes have been regularly criticized by many of the WTO's developing-country members who are often excluded from these negotiations.

The WTO oversees about 60 different agreements that have the status of international legal texts. Member countries must sign and ratify all

WTO agreements on accession. Some of the most important agreements concern agriculture, services, and intellectual-property rights.

Regional arrangements such as Mercosur in South America; the North American Free Trade Agreement (NAFTA) between the United States, Canada, and Mexico; ASEAN in Southeast Asia; and the European Union (EU) between 27 independent states constitute a second dimension of the international trade regulatory framework.

The *EU* is an economic and political union of 27 member states. Committed to regional integration, the EU was established by the Treaty of Maastricht on November 1, 1993, upon the foundations of the pre-existing European Economic Community. With almost 500 million citizens, the EU combined generates an estimated 30% share of the nominal gross world-product.

The EU has developed a single market through a standardized system of laws that apply in all member states, ensuring the freedom of movement of people, goods, services, and capital. It maintains common policies on trade, agriculture, fisheries, and regional development. A common currency, the euro, has been adopted by 16 member states known as the Eurozone. The EU has developed a limited role in foreign policy, having representation at the WTO, G8 summits, and at the UN. It enacts legislation in justice and home affairs, including the abolition of passport controls between many member states. Twenty-one EU countries are also members of NATO, those member states outside NATO being Austria, Cyprus, Finland, Ireland, Malta, and Sweden.

Mercosur is a regional trade agreement among Argentina, Brazil, Paraguay, and Uruguay, founded in 1991 by the Treaty of Asunción, which was later amended and updated by the 1994 Treaty of Ouro Preto. Its purpose is to promote free trade and the fluid movement of goods, people, and currency.

Bolivia, Chile, Colombia, Ecuador, and Peru currently have associate-member status. Venezuela signed a membership agreement on June 17, 2006, but before becoming a full member, its entry has to be ratified by the Paraguayan and the Brazilian parliaments.

The *NAFTA* is an agreement signed by the governments of the United States, Canada, and Mexico, creating a trilateral trade bloc in North America. The agreement came into force on January 1, 1994. It superseded the Canada–United States Free Trade Agreement. In terms of combined purchasing power, parity GDP of its members, as of 2007 the trade block, is the largest in the world and second largest by nominal GDP comparison. NAFTA has two supplements: the North American Agreement on Environmental Cooperation (NAAEC) and the North American Agreement on Labor Cooperation (NAALC).

The *Association of Southeast Asian Nations*, commonly abbreviated *ASEAN*, is a geopolitical and economic organization of 10 countries located in Southeast Asia, which was formed on August 8, 1967, by Indonesia, Malaysia, the Philippines, Singapore, and Thailand. Since then, membership has expanded to include Brunei, Burma (Myanmar), Cambodia, Laos, and Vietnam. Its aims include the acceleration of economic growth, social progress, cultural development among its members, and the protection of the peace and stability of the region.

APPENDIX B

Suggested Cases

This appendix lists suggested cases for each chapter of this book. All can be ordered through Harvard Business School Publishing.

Chapter 1

Ghemawat, P., Rukstad, M. G., & Illes, J. L. (2009). *Arcor: Global strategy and local turbulence* (abridged).

Jones, G. G., & Lefort, A. (2009). *McKinsey and the globalization of consultancy.*

McKern, B., & Palma, M. V. (2006). *Confectionary industry: Latin America and the global industry in 2006.*

Chapter 2

Alafaro, L. (2002). *Brazil: Embracing globalization?*

Bartlett, C. A. (2009). *Global wine war 2009: New world versus old.*

Ghemawat, P., & Matthews, J. L. (2004). *Globalization of CEMEX.*

Chapter 3

Inkpen, A. C. (2000). *Whirlpool corporation's global strategy.*

Ramaswamy, K. (2003). *Louis Vuitton Moet Hennessy: In search of synergies in the global luxury industry.*

Chapter 4

Bartlett, C. A. (2003). *BRL Hardy: Globalizing an Australian wine company.*

Roberto, M. A. (2005). *Robert Mondavi and the wine industry.*

Tan, D., & Tan, J. (2004). *Amway in China (A): A new business model.*

Chapter 5

Azhar, W., & Drabkin, D. (2008). *Pepsi Cola Pakistan: Franchising & product line management.*

Getaway, P., & Khanna, T. (2009/1999). *Tricon Restaurants International: Globalization re-examined.*

Roberts, J., & Doornik, K. (2007). *Nokia Corp: Innovation and efficiency in a high-growth global firm.*

Chapter 6

Bartlett, C. A. (2004). *P&G Japan: The SK-II globalization project.*

Khanna, T., Vargas, I., & Palepu, K. G. (2006). *Haier: Taking a Chinese company global.*

Ramaswamy, K. (2007). *LG Electronics: Global strategy in emerging markets.*

Chapter 7

Quelch, J. A. (2008). *BBC worldwide: Global strategy.*

Quelch, J. A. (2006). *Lenovo: Building a global brand.*

Quelch, J. A., & Harrington, A. (2008/2004). *Samsung Electronics Co: Global marketing operations.*

Chapter 8

Goldberg, R. A., & Clay, T. (1997). *Royal Ahold NV: Shopkeeper to the global village.*

Ichijo, K., & Radler, G. (2006). *Toyota's strategy and initiatives in Europe: The launch of the Aygo.*

Ko, S., & Loo, G. (2009). *Li & Fung: Growth for a supply-chain specialist.*

Chapter 9

Lee, H., Hoyt, D. W., & Singh, S. (2007). *Rio Tinto Iron Ore: Challenges of globalization in the mining industry.*

Marks, M., Holloway, C., Lee, H., Hoyt, D. W., & Silverman, A. (2009). *Crocs: Revolutionizing an industry's supply chain model for competitive advantage.*

Nielsen, B., Pedersen, T., & Pyndt, J. (2008). *ECCO A/S: Global value chain management.*

Pisano, G. P., & Adams, A. (2009). *VF Brands: Global supply chain strategy.*

Chapter 10

Mandviwalla, M., & Palmer, J. W. (2008). *Globalization of Wyeth*.

Paine, L. S., & Wruck, K. H. (2006). *Sealed Air Corp: Globalization and corporate culture* (abridged).

Notes

Chapter 1

1. Levitt (1983, May–June).
2. Ghemawat (2007a), p. 9.
3. Friedman (2007), p. 50.
4. Friedman (2007), p. 205.
5. Ghemawat (2007b).
6. Moore and Rugman (2005a); see also Moore and Rugman (2005b).
7. The Toyota, Wal-Mart, and Coca-Cola examples are taken from Ghemawat (2007a), chap. 1.
8. This mini case study was first published in de Kluyver and Pearce (2009), chap. 8.
9. Sirkin, Hemerling, and Bhattacharya (2008).
10. Gupta, Govindarajan, and Wang (2008), p. 28.
11. Fishbein (2008, January 17).
12. Gupta, Govindarajan, and Wang (2008), p. 7
13. Ghemawat (2001).
14. http://german.about.com
15. This section draws on Behrendt and Khanna (2004).

Chapter 2

1. Farrell (2004, December 2).
2. Hamel and Prahalad (1985, July-August).
3. Lindquist (2002, November 1); and http://www.cemex.com/
4. Krugman (1993).
5. Porter (1990).
6. Oster (1994).
7. Oster (1994).
8. George S. Yip first developed this framework in his book *Total global strategy: Managing for worldwide competitive advantage* (1992), chaps. 1 and 2.
9. Sturgeon, Van Biesebroeck, and Gereffi (2009).
10. Yoffie (1993), chaps. 1 and 10. The reader is encouraged to consult this excellent book for further details.
11. Yoffie (1993), 432.
12. Yoffie (1993), 433, 434.

Chapter 3

1. This chapter draws substantially on Ghemawat (2007b).
2. Mucha and Scheffler (2007, April 30).
3. http://www.whirlpoolcorp.com/about/history.aspx
4. Ghemawat (2007a), chap. 6.
5. Ghemawat (2007a), chap. 6.
6. Dickerson (2007, June 9).
7. This discussion draws on Ghemawat (2007b), Chapter 7.
8. http://www.vizio.com/
9. Citibank's Co-Operative Strategy in China (2009).

Chapter 4

1. Kirkpatrick (2007, July 17).
2. This section is based on Treacy and Wiersema (1993).
3. www.airarabia.com
4. Martin (2007).
5. Morrison (2009, August 10).
6. Treacy and Wiersema (1993).
7. Chai (2008, October 27).

Chapter 5

1. Ghemawat (2001).
2. Quelch (2003, August); Holt, Quelch, and Taylor (2004, September).
3. Khanna, Palepu, and Sinha (2005).
4. Haddock and Jullens (2009).
5. Arnold (2004), p. 34.
6. Chow (2008, April 28).
7. http://www.thecoca-colacompany.com/; http://www.illycaffeé.com/
8. For a more detailed discussion, see Tellis, Golder, and Christensen (2001).
9. Starbucks: A Global Work-in-Process (2006); http://www.starbucks.com/.

Chapter 6

1. Jargon (2008, May 1).
2. Palmeri and Balfour (2009, September 7).
3. http://www.kfcbd.com/aboutus_kfcbang.htm
4. Power (2009, June 1).
5. Buss (2009).

6. Eppinger and Chitkara (2006).
7. Santos, Doz, and Williamson (2004, Summer).
8. Santos, Doz, and Williamson (2004, Summer).
9. Jana (2009, March 31).

Chapter 7

1. Brand managers' high-wire act (2007, October 31).
2. http://www.leadingglobalbrands.com/
3. Arnold (2007); Schroiff and Arnold (2004).
4. Douglas, Craig, and Nijssen (2001).
5. Bartlett and Ghoshal (1989).
6. Douglas, Craig, and Nijssen (2001), p. 101.
7. Douglas, Craig, and Nijssen (2001), p. 103.
8. Silverstein (2008, November 24).
9. Douglas, Craig, and Nijssen (2001), p. 104.
10. Holt, Quelch, and Taylor (2004, September).
11. http://www.Interbrand.com/ (2009).

Chapter 8

1. Prahalad and Hamel (1990, May/June).
2. Special report on outsourcing (2006, January).
3. Myers and Cheung (2008, Summer).
4. Bliss, Muelleer, Pfitzmann, and Shorter (2007).
5. Special report on outsourcing (2006, January).
6. Raiborn, Butler, and Massoud (2009)
7. http://www.nokia.com/search?qt=Innovation&GO.y=0&GOx=0&GO=GO
8. KPMG (2009).
9. KPMG (2009).
10. Aris (2006, December 18).
11. Harbison (1993).
12. Cools and Roos (2005).
13. http://corporate.airfrance.com/; http://corporate.klm.com/; http://news.delta.com/
14. GE money to form a joint venture (2007, February 28).

Chapter 9

1. Lee (2004, October).

2. Myers and Cheung (2008, July).

3. Capell, Kamenev, and Saminather, N. (2006, September 4).

4. Lambert and Cooper (2000, January).

5. Lambert , Guinipero, and Ridenhower (1998).

6. Lee (2004, October).

7. Sheffi (2005, October).

8. Sheffi (2005, October).

9. http://www.ups-scs.com/solutions/case_studies/cs_nikon.pdf

10. Steinert-Threlkeld (2006, January).

Chapter 10

1. Huggett (2002, April 4).

2. Paul (2000).

3. Paul (2000).

4. Prahalad and Lieberthal (1998).

5. Paul (2000).

6. This section draws substantially on Aboy (2009).

7. See, for example, Bartlett and Ghoshal (1987a, 1987b, 1988, 1992, 2000).

8. Bartlett and Ghoshal (1987a, 1987b).

9. See, for example, G. S. Yip (1981, 1982a, 1982b, 1989, 1991a, 1991b, 1994, 1996, 1997); Yip and Madsen (1996).

10. Ohmae (2006).

11. Aboy (2009), p. 3

12. http://news.primerica.com/public/news/citi-announces-new-corp -organizational-structure.html

Appendix A

1. Mercantilism is an economic theory that holds that the prosperity of a nation is dependent upon its supply of capital, and that the global volume of trade is "unchangeable." Economic assets or capital are represented by bullion (gold, silver, and trade value) held by the state, which is best increased through a positive balance of trade with other nations (exports minus imports). Mercantilism suggests that the ruling government should advance these goals by playing a protectionist role in the economy through encouraging exports and discouraging imports, especially through the use of tariffs. Mercantilism was the dominant school of thought from the 16th to the 18th centuries. Domestically, this led to some of the first instances of significant government intervention and control over the economy, and it was during this period that much of the modern capitalist system was established. Internationally, mercantilism encouraged the many

European wars of the period and fueled European imperialism. Belief in mercantilism began to fade in the late 18th century, as the arguments of Adam Smith and the other classical economists won out. Today, mercantilism (as a whole) is rejected by economists, though some elements are looked upon favorably by noneconomists.

2. Friedman and Friedman (1980).

3. Krugman (1987).

4. Bhagwati (2004).

5. Daly (2007).

6. Roberts (2005, July 26).

References

Aboy, M. (2009). The organization of modern MNEs is more complicated than the old models of Global, Multidomestic, and Transnational. *Working Paper Series: International Business Strategy–Social Science Research Network*, 1–5.

Aris, A. (2006, December 18). Special report: Capturing the global halal food market. http://www.theedgemalaysia.com/

Arnold, D. (2004). *The mirage of global markets*. FT Prentice Hall, Pearson Education, Upper Saddle River, New Jersey.

Arnold, D. (2007). "Think global, act local": A modularization of marketing and marketing organizations. *Globe Management Review, 1*(1), 5.

Bartlett, C. A., & Ghoshal, S. (2000). Going global. *Harvard Business Review, 78*(2), 132–142.

Bartlett, C. A., & Ghoshal, S. (1992). What is a global manager? *Harvard Business Review, 70*(5), 124–132.

Bartlett, C. A., & Ghoshal, S. (1989). *Managing across borders*. Boston, MA: Harvard Business School Press.

Bartlett, C. A., & Ghoshal, S. (1988). Organizing for worldwide effectiveness: The transnational solution. *California Management Review, 31*(1), 54–72

Bartlett, C. A., & Ghoshal, S. (1987a). Managing across borders: New organizational responses. *International Executive, 29*(3), 10–13.

Bartlett, C. A., & Ghoshal, S. (1987b). Managing across borders: New strategic requirements. *Sloan Management Review, 28*(4), 7–17

Behrendt, S., & Khanna, P. (2004). Risky business: Geopolitics and the global corporation. *Strategy & Business, 32*(2).

Bhagwati, J. (2004). "Protectionism." In David R. Henderson (Ed.), Concise encyclopedia of economics. http://www.econlib.org/library/Enc/Protectionism.html

Bliss, C., Muelleer, C., Pfitzmann, M., & Shorter, D. (2007). *Make manufacturing and supply chain a winning pair*. McLean, VA: Booz Allen & Hamilton.

Brand managers' high-wire act: Going global and staying local. (2007, Oct. 31). http://knowledge.wharton.upenn.edu/

Buss, D. (2009). Creating the perfect fit: New car seat design. Trying to please all of the people, all of the time. Retrieved from http://www.edmunds.com/advice/buying/articles/121813/article.html

Capell, K., Kamenev, M., & Saminather, N. (2006, September 4). Fashion conquistador; Zara's quick turnover lures shoppers, but global expansion could be a strain. *BusinessWeek*, 38.

Chai, W. (2008, October 27). Dell puts on a new game face in Asian market: Its design philosophy now emphasizes form as opposed to functional and low-cost attributes in the past. *Business Times Singapore, 4.*

Chow, N. (2006, April 28). India's Tata AutoComp making inroads to China. *Plastic News*, p. 17.

Citibank's co-operative strategy in China: The Renminbi debit card. (2009). Case 09/412C, Poon Kam Kai Series. Asia Case Research Center, University of Hong Kong.

Cools, K., & Roos, A. (2005). *The role of alliances in corporate strategy.* Boston, MA: The Boston Consulting Group.

Daly, H. (2007). *Ecological economics and sustainable development: Selected essays of Herman Daly.* Northampton, MA: Edward Elgar.

de Kluyver, C. A., & Pearce, J. A., II. (2009) *Strategy: A view from the top* (3rd ed.). Upper Saddle River, NJ: Prentice Hall.

Dickerson, M. (2007, June 9). Latin America attracting investors from India: Similarities in consumer bases help make the region a natural market. *Los Angeles Times.*

Douglas, S., Craig, C. S., & Nijssen, E. J. (2001). Executive insights: Integrating branding strategy across markets. Building international brand architecture. *Journal of International Marketing, 9*(2), 97–11.

Eppinger, S. D., & Chitkara, A. R. (2006). The new practice of global product development. *MIT Sloan Management Review, 47*(4), 22–30.

Farrell, D. (2004, December 2). Beyond offshoring: Assess your company's global potential. *Harvard Business Review.* 82–90.

Friedman, M., & Friedman, R. (1980), *Free to choose: A personal statement,* Hartcourt Books, Chicago.

Friedman, T. L. (2007). *The world is flat: A brief history of the twenty-first century.* New York, NY: Farrar, Strauss and Giroux.

GE Money to form a joint venture with Colombia's Banco Colpatria. (2007, February 28). *Business Wire.*

Ghemawat, P. (2007a). Why the world isn't flat. *Foreign Policy, 159,* 54–60.

Ghemawat, P. (2007b). Redefining global strategy: Crossing borders in a world where differences still matter. Harvard Business School Press, Boston.

Ghemawat, P. (2001). Distance still matters: The hard reality of global expansion. *Harvard Business Review, 79*(8), 137–147.

Gupta, A. K., Govindarajan, V., & Wang, H. (2008). *The quest for global dominance* (2nd ed.). San Francisco, CA: Jossey-Bass.

Haddock, R., & Jullens, J. (2009). The best years of the auto industry are still to come: Even as they struggle through the economic meltdown, vehicle makers can look ahead to a high-growth, flexible, global future. http://www.strategy-business.com/media/file/sb55_09204.pdf

Hamel, G., & Prahalad, C. K. (1985, July–August). Do you really have a global strategy? *Harvard Business Review*, pp. 139–148.

Harbison, John R. (1993). *A practical guide to alliances: Leapfrogging the learning curve*. Los Angeles, CA: Booz Allen & Hamilton.

Holt, D. B., Quelch, J. A., & Taylor, E. L. (2004, September). How global brands compete. *Harvard Business Review*, pp. 69–75.

Huggett, P. (2002, April 4). When global strategy goes wrong. *The Asian Wall Street Journal.*

Interbrand. (2009). The definitive guide to the world's most valuable brands. http://www.interbrand.com/images/studies/-1_BGB2009_Magazine _Final.pdf

Jana, R. (2009, March 31). P&G's trickle-up success: Sweet as honey. Retrieved from http://www.businessweek.com/

Jargon, J. (2008, May 1). Kraft reformulates Oreo, scores in China. Retrieved from http://www.wallstreetjournal.com/

Khanna, T., Palepu, K. G., & Sinha, J. (2005). Strategies that fit emerging markets. *Harvard Business Review, 83*(6), 63–76.

Kirkpatrick, D. (2007, July 17). How Microsoft conquered China, http://money .cnn.com/magazines/fortune

KPMG Peat Marwick (2009). *Global location strategy for automotive suppliers*. http://www.kpmg.com/Global/en/IssuesAndInsights/ArticlesPublications/ Pages/default.aspx

Krugman, P. R. (1987). Is free trade passe? *Journal of Economic Perspectives, 1*(2), 131–144. Retrieved from http://www.jstor.org/pss/1942985

Krugman, P. R. (1993). *Geography and trade*. Cambridge, MA: MIT Press.

Lambert, D. M., & Cooper, M. C. (2000, January). Issues in supply chain management. *Industrial Marketing Management, 29*(1), 65–83.

Lambert, D. M., Guinipero, L. C., & Ridenhower G. J. (1998*). Supply chain management: A key to achieving business excellence in the 21st century*. Unpublished manuscript, referred to by D. M. Lambert, J. R. Stock, & L. M. Ellram (Eds.), *Fundamentals of logistics management*. Burr Ridge, IL: Irwin/ McGraw-Hill.

Lee, H. L. (2004, October). The triple-A supply chain. *Harvard Business Review*, 102–112.

Levitt, T. (1983, May–June). The globalization of markets. *Harvard Business Review.*

Lindquist, D. (2002, November 1). From cement to services: Cemex's Lorenzo Zambrano revolutionized the low-tech cement business by investing in technology. Now companies want to buy that expertise. *Entrepeneur*. Chief Executive (U.S.). Retrieved from http://www.entrepreneur.com/tradejournals/ pub/4070.html/

Martin, R. (2007). *The opposable mind: How successful leaders win through integrative thinking.* Boston, MA: Harvard Business School Press.

Moore, K., & Rugman, A. (2005). Globalization is about regionalization. *McGill International Review, 6* (1) 37–45

Moore, K., & Rugman, A. (2005, Summer). The myth of global business. *European Business Forum.*, http://www.europeanbusinessforum.com

Morrison, C. (2009, August 10). How to innovate like Apple. Retrieved from http://www.BNET.com/

Muccha, T., & Scheffler, M. (2007, April 30), Outsurcing, Inc. Retrieved from http://www.chicagobusiness.com/

Myers, M. B., & Cheung, M.-S. (2008, July). Sharing global supply chain knowledge. *Sloan Management Review, 49*(4), 67–73.

Ohmae, K. (2006). Growing in a global garden. *Leadership Excellence, 23*(9), 14–15.

Oster, S. M. (1994). *Modern competitive analysis* (2nd ed.). Oxford, UK: Oxford University Press.

Palmeri, C., & Balfour, F. (2009, September 7). Starwood is blanketing China. *BusinessWeek*, p. 56.

Paul, H. (2000, March/April). Creating a mindset. *Thunderbird International Business Review, 42*(2), 187–200.

Porter, M. (1990). *The competitive advantage of nations.* New York, NY: The Free Press.

Power, C. (2009, June 1). Buying Muslim. *Time.* http://www.time.com/

Prahalad, C. K., & Lieberthal, K. (1998). The end of corporate imperialism. *Harvard Business Review.* 109–117.

Prahalad, C. K., & Hamel, G. (1990, May/June). The core competence of the corporation. *Harvard Business Review*, pp. 79–93.

Quelch, J. A. (2003, August). The return of the global brand. *Harvard Business Review*, pp. 22–23.

Rayborn, C. A., Butler, J. B., & Massoud, M. F. (2009). Outsourcing support functions: Identifying and managing the good, bad, and ugly. *Business Horizons, 52*, 347–356.

Roberts, P. C. (2005, July 26). U.S. falling behind across the board. *VDARE.com.* Retrieved from http://www.vdare.com/roberts/050726_behind.htm

Santos, J., Doz, Y., & Williamson, P. (2004, Summer). Is your innovation process global? *MIT Sloan Management Review, 45*(4), 31.

Schroiff, H.-W., & Arnold, D. (2004). Strategies for managing brand and product in international markets. In J. Quelch & R. Deshpande (Eds.), *The Global Market.* San Francisco, CA: Jossey-Bass.

Sheffi, Y. (2005, October). Building a resilient supply chain. *Harvard Business Review Supply Chain Strategy, 1*(5), 1–4.

Silverstein, B. (2008, November 24). Older and wiser: How brands stand the test of time. http://www.brandchannel.com/features_effect.asp?pf_id=421

Sirkin, H. L., Hemerling, J. W., & Bhattacharya, A. K. (2008). *Globality: Competing with everyone from everywhere for everything*. New York, NY: Business Plus.

Special report on outsourcing. (2006, January). *BusinessWeek*. Retrieved from http://www.businessweek.com/magazine/toc/06_05/B39690605outsourcing .htm/

Somjen, A., Davila, A., Foster, G., & Putt, C. (2006). Starbucks: A global work-in-process. Case IB-74. Stanford Graduate School of Business, Stanford University. Retrieved from https://gsbapps.stanford.edu/cases/detail1 .asp?Document_ID=3032/

Steinert-Threlkeld, T. (2006, January). Nestlé pieces together its global supply chain. *Baseline*. Retrieved from http://www.baselinemag.com/

Sturgeon, T., Van Biesebroeck, J., Gereffi, G. (2009). Value chains, networks, and clusters: Reframing the global automotive industry. *Journal of Economic Geography 8(3) 297-321*

Tellis, G. J., Golder, P. N., & Christensen, C. M. (2001) *Will and vision: How latecomers grow to dominate markets*. Princeton, NJ: McGraw-Hill.

Treacy, M., & Wiersema, F. (1993). Customer intimacy and other value disciplines. *Harvard Business Review, 71*(1) 84–93.

Yip, G. S. (1997). Patterns and determinants of global marketing. *Journal of Marketing Management, 13*(1–3), 153–164.

Yip, G. S. (1994). Industry drivers of global strategy and organization. *International Executive, 36*(5), 529–556.

Yip, G. S. (1992). *Total global strategy: Managing for worldwide competitive advantage*. Upper Saddle River, NJ: Prentice Hall.

Yip, G. S. (1991a). A performance comparison of continental and national businesses in Europe. *International Marketing Review, 8*(2), 31–43

Yip, G. S. (1991b). Strategies in global industries: How U.S. businesses compete. *Journal of International Business Studies, 22*(4), 749–753.

Yip, G. S. (1989). Global strategy a world of nations? *Sloan Management Review, 31*(1), 29–41.

Yip, G. S. (1982a). Diversification entry: Internal development versus acquisition. *Strategic Management Journal, 3*(4), 331–345.

Yip, G. S. (1982b). Gateways to entry. *Harvard Business Review, 60*(5), 85–92.

Yip, G. S. (1981). *Market selection and direction: Role of product portfolio planning*. Boston, MA: Harvard Business School.

Yip, G. S., & Madsen, T. L. (1996). Global strategy as a factor in Japanese success. *International Executive, 38*(1), 145–167.

Yip, G. S., & T. L. Madsen, (1996). Global account management: The new frontier in relationship marketing. *International Marketing Review, 13*(3), 24–33.

Yoffie, D. B. (Ed.). (1993). *Beyond free trade: Firms, governments, and global competition.* Boston, MA: Harvard Business School Press.

Index

CPSIA information can be obtained at www.ICGtesting.com
Printed in the USA
BVOW020619120912

300038BV00005B/2/P